Praise for

The Free Market Existentialist

"Ever since the Enlightenment the long arc of moral progress that has created the modern world has had at its core the central tenet of individual freedom and autonomy against the collectivist and authoritarian dogmas of church and state. The two most extreme defenders of this individualism are libertarians and existentialists, two groups one never finds discussed in the same sentence. Until now. William Irwin has transcended ideology and tribalism to unite a set of ideas that, for the first time, could end the rancor between the Left and the Right by reminding each of their shared values. This book will change the thinking of everyone interested in politics, economics, or religion—a game-changing work."

—**Michael Shermer**, *Publisher of* Skeptic *magazine, Presidential Fellow, Chapman University, and author of* The Moral Arc

"Irwin offers a defense of free market existentialism that is very readable and refreshingly humble. He is not trying to prove that we all ought to be free market existentialists. Instead he is simply presenting us with various considerations, first to show that existentialism in a plausible interpretation is compatible with favoring a capitalist regime, and then to make their pairing seem attractive to us. But in the end, he acknowledges, it is a matter of preference."

—*Joel Marks*, *Professor Emeritus of Philosophy, University of New Haven and author of* Ethics without Morals: In Defence of Amorality *and* Bad Faith: A Philosophical Memoir

"In *The Free Market Existentialist*, William Irwin skillfully rescues existentialism from the specter of collectivism, with which it never sat easily. He highlights the affirmative individualism within existentialism that aligns it more closely with minimal-state capitalism, and explores the responsibilities we all have to choose for ourselves who we want to be and to resist our conformist mass culture of consumerism."

—**Mark D. White**, *chair of the Department of Philosophy, College of Staten Island/CUNY and author of* Kantian Ethics and Economics: Autonomy, Dignity, and Character

"This is a first-rate book; gutsy and charmingly written, with a genuinely exciting central argument. Amoral-atheist-existentialist capitalism is compelling and ahead of its time. Irwin has crystallized our forbidden thoughts, articulating them in an accessible way, showing why we should no longer keep quiet about them."

—*Sharon M. Kaye*, *Professor of Philosophy, John Carroll University and author of* Philosophy: A Complete Introduction

The Free Market Existentialist

Capitalism without Consumerism

William Irwin

WILEY Blackwell

This edition first published 2015
© 2015 John Wiley & Sons Ltd.

Registered Office
John Wiley & Sons Ltd, The Atrium, Southern Gate, Chichester,
West Sussex, PO19 8SQ, UK

Editorial Offices
350 Main Street, Malden, MA 02148-5020, USA
9600 Garsington Road, Oxford, OX4 2DQ, UK
The Atrium, Southern Gate, Chichester, West Sussex, PO19 8SQ, UK

For details of our global editorial offices, for customer services, and for information about how to apply for permission to reuse the copyright material in this book please see our website at www.wiley.com/wiley-blackwell.

The right of William Irwin to be identified as the author of this work has been asserted in accordance with the UK Copyright, Designs and Patents Act 1988.

Library of Congress Cataloging-in-Publication Data

Irwin, William, 1970–
  The free market existentialist : capitalism without consumerism / William Irwin.
    pages cm
  Includes bibliographical references and index.
  ISBN 978-1-119-12128-2 (pbk.)
  1. Existentialism.   2. Free enterprise.   3. Capitalism.   4. Consumption
(Economics)   5. Anti-realism.   I. Title.
  B819.I77 2015
  142'.78–dc23
                                                              2015016326

A catalogue record for this book is available from the British Library.

Cover design by Cyan Design

Set in 10.5/12.5pt Palatino by Aptara Inc., New Delhi, India

Printed and bound in Malaysia by Vivar Printing Sdn Bhd

1   2015

Contents

Contents

Acknowledgments

Writing a book can be a solitary process. Not so in this case. I received welcome support from friends, family, and colleagues. Indeed, it would have been a very different book were it not for the comments, corrections, leads, suggestions, and recommendations of the great many people I consulted.

It has become cliché for an author to absolve those he thanks in the acknowledgments from any possible faults in the book that follows. But in this case I really mean it. None of the people I thank should be taken as agreeing with my arguments. In fact, none of them fully agree with all the arguments in this book and many of them vehemently disagree. With that said, I especially thank Eric Bronson, Joel Marks, and Trip Johnson, who read and commented extensively on the whole manuscript.

Eric is an old and dear friend, whose support throughout the project meant more to me than he could realize. It is not easy to give feedback that is at the same time seriously critical and greatly encouraging. Eric managed to do that with every chapter.

Joel Marks is not an old friend. In fact, I've never met him in person. Just as I was beginning work on this book I struck up an e-mail correspondence with Joel concerning his excellent book *Ethics without Morals: A Defense of Amorality*. Joel has been exceedingly patient,

Acknowledgments

kind, and generous, reading the entire manuscript twice and several chapters three or four times, providing invaluable comments. He is the nicest and smartest amoralist I have never met.

Trip Johnson is my Facebook friend, currently a medical doctor serving in Army Special Forces, formerly a student at King's College. I did not have the good fortune to teach Trip when he was at King's, but I did have the good fortune of learning from him when he commented insightfully on my manuscript. Ryan Klubeck is another King's alumnus who I did not have the good fortune to teach. Nonetheless, in working as an intern for the philosophy department, Ryan proofread the entire manuscript and saved me from some serious flubs.

My wife, Megan Lloyd, has been my constant discussion partner since the conception of this project. Additionally she read several parts of the manuscript and offered very helpful feedback in addition to bountiful love and support.

Other friends and colleagues read or discussed parts of the manuscript, providing vital feedback and frequently helping me to rethink my arguments. Those folks include: Leslie Aarons, Dave Baggett, Greg Bassham, Kimberly Blessing, Bill Bolan, Paul Cantor, Alan Clune, Shane Courtland, David Detmer, Kimberly Engels, Jerry Erion, Richard Garner, David Glick, R. Kevin Hill, Kyle Johnson, Alan Kahan, Ed Romar, Aeon Skoble, James South, Janice Thompson, Mark White, and Gloria Zuniga. No doubt I have absentmindedly neglected to include some names. If yours is one of them, please forgive me.

I presented part of a draft of chapter 4 at the 40th Conference on Value Inquiry at Neumann University in May 2014 and revised the chapter in light of very helpful feedback there. I wish to thank all the conference participants, especially Jake Davis, Jorge Oseguera Gamba, David Kaspar, John Lemos, Justin Morton, John Park, and Eric Sampson.

Two people who mean a great deal to me were spared from reading the manuscript but will not be spared the embarrassment of my thanks. Jorge J.E. Gracia would have read the manuscript if I had asked, and he would have supported me even though he disagreed with it. I am proud and fortunate to call him my mentor. Jim Lawler first took me through *Being and Nothingness* and has always been a supportive and insightful critic of my work. Because this book would have tested the limits of even his kindness and support I did not ask him to read it. Nonetheless I heard his voice in my head as I took aim at Marxism.

It has been a true pleasure to work with Liam Cooper, my editor at Wiley Blackwell. His support and enthusiasm for the project began with my initial query and have not faded. Liam lined up three anonymous reviewers for the manuscript, all of whom provided helpful comments and criticisms that pushed me to improve the book. I am grateful to those anonymous, unsung heroes. Working with Liam, Sian Jones has been incredibly helpful in getting all of the details right, from the front cover artwork to the back cover testimonial blurbs. With a light hand and a keen eye, Louise Spencely is the best copyeditor in the business. I am grateful to her for improving my writing. Allison Kostka and the production team were the picture of diligence and efficiency, guiding me through the tangled process leading from Word document to printed book.

As you can see, this book really was not a solitary experience. With that, in closing, let me say that I am also grateful to you, the reader, and I would welcome your comments and criticisms.

Introduction

Philosophies of Individualism

I am all alone, not in a despairing existentialist place, though sometimes I go there. No, I am all alone in the intersection of circles in
a Venn diagram. The first circle represents the set of free market
philosophers and the second circle represents the set of existentialist
philosophers. Free market existentialism? The very idea makes some
people cringe. Academic philosophy in the English-speaking world
is dominated by the analytic school, which is often openly hostile to
continental philosophy in general and existentialism in particular.
There is, though, at least one thing that the vast majority of academic
philosophers of both the analytic and continental schools agree on:
the free market is bad. The few defenders of the free market in academic philosophy are all analytic. Indeed, to my knowledge, I am
the only existentialist defender of the free market. So this book is an
attempt to synthesize views that don't often relate. It aims to show
that existentialism and free market thinking can not only associate
but can do so very well.

By the free market I do not mean the crony capitalism or "crapital-
ism" one finds in the United States, but rather an economic system

The Free Market Existentialist: Capitalism without Consumerism, First Edition. William Irwin.
© 2015 John Wiley & Sons, Ltd. Published 2015 by John Wiley & Sons, Ltd.

in which the government plays no role aside from providing rule of law and protecting property rights. I also use the term "free market" more broadly as shorthand for libertarian political philosophy: briefly, the view that the proper role of government is limited to the prevention of force, fraud, and theft. Though I think the free market has many advantages, it is not the purpose of this book to argue for the superiority of the free market. Rather, the purpose of the book is to show that capitalism and existentialism are compatible and to argue modestly that a minimal state with a truly free market would be a worthwhile option among liberal states.

The main link between existentialism and libertarianism is individualism. The individual is primary and the individual is responsible. Granted, the sense of individualism characteristic of existentialism is not exactly the same as the sense of individualism characteristic of libertarianism, but they are not foreign to each other, inasmuch as both strive for genuine autonomy. Libertarians have long recognized the importance of strong property rights in securing autonomy, and existentialists have long recognized the importance of choosing meaning and subjective values for oneself in developing authenticity. One sense does not necessarily imply the other, but they do fit together well. Existentialists emphasize the importance of subjectively choosing one's values and making one's meaning, and libertarians champion the individual's prerogative to live in any way that does not cause harm to others.

Existentialism and libertarianism both value freedom and responsibility. As with individualism, the sense of freedom characteristic of existentialism is not exactly the same as the sense of freedom characteristic of libertarianism, but they are not foreign to each other. The entrepreneurs whom libertarians celebrate are risk takers and often rebels who feel a sense of exhilaration in taking chances. Existentialists, though, because of their largely negative view of capitalism, have typically ignored or dismissed such entrepreneurs as not genuine examples of individuals exercising their freedom. Sartre and the French existentialists were tenderhearted, with great care and concern for oppressed groups, and thus did not extend their concern for freedom into the economic realm as a concern for freedom from government interference. Instead, they championed freedom in the economic realm in terms of improving equality of opportunity.

One of the great fears of the political left is that capitalism deprives us of freedom, that, among other things, it makes us into mindless drones who simply buy and consume. Of course capitalism provides circumstances that make it easier for a person to live that way, but capitalism can't make you do anything. It is possible to have capitalism without consumerism. Existentialism is actually the ideal balancing agent, the perfect accompaniment to capitalism, allowing us to reap the benefits of a free market while encouraging us to resist crass consumerism.

Existentialism highlights the individual's ontological freedom. The individual is never compelled to do anything she does not want to do; and she is urged to make and create herself. Just as the individual is ill-advised to let family, church, or government dictate who she is, so too she is ill-advised to let the economic system dictate who she is. Family, church, and government may provide good resources and worthwhile pieces of identity as long as they are reflectively chosen. Likewise, the capitalist system not only brings benefits in terms of wealth but in terms of opportunities for free expression. This is all desirable, and with the existentialist imperative to define oneself, the negative of crass consumerism can be avoided. As I say, this is desirable, but it is not strictly necessary. The argument of this book is not that all libertarians should become existentialists or that all existentialists should become libertarians. The argument is simply that the two fit together well, better than either libertarians or existentialists might have realized. Indeed, free market existentialism is a view worthy of consideration in the marketplace of ideas.

The Free Market Existentialist is divided into seven chapters and addresses three main issues. Chapters 1–3 address the nature of existentialism, its relationship to Marxism, and the way existentialism can be reconciled with capitalism. Chapters 4 and 5 make a case for an existentialist moral anti-realism. And chapters 6 and 7 argue, on the basis of existentialist moral anti-realism, for strong property rights and a minimal state.

Chapter 1 "Out, out, Brief Candle!": What Do You Mean by Existentialism?" addresses its subtitle's question. Because existentialism has regularly been associated with Marxism, the reaction to combining existentialism and free market thinking may be one of disbelief. Once the disbelief fades, though, the admission follows that "it depends on what you mean by existentialism." I agree. In this chapter, I argue that existentialism is best understood as a family resemblance concept with no necessary and sufficient conditions, just an overlapping set of characteristics among its instances. Without attempting to defend my account against all comers or establish necessary and sufficient conditions, I define existentialism as a philosophy that reacts to an apparently absurd or meaningless world by urging the individual to overcome alienation, oppression, and despair through freedom and self-creation in order to become a genuine person. I then elaborate on the elements of the definition with reference to the canonical existentialist philosophers.

Chapter 2, "Like Cigarettes and Existentialism: Why There Is no Necessary Connection between Marxism and Sartre," considers the question: Why was Jean-Paul Sartre a Marxist? Sartre's great emphasis on individual freedom and responsibility in *Being and Nothingness* seems an unlikely match for Marxism. A look at the historical record reveals that Sartre's existentialism was, in fact, rejected as "bourgeois" by the leading French Marxists of the day. Sartre was never an orthodox Marxist, but he was an unorthodox Marxist in his later work, most notably the *Critique of Dialectical Reason*. The reason for Sartre's move to Marxism, it is averred, lies in the cultural milieu of post-war France.

Chapter 3, "To Consume or not to Consume?: How Existentialism Helps Capitalism," makes the positive case for a link between existentialism and the free market. Both, of course, stress the importance of the individual and freedom. Beyond that, however, existentialism actually helps the individual to deal with capitalism's potential pitfalls. For the free market existentialist, alienation is not something that just happens to a person but rather is something the person must avoid. The free market existentialist must take responsibility to choose work that she finds meaningful rather than aimlessly drifting into work that is alienating. And even when she is compelled to do work that is dull, repetitive, and potentially alienating, the existentialist, like Camus' Sisyphus, can make meaning and soar above her fate.

As with alienation, so with consumerism, the free market existentialist does not see herself as a victim. By consumerism I mean the addictive drive and desire for the newest and latest goods and services for the sake of deriving self-worth and for signaling one's worth to others. Existentialism calls for us to define ourselves as individuals and to resist being defined by external forces. The self-defining existentialist will find consumer culture crass without necessarily rejecting the free market that makes it possible. Indeed, the existentialist may choose to practice voluntary simplicity so as not to contract affluenza, "a painful, contagious, socially transmitted condition of overload, debt, anxiety, and waste resulting from the dogged pursuit of more."[1] One size does not fit all, though. Ultimately, guided by prudence, the free market existentialist will pursue whatever she deems to be desirable and in her enlightened self-interest.

Chapter 4, "Why Nothing Is Wrong: Moral Anti-realism," takes up the existentialist denial of objective moral values. Here I make another unexpected connection, that between existentialism and evolutionary theory. At first glance, the two are incompatible because existentialism holds that there is no human essence or nature, whereas evolutionary theory holds that human nature is in our genes. Upon closer inspection, though, it becomes clear that the human nature dictated by our genes is loose and fluid. It is not constraining in a way that would eliminate freedom. To the contrary, our genetic inclinations and limitations simply provide the context that we can interpret to make free choices. Having reconciled existentialism and evolutionary theory, the chapter considers the evolutionary evidence against moral realism and in favor of moral anti-realism. Drawing on work by Richard Joyce, Sharon Street, Alex Rosenberg, and others, the chapter argues that the best atheistic explanation for our moral feelings is evolutionary adaptation.[2] The development of moral feelings, a kind of "core morality" rooted in reciprocity, was adaptive for humans living in groups. Moral realist theories, which argue that our moral feelings track a metaphysical moral reality, are not parsimonious and are to be rejected.

Chapter 5, "Not Going to Hell in a Handbasket: Existentialism and a World without Morality," considers the options and implications for accepting moral anti-realism. Richard Joyce, a moral anti-realist, has argued in favor of "moral fictionalism" in which a person accepts morality without believing in its metaphysical reality.[3] Thus, much as we accept the action on the screen while watching a movie without believing that it is actually occurring in the real world, so too the moral fictionalist acts as if it is true that, for example, gratuitously kicking a dog is morally wrong while not really believing it. Joyce argues that such moral fictionalism can be helpful to us in taking the actions we most want to take; the relevant fictional moral propositions act as bulwarks, providing reinforcement when habits and non-moral prudence fail.

Against Joyce, chapter 5 argues that moral fictionalism is disingenuous, and, beyond that, moral fictionalism is unlikely to be effective for highly reflective people. When push comes to shove in the fray of decision making, such people will realize that they regard moral propositions as literally false, and so the propositions will not be effective as bulwarks.

Some may be concerned that a moral anti-realist unaided by moral fictionalism is apt to do the kind of harmful things that morality calls wrong. Chapter 5 argues that this concern is largely unwarranted. Yes, in getting accustomed to moral anti-realism, some people may abuse their existential freedom like the student away at college for the first time who abuses her freedom by overindulging in pleasures and underperforming in the classroom due to lack of preparation. But much as the student is likely to settle down into more responsible behavior, so too is the moral anti-realist likely to settle down into responsible behavior as dictated by non-moral prudence. Endorsing the views of Hans-Georg Moeller, the chapter argues that love and the law can largely replace the motivating role of morality.[4] It remains an open empirical question what an amoral world would look like. Opponents fear the worst, whereas some advocates, such as Ian Hinckfuss, predict that the world would likely be more peaceful and less conflict-ridden.[5] Splitting the difference, I argue that an agnostic position is warranted.

Chapter 5 concludes by endorsing a version of Joel Marks's amoralist philosophy of desirism, which counsels individuals to reflect rationally on what they, all things considered, desire, and then act to satisfy their desires.[6] The free market existentialist will rely on non-moral prudence to make decisions and take actions in accord with desirism. This prudence is itself relative to the individual and her circumstances; it fits the existentialist paradigm by working within the confines of the individual's situation and allowing for free choice, ultimately posing the question: "Can you live with it?"

The moral anti-realist is likely to be left with vestiges of her previous morality in the form of guilt, and so part of the prudential decision making will involve considering whether she can live with the guilt that follows from an action.

Chapter 6, "What's Mine Is Mine: Moral Anti-realism and Property Rights," argues that, from a moral anti-realist perspective, there are no natural rights. All rights, including property rights, are contractual, which is not to say that they are granted by the state or necessarily require the state for their protection. The chapter considers the way that property rights could develop in the state of nature, beginning with property claims that are contested, negotiated, and eventually agreed to contractually. Spontaneous development is likely to produce appropriate laws, and it will likely become attractive to leave the state of nature to obtain the stability provided by rule of law provided by government. Among other topics, the chapter considers first appropriation, the Lockean proviso, and intellectual property. While a moral anti-realist will reject any realist conception of justice, Nozick's conceptions of justice in acquisition, justice in transfer, and justice in rectification can be pragmatically agreed to, shorn of any moral realism.

She who has decided she can live without God and morality must next decide if she can live without the nanny state. The free market existentialist calls for internalizing responsibility as much as possible. Chapter 7, "Who's Afraid of the Free Market?: Moral Anti-realism and the Minimal State," thus considers the possibility of a minimal state that is restricted to protecting citizens against force, fraud, and theft. Exposing the fallacies of the scarcity mentality that characterizes the proponents of redistribution, the chapter argues for the spillover benefits of economic growth.

For the free market existentialist, capitalism provides a large array of choices and opportunities conducive to self-definition. Dealing with consumer culture may be difficult, but it is just the kind of challenge the existentialist should relish for its opportunity to exercise responsibility and to grow through challenge. Fear of the free market is just fear that people can't be trusted to think and act for themselves, a proposition that the existentialist roundly rejects along with the proposition that freedom must sometimes be restricted in the name of freedom. Because of our radical individuality, no person or persons could ever know enough about individuals and the societies they form to make good top-down decisions for all. Knowledge, as F.A. Hayek argues in "The Uses of Knowledge in Society," is widely dispersed and localized.[7]

To fund the minimal services of the minimal state, the free market existentialist rejects the income tax, arguing that it is tantamount to theft. The "equal tax" is presented as an attractive alternative. The state is conceived as a club in which members pay equal dues for equal benefits, "from each the same, to each the same." No one would be compelled to join the club, but there would potentially be adverse effects for those who were not club members. For example, others might be less likely to hire them or patronize their businesses. The minimal state is not an historical inevitability, but it is a viable option—one that ideally would be offered as a choice among liberal states that share in common the right to exit.

To begin this introduction I stood alone in the intersection of a Venn diagram, its circles representing the set of free market philosophers and the set of existentialist philosophers. In fact, the space is even lonelier than that, for I am a moral anti-realist in addition to being a libertarian and an existentialist. So there are actually three circles. While historically there have been some existentialists who arguably were moral anti-realists, I know of none but myself living today. And I know of no other libertarians who are moral anti-realists. So I find myself alone where the three circles overlap, and I worry that it is not a Venn diagram that I have drawn in my mind, but instead a target on my back. I realize that I do not have a popular view, but I do not think that I am terminally unique. My conjunction of commitments is logically possible and, I hope, philosophically attractive.

In closing this introduction I should say something about my writing style. This book is intended to be of interest to both a scholarly audience and a general audience. For that reason, some parts are more formal and others are more informal. Not all parts will necessarily be of interest to all readers, and so you should feel free to skip parts that do not suit your interest. I hope that by the end of the book you will join me in the intersection of the Venn diagram, or, if not, that at least you won't think that I *deserve* to be alone. I hope to start a conversation, not to conclude an argument.

Notes

1 John de Graaf, David Waan, and Thomas H. Naylor, *Affluenza: The All-Consuming Epidemic* (San Francisco: Berrett-Koehler Publishers, 2001), p. 2.

2 Richard Joyce, *The Evolution of Morality* (Cambridge: MIT Press, 2007); Sharon Street, "A Darwinian Dilemma for Realist Theories of Value," *Philosophical Studies* 127 (2006): 109–66; Alex Rosenberg, *The Atheist's Guide to Reality: Enjoying Life without Illusions* (New York: Norton, 2011).

3 Richard Joyce, *The Myth of Morality* (Cambridge: Cambridge University Press, 2001), pp. 206–31.

4 Hans-Georg Moeller, *The Moral Fool: A Case for Amorality* (New York: Columbia University Press, 2009).

5 Ian Hinckfuss, *The Moral Society—Its Structure and Effects* (1987). http://philosophy.ru/lib/fortext/fortext_2075.html.

6 Joel Marks, *Ethics without Morals: A Defense of Amorality* (New York: Routledge, 2013).

7 F.A. Hayek, "The Uses of Knowledge in Society," *American Economic Review* 35 (1945): 519–30.

1

"Out, out, Brief Candle!"

What Do You Mean by Existentialism?

"Let us imagine a number of men in chains, and all condemned to death, where some are killed each day in the sight of the others, and those who remain see their own fate in that of their fellows and wait their turn, looking at each other sorrowfully and without hope. It is an image of the condition of men."[1]

Blaise Pascal, *Pensées*

Existentialism and free market thinking are not often found together, and so I have met with some disbelief when I have proposed combining them.[2] The strength of the connection between the two depends on the conception of existentialism. The aim of this chapter is thus to articulate my account of existentialism, which is an atheistic and highly individualistic, rather than social, philosophy. I do not seek to defend my account of existentialism or my interpretation of particular existentialists against competing accounts, nor do I attempt to establish the truth of my account. The aim of this chapter is

The Free Market Existentialist: Capitalism without Consumerism, First Edition. William Irwin.
© 2015 John Wiley & Sons, Ltd. Published 2015 by John Wiley & Sons, Ltd.

predominantly explanatory, not argumentative. The relevant arguments come in chapters 2 and 3. The existentialist I describe may be a figure in whom you recognize yourself or others, but even if you do not, the description will serve as the foundation for the larger project of this book, namely articulating and defending free market existentialism.

Defining Existentialism

Those who do not appreciate existentialism often seek to dismiss it as a passing fad or a moment in time characteristic of post-war France. This is misguided. Existentialism crystallizes an insight or impulse that has always been with us to recognize the importance of individual, lived, concrete experience. We see this tendency in many places, from the Old Testament books of *Job* and *Ecclesiastes* to elements of Buddhism and stoicism, to Pascal, to Shakespeare, and beyond. In my view, existentialism is expressed hauntingly in Macbeth's musing:

> Out, out, brief candle!
> Life's but a walking shadow, a poor player
> That struts and frets his hour upon the stage
> And then is heard no more. It is a tale
> Told by an idiot, full of sound and fury
> Signifying nothing.[3]

Not all existentialists have been as gloomy and pessimistic as Macbeth at that moment, but human beings from any time or place could comprehend the significance of this image: the absurdity, the meaninglessness, the deception, the pointless striving, the anxiety, the despair, the urgency, and the sense of ever-impending death.[4]

Existentialism resists definition because there is nothing essential that the philosophers and artists grouped together as existentialists share in common. Indeed, existentialism is best thought of as a family resemblance concept with an overlapping set of characteristics but no necessary or sufficient conditions.

If there were an existentialist's club, no one would join.[5] Existentialists aren't joiners; they're individualists. And they certainly don't like labels, including "existentialist." Nearly all the philosophers who are usually considered existentialists did not accept the label at one point. Two of the major figures we will consider, Søren Kierkegaard and Friedrich Nietzsche, pre-date the term and are often referred to as forerunners or fathers or grandfathers of existentialism rather than as existentialists themselves. Martin Heidegger purposely disavowed the existentialist label, and Albert Camus saw himself as being in opposition to existentialism. Jean-Paul Sartre rejected the label at first before later accepting it. Among the big four of existentialism—Kierkegaard, Nietzsche, Heidegger, and Sartre—only Sartre can unquestionably be called an existentialist. Labeling any of the other three as an existentialist will result in a scholarly fight, and even Sartre's relationship to existentialism is ambiguous. As I will argue in chapter 2, Sartre's adoption of Marxism after the publication of *Being and Nothingness* sits in uncomfortable tension with the existentialism articulated in his *magnum opus*.

Clearly, whatever I claim existentialism is will meet with disagreement. Because my aim is not primarily historical, nor to articulate what is common to the canonical existentialists, but rather to present a view that I want to advance and apply in subsequent chapters, I will start with a definition that I will unpack briefly here and in more detail throughout the chapter. This is a definition that highlights elements of existentialism that I find appealing and that fit with my project of defending the free market. Please note that this definition does not attempt to specify a set of necessary and sufficient conditions. Without further ado, here it is: Existentialism is a philosophy that reacts to an apparently absurd or meaningless world by urging the individual to overcome alienation, oppression, and despair through freedom and self-creation in order to become a genuine person.

To say the world is absurd is to say with Camus that it defies our hopes and expectations. Truly speaking, as Camus notes, it is our relationship to the world that is absurd, not the world itself. "The world in itself is not reasonable, that is all that can be said. But what is absurd is the confrontation of this irrational and … wild longing for clarity whose call echoes in the human heart. The absurd depends as much on man as on the world."[6] We are thus called to make an adjustment, to recognize the world for what it is and to not expect it to be anything else. The world is not hostile, but the world is meaningless, at least for the atheistic existentialist who sees the world and life itself as being without pre-given meaning.[7]

Existentialism speaks to the individual rather than to the group.[8] Dealing with absurdity and meaninglessness is an individual endeavor. The individual seeks to overcome alienation, the sense of being "other," of being excluded, of being not at home. The existentialist response to alienation is not to join a group but to create the self. The individual seeks to overcome oppression, the feeling that others are keeping you down or controlling you. Again, the existentialist response is not to join the oppressors, nor is it necessarily to join together with others against the oppressors. It is to refuse to be oppressed; it is akin to the stoics' assertion of the freedom of one's own mind.

The individual seeks to overcome despair. In Kierkegaardian terms, Hubert Dreyfus says, "Despair is the feeling that life isn't working out for you and, given the kind of person you are, it is impossible for things to work for you; that a life worth living is, in your case, literally impossible."[9] Existentialism does not glorify despair. Rather, it recognizes despair as a common part of the human experience, urging us to overcome it. Again, the key to overcoming is freedom and self-creation. I do not need to be who I have been or who others have defined me as. Instead, I need to be a genuine person, what existentialists call authentic. This means someone who takes responsibility for his or her free actions and the self he or she creates. We will say more about the authentic ideal later.

Inspired by Heidegger, Sartre famously defined existentialism as the doctrine that existence precedes essence.[10] In other words, unlike many things, which have their essence pre-given, human beings construct and create their own essence through their free choices. So, for example, a tree has its essence or nature set by its DNA, and a teapot has its essence or nature set by its manufacturer.[11] According to Sartre, we are radically free because we are unconstrained by an essence. Sartre, though, is too extreme in his denial of a human nature, not properly recognizing the limitations that biology places on human nature. As we will see and discuss in chapter 4, this is a way in which his existentialism needs to be revised and brought into line with science, particularly concerning evolution, which gives humans a loose-fitting nature.

13

Concrete Individual Existence

Philosophy has a tendency to get caught up in abstract concepts and unlikely thought experiments while forgetting concrete lived existence. Here the existentialist connection with literature and other arts is salutary for its attempt to depict and describe human experience. Existentialism recognizes the validity and importance of first-person experience. Each existing individual experiences the world differently, and the differences can be as important, or more important, than detached, objective, scientific description and analysis. Ironically, in describing what it is like for me to exist as an individual, something universal is communicated, namely the uniqueness of our individual experiences and the sense in which we are ultimately "alone with others."[12] No one can ever know or experience the world the way I do, and I can never know or experience the world the way another person does. We are divided by the gulf of subjectivity between us, and yet, recognizing this, we can feel some solidarity with one another. We are inescapably locked up in ourselves, yet we are social creatures who inevitably interact with others and are concerned with the way others think and feel and the way others perceive us.[13]

Sartre takes "the look" of the other, the way the other makes me a thing with his stare, to be such a strong experience as to erase any doubt as to whether other people have minds like ours; their minds are felt in our experience. The other person attempts to define me, and the other person also attempts to compel me to accept his or her own self-definition. I respond in kind. Hence the nature of interpersonal relationship is conflict: "Hell is other people."[14] Yet we do not want to be completely alone; we want recognition and validation from others. This is one of the many elements of ambivalence in the human condition. Other people—can't live with 'em, can't live without 'em.

Sartre says, "But, given that man is free and that there is no human nature for me to depend on, I can not count on men whom I do not know by relying on human goodness or man's concern for the good of society."[15] This line from the 1946 public lecture "Existentialism Is a Humanism" is aimed at Marxism. Shortly after this, however, Sartre became a Marxist, albeit an unorthodox one, and began to view the issue of freedom and others differently. In chapter 2 we will examine Sartre's changes in detail.

Kierkegaard's greatest contribution to existentialism was his recognition that philosophy had become so abstract as to lose sight of the existing individual. A map posted in a park that doesn't have a locator saying "you are here" can be practically useless. Likewise, an abstract metaphysical system that does not locate the existing individual is useless. Along these lines, existentialism validates the archetypal storyline of the hero's journey of self-discovery. The individual finds the confines of her upbringing to be constricting or absurd. With some level of awakening or realization, she must leave or reject what was familiar to her and face new challenges. In the process she discovers or creates her true identity, and ultimately she returns home to tell those she left what she has discovered. Thus Kierkegaard both loves and hates his native Copenhagen. He finds its institutional Christianity to be stifling and un-Christian. In the course of his journey of self-discovery he enters a deeply personal and paradoxical relationship with the divine and breaks his engagement with Regine Olsen. Although he leaves Copenhagen for a short time, he returns and taunts his fellow citizens as a gadfly.

The self-discovery is not enough; it must be shared. Nietzsche too, despite his solitary lifestyle, wrote to be read, wrote to provoke. So although the individual is paramount, there is an inescapable desire to communicate individuality to others, not so that they will imitate one's own individuality but so that they will seek individuality for themselves. In this way, the existentialists are *provocateurs par excellence*, and in many cases they write to be read by regular people, not just professors. Most are not dry and dusty, but, at their best, vivid and vital.

Kierkegaard reacted most directly to Hegel, but his point applies to much of Western philosophy. It had begun with Socrates among the people, ultimately facing his own execution, but from Plato onward philosophy became more and more a matter of abstract metaphysical speculation. Socratic philosophy begins with the question "What should I do?" To answer the question, it finds that it must answer the questions "What is real?" and "How can I know?" But these questions of metaphysics and epistemology become ends in themselves rather than means to the end of answering the question

"What should I do?" And answers to the question "What should I do?" are actually given as answers to the question "What should *we* do?" or "What would or should *the ideal person* do?" Kierkegaard draws us back to the very personal and individual way of answering the question "What should I do?" The answer for me will not be exactly the same as the answer for you, because we are all unique individuals who find ourselves in unique circumstances.

Although the modern age has seen the rise of individualism, it has also paradoxically seen the rise of mass society and mass culture. The result is that the individual gets swallowed up; even ways of "acting out" individually fit templates and become clichés of rebellion. Existentialism seeks to counteract that, to make a place for unique individuals. The crowd tries to suck you in. There is no grand conspiracy to obtain your conformity, but the pressure of the crowd is great nonetheless. And this is one reason why we should resist thinking of ourselves as part of a group.

God

Nathaniel Hawthorne said of Herman Melville, "He can neither believe, nor be comfortable in his unbelief; and he is too honest and courageous not to try to do one or the other."[16] To the extent that he fits this description, Melville is an existentialist. Existing in a state of doubt, uncertainty, and ambivalence about the existence of God marks his honest individual appraisal of life. An existentialist refuses to accept easy answers from a group and refuses to pretend there are no unpleasant consequences from decisions or conclusions; an existentialist recognizes undeniable personal responsibility.

Anyone who does not occasionally worry that he may be a fraud almost certainly is. Nor does the worry absolve one from the charge; one may still be a fraud, just one who rightly worries about it on occasion. Likewise, anyone who does not occasionally worry that he is wrong about the existence or non-existence of God likely has a fraudulent belief. Worry can make the belief or unbelief genuine, but alas it cannot make it correct.

Existentialists do not usually produce formal arguments for or against the existence of God. Kierkegaard had faith in the God of Christianity, but this faith was not the kind of belief that results from careful rational analysis or a weighing of the arguments for and against the existence of God. No, for Kierkegaard faith was separate from, and even opposed to, reason. Obviously, reason could not conclusively prove the existence of God. So what? According to Kierkegaard, God is not known through reason but through faith. Viewed through the lens of reason, the story of covenants, atonement, and salvation is absurd: an eternal being who is both God and man somehow enters time and space to save humanity. Of course that doesn't make sense through reason, but nonetheless it can and should be believed through faith according to Kierkegaard. Faith— not some received doctrine, but an active passionate belief—tells us it is true.

Still, despite the importance of what Kierkegaard would call the subjective *how of truth*, we need to be concerned with the objective *what of truth* as well. The problem with focusing on the subjective "how of truth" is that it seems to give us permission to believe whatever we want. This is dangerous. So while I agree that it is often important to find something that one can be deeply, personally committed to, I think it is even more important to be committed to the objective *what of truth*. Without an objective orientation we will not make decisions based on accurate information. And though some objective information may seem trivial and mundane, it is crucial for making bigger, more profound decisions. That is why I part company with Kierkegaard on God.

Nietzsche and Sartre focus on the subjective sense in which we feel forlorn with the loss of God. Perhaps the day will come when people will not feel forlorn; perhaps it has even come now for some who have been raised without God or religion. But for those of us who were raised to believe in God and religion, the loss is immense. By comparison, the loss felt upon discovery that there is no Santa Claus is trivial. This is something that the New Atheists have missed. Not only does the loss of God have huge implications for morality, as we will discuss in chapter 4, but there is a great sadness that comes as well, like the sadness we feel at the death of a friend or family member. We must grieve the loss, and we will perhaps never fully overcome it.

Nietzsche and Sartre drew out the implications of the death of God, making clear that without God we are without a source of objective values. As opposed to the New Atheists like Dawkins and

Dennett, the Good Old Atheists like Nietzsche and Sartre (at least some of the time) saw the loss of God as disturbing and challenging. We cannot just pretend that life goes on in the same way without God. Values can no longer be found or discovered; without God, they have to be invented and created. Indeed, the question of what values to invent and create is a prime issue in subsequent chapters of this book.

Meaning

We can distinguish between the meaning *of* life and meaning *in* life.[17] Of course, in many cases the two are directly connected. Most religions will tell you what the meaning *of* life is (e.g., to serve God) and they will also tell you how to have meaning *in* life (e.g., how best to serve God). From my existentialist perspective, without God there is no meaning of life, but there can still be meaning in life. That is, there is no pre-given purpose to life, but there can still be things to do that make the experience of life fulfilling, rewarding, and purposeful. So, without God, life is meaningless in one sense but not necessarily in another.

In "Pyrrhus and Cineas," Simone de Beauvoir retells a story from Plutarch in which Pyrrhus is asked by his advisor Cineas what he will do after he conquers the world. Pyrrhus replies that he will rest. Cineas then asks him: why not rest now?[18] This little exchange nicely frames the existentialist approach to the meaning of life. If life has no pre-given meaning, we can only give it meaning through our own chosen goals and projects. But what is the payoff for achieving and completing those goals and projects? Presumably, satisfaction. But why not just be satisfied now? Why not "rest" content now? Perhaps some people can. Good for them. For most of us, though, a rest only feels good after exertion. It is pleasant to be tired and fall asleep at night after a hard day's work, but a day of idleness may conclude with tossing and turning in trying to fall asleep. So satisfaction does not come with the flip of a switch or as a result of changing one's mind. Satisfaction typically comes after struggle and striving. This is the existentialist answer to the meaning of life: it is whatever you choose it to be, but choosing something that forces you to struggle and grow will likely produce a greater satisfaction in its accomplishment. Struggle and effort do not convey meaning and value, but they make it easier to appreciate the meaning and value that one places on one's goals and achievements.

Nietzsche's concept of the will to power sheds light on why we do not want to rest now, rather than conquer the world first. The process matters more than the product. Even if we conquer the world we will not rest long before looking for the next challenge—perhaps the next world to conquer. Maybe it makes sense that we do not want to rest now, since we are mistaken in thinking that we will want to rest later. To be sure, we will probably rest for a moment, but it will not be long before the restlessness will stir us to action again. We do not have to buy Nietzsche's concept of the will to power in order to see this. Perhaps, though, this incessant striving itself is something to be overcome; perhaps we even need to struggle to overcome it.[19]

Free Will

Just as God and the meaning of life are subjects of concern for existentialism, so is free will.[20] If we assume a materialist worldview, then freedom of the will as traditionally conceived appears to be impossible. There is no place in the causal chain of physical things for the will to act in an uncaused way. What people have traditionally thought of as freedom of the will is impossible unless there is a non-physical soul or a non-physical mind that somehow interacts with the material universe and is itself uncaused. This view of the soul (or mind) and the will was put forward by Augustine and it was affirmed centuries later by Descartes. To this day, it is the natural assumption of most Christians. Of course, it may turn out to be correct, but everything we know about the brain suggests that it performs all the functions that were formerly attributed to the non-physical soul or mind.[21] This puts the existentialist in a strange position, for the overriding assumption of existentialism is freedom of the will.[22] It will not work to adopt a compatibilist solution, according to which the will is caused and determined and yet can be regarded as free so long as it plays a role and is not subject to coercion and constraint. This is not what has traditionally been meant by freedom of the will, and it is not the kind of freedom that

19

experience tells us we have. Rather, experience suggests that we are ultimately free in making decisions and choices.

Most of us do not experience our "selves" as caused; we experience our selves as radically free. We find ourselves in a situation in which circumstances provide reasons for acting one way, but we remain completely free to act in another way. Sartre is not a materialist.[23] According to Sartre, the self is not caused to do anything, because the self is a no-thing and only things are within the causal chain. While we might want to take issue with Sartre's ontology and reasoning, his insight fits the phenomenology of freedom. Most of us do not experience ourselves as algorithmic in our choices, as input-output functions. We experience ourselves as free to make even the most unlikely choices in all circumstances.

Strangely, even if we become convinced by the argument against freedom of the will, most of us cannot help but feel as though we nonetheless have freedom of the will. Upon reflection we may conclude that we probably have no freedom of the will, but we may still find it impossible to believe this in a way that translates into action or non-action. So, because freedom of the will is at least possible, and for the sake of remaining true to lived experience, I will assume in this book that we do have freedom of the will as traditionally understood. Pascal's Wager addresses the issue of whether or not it makes sense to bet on belief in God. We need a kind of "Pascal's Wager on Free Will." Along those lines, William James famously remarked that his first act of free will would be to believe in free will.[24] Because we cannot conclusively establish the negative conclusion that we have no freedom of the will, the door is left open to believing and acting as if we do have freedom of the will.

What would it mean to act as though one had become convinced that there is no free will? Some people imagine that the result would be to sit idly and slothfully by as the world turns. But there is no reason to think you would act that way if you did not have free will. In fact, that kind of non-action would be more indicative of a free choice to do nothing. Really, without free will you would simply act in the way that you were pre-determined to act, and that would probably not be to sit idly by. On the other hand, if you became convinced that there was no free will and you were wrong, you might freely choose to sit idly by for the most part. And that would likely be regrettable.

A fictionalist approach to free will is probably unavoidable and involuntary for most people who have become convinced that free will is impossible. Following a fictionalist account of free will, we would *accept free will* while *not believing* in free will. The upshot would be that in almost all situations we would act as if we have free will, but when we were pushed to give our answer to the theoretical, philosophical question of whether we have free will, we would respond that "no, we probably do not have free will." Yet our lack of belief would not manifest itself in action or attitude in the next moment. We would go right back to acting as if we had free will. In this sense, free-will fictionalism may be like Humean cause-and-effect fictionalism. The Humean is convinced by the arguments against cause and effect, yet she accepts cause and effect in daily life. It is only when she considers the philosophical question of whether there is cause and effect that she says "no, I don't believe there is." Right after giving this answer she returns to living as if there is cause and effect. To recap, the working assumption of this book will be that we do have free will. Free will is worth betting on despite the odds against it. For my part, even at times when I am inclined to bet against free will theoretically I find myself involuntarily engaging in free-will fictionalism.

Freedom, Responsibility, and Excuses

We live in an excuse culture. Not only are we inclined to make excuses for ourselves, but others are inclined to accept them and sometimes even make them for us. Of course, life is not easy and there are factors that provide the context for bad decisions and actions. But the pendulum has swung too far in the direction of not holding ourselves and others responsible. Because the extent to which mitigating factors are relevant is a matter we can only truly know of ourselves, responsibility needs to begin with ourselves. We may want to be kind in offering someone else the benefit of the doubt and we may want to forgive ourselves when we act regrettably, but we need to take responsibility for ourselves. We lead by example that way.

At the risk of sounding cliché, some of what is most attractive about existentialism for me is its attitude of "no excuses."[25] Other people who adopt free-will fictionalism may have a quite different reaction to the "no excuses" attitude. For me, betting on the existence of free will makes sense because there is nothing to lose and much to gain from the wager. With its uncompromising insistence on the ever-presence of freedom, the heroic view of existentialism is the freedom to say "no" even at the point of a gun. Circumstances may be difficult and conspire against us, but we always have responsibility and we never have excuses, because we are always ultimately free. Only two options are needed for freedom, and there are always at least two options. As we will discuss in greater detail in chapter 2, for Sartre freedom, in the ontological sense, does not come in degrees; there is never a decrease in ontological freedom, just an increase in the difficulty of circumstances. Having fewer good options does not make you less free in the ontological sense, only in the practical sense. It is this ontological sense of freedom that I am willing to bet on despite the case against it.

"The environment can act on the subject only to the exact extent that he comprehends it; that is, transforms it into a situation."[26] Here we see Sartre's stoicism. Of course, some circumstances give us more favorable material to work with than others, but it is still up to us to construct what we will and determine the situation we are in. We are always completely free ontologically, but our circumstances are sometimes unfortunate and act as limits to our practical freedom. Sartre thus characterizes his existentialism as a philosophy of "optimistic toughness."[27] It is a stoicism without quietism. We are not doomed or determined by our circumstances, and though life is difficult, we can make of our lives what we will.

The stoicism of existentialism is actually best encapsulated by an insight from the pragmatist William James: "My experience is what I agree to attend to."[28] We create and construct our situation by interpreting our circumstances. Of course some circumstances will force themselves on our attention like the scream of a siren, but with effort and practice we can come to choose what we will give our attention to and how we will conceive it. This is not easy, of course, but the world is one of our making, first in our minds and later in our actions that can transform the reality outside our minds. This is not to say we are unlimited in such power, but rather just to suggest that we often leave such power largely untapped.

The matter of what we agree to attend to resonates with the stoic Epictetus' judgment that it is not the man who reviles or strikes you who harms you but your own judgment that harms you.[29] Epictetus is likely sincere even if he is overstated. Likewise, so are James and Sartre. Still, it is usually better to err on the side of overestimating the extent to which we determine our own experience than to underestimate it and see ourselves as victims of a world outside our control.

Sometimes excuses take the form of a false honesty, as when a person admits with a what-can-you-do attitude that he is lazy or cowardly or impatient or whatever. Sartre argues, though, that no one is any of those things in a fixed sense, and we all have the freedom to change ourselves and act against the tendencies we have developed. In fact, however, most people don't want freedom. As Dostoevsky brilliantly illustrated in his story of "The Grand Inquisitor" in *The Brothers Karamazov*, people would prefer to have most decisions made for them; they want simple rules to obey. People want to pretend that they have roles to play that bind them. They engage in Sartrean bad faith, acting as if they really were a teacher, student, waiter, or bus driver in the way a rock is a rock. It is a subtle self-deception by which they focus on an undeniable aspect of themselves, namely that they are in the role of teacher, waiter, or what-have-you while conveniently ignoring the fact that they are not just that role. They ignore the fact they are free and can make choices not in conformity with the expectations for the role they are playing.

We are, as Sartre says, "condemned to be free."[30] We have a purpose or plan only to the extent that we give it to ourselves. This can all be too much to bear. We would often like to hide from or deny our freedom, and in bad faith this is precisely what we do. To be clear, this is different from involuntary free-will fictionalism in which the fictionalism is not consciously chosen. Even when there is a conscious choice to hide from freedom in bad faith, it is a free choice; we can never escape it. Freedom is something to be sought and celebrated, but it is also a heavy burden.

In *The Ethics of Ambiguity* Beauvoir nicely observes that we are all free, but some of us, perhaps most of us, do not fully recognize and act on our freedom. We hide from our freedom to one extent or another. The existentialist ideal is to recognize our full freedom, choose a goal or project, and struggle to achieve it. While political action may be important and helpful in securing for people practical freedom from the oppression of others, it is also important to wake people up to the freedom they already have in all circumstances, the freedom to choose and to act.

In *The Second Sex*, Beauvoir famously says that "One is not born, but rather becomes woman."[31] With the passage of time and social progress, this has become obvious, but it continues to express the fundamental existentialist insight that existence precedes essence. No one can force you to be or live a certain way based on the genitalia you are born with. Society, though, will try to force you, however gently or subtly, into certain roles. Here, it is possible to resist. The temptation may be to drift along with what is expected of you, but you remain free to make yourself, to create your essence through your own free choices.

Compared to Sartre and Beauvoir, Heidegger is much more constrained in his view of freedom, depicting us as thrown into a world that constricts our possibilities. In *The Jerk*, Steve Martin's title character tells us, "I was born a poor black child." Well, he was born poor, but much to his dismay it turns out that he is not black, never was, never will be. There are things about us that we cannot change; our race is one example. Likewise, some possibilities are closed off to us. Given my age, height, and lack of athletic ability, it is not a genuine possibility that I may some day play in the NBA. Nor will I ever be a court jester—since no such jobs are available in our day and age. Sartre believes we have the *freedom to try*, though not the *freedom* to *succeed*. So I do have the freedom to try to become an NBA player even though I have no real chance of succeeding; likewise, I have the freedom to jump out the window and flap my arms in an attempt to fly. My ontological freedom is unlimited no matter how limited my practical freedom is. Despite his hyperbole, Sartre is closer to the truth and certainly more inspiring than Heidegger. The temptation is great to rule out possibilities based on circumstances. Think of the young person who lacks the confidence to pursue a career in medicine. No short, unathletic, middle-aged man needs to be told that he will not succeed in making it to the NBA, and no sane person needs to be told that he will not succeed if he tries to fly from the window by flapping his arms. But many young people may need to be told that they can make a career in medicine (or some other field) if they apply themselves and persevere.

Maurice Merleau-Ponty criticized Sartre for his conception of absolute freedom, which suggests that even physical disabilities do not limit our freedom. Of course, in a way they do. They limit our practical freedom, though not our ontological freedom. No blind person is ever going to play major league baseball, but Sartre would respond that blind people are still free to try. For Sartre, we are limited by our facticity, the sum of all facts that are true of us. But we remain free to interpret our facticity and thus construct the situation in which we find ourselves. It is along these lines that Sartre hyperbolically says that "the slave in chains is as free as his master."[32] And it is in this way that existentialism is a kind of empowered stoicism. Rather than counseling resignation and acceptance à la stoicism, existentialism à la Sartre urges us to be bold and to refuse to see our facticity as limiting, as much as it is enabling, calling for us to react to life's pain and difficulty with creativity. Nietzsche likewise argues that Greek tragedy resulted, in part, from the reaction to life's pain and difficulty. The response is not one of despair or resignation but rather of creativity, as the oyster makes a pearl in response to irritation and infection. Certainly this is a more optimistic and more welcome message than we get from the recognition of limitations in Heidegger and Merleau-Ponty.

In addition to "no excuses," another resonant existentialist maxim is "get over it." Existentialism is a philosophy of action, not of wallowing in despair. For the existentialist, there is always something to complain about and bemoan, but there is no value in despair, only in overcoming despair. "Get over it" is not a mere platitude. Implicit in the injunction is acceptance that life is not fair. "That's not fair" is one of the first complaints that children learn to make, but of course, life really is not fair, as reflected in the retort "Whoever told you that life was fair?" We may struggle to make things as fair as possible but we will never succeed fully. Life is what you make of what you have in the place that you are. It is not about what you could have done if you had different assets or opportunities in a different situation. What did you actually do? That is all that matters. As Sartre says, "A man is involved in life, leaves his impress on it, and outside of that there is nothing."[33]

Anguish

Choices made today will have effects long after tomorrow, and most significant choices cannot be made with certainty of their effects. In fact many choices must be made in the midst of deep uncertainty as to their long-term effects. It is partly for this reason that existentialism puts a premium on the subjective quality of one's beliefs. It's not that truth is subjective, but that things worth believing, choosing, and risking require some passion.

Sartre conceives of consciousness as nothingness, implying the dictum that "existence precedes essence." The self does not pre-exist but must be created, an idea intimately tied to Sartre's radical freedom. My actions do not result from decisions of a self in the cause and effect fashion of objects in the world. For Sartre, there are never motives *in* consciousness, but only *for* consciousness.[34] This means that consciousness can choose to act on those motives or not; it is not driven or caused by them. Anguish starts with consciousness of this freedom. I am in anguish when I recognize that the decision and action I am about to make and initiate is not caused or determined by my past. Hence we get Sartre's famous example of the gambler in anguish. He has resolved to gamble no more, but when he is confronted with the gambling table he realizes that the past resolution has no binding or causal power. He must freely decide again to gamble or not.[35] Sartre's other paradigmatic example of anguish involves the realization that I am free to fling myself from the precipice on which I am walking. I fear that the precipice may crumble and so I may fall, but I have anguish concerning what I may do with my own freedom.[36] Anguish, therefore, is not just consciousness of my freedom but fear of what I may do with it.

Choices are inevitable, as even the failure to choose is tantamount to a choice. So to avoid the anguish that comes with the inevitability of choice we adopt conventional morality and develop habits. Both routes allow us to operate on automatic pilot and pretend that there is no choice to be made. Habit is particularly powerful when built into a routine, which is described by the character Odintsova in Turgenev's *Fathers and Sons* as being indispensable for life in the country.[37] Habit and routine allow one to pretend that certain things simply have to be done, thus avoiding anguish by concealing choice. Likewise, conventional morality and manners tell our id

26

and impulses that our desires are simply unacceptable, out of the question, and thus easily dismissed. Take away conventional morality and manners, and we are left confronting our own freedom and worrying that we may make a choice that will bring pleasure in the moment but bring pain in the long run.

This desire to avoid anguish can also be seen in the desire to construct a fixed and stable identity. If I can simply tell myself that I am a father and a father takes care of his children, then certain temptations are disqualified. But, of course, Sartre's reply is that I am not a father, not in the way a pen is a pen. I have no fixed and stable nature; I simply pretend to for the sake of minimizing anguish. Thankfully we are not always in a state of anguish. We sometimes avoid anguish through bad faith in which we deny our freedom and conceive of ourselves as things with a fixed and stable nature. But more often we are not in anguish because we are absorbed in the world. We are not self-reflectively aware. In Sartre's example, no self inhabits my experience of running to catch a streetcar. My consciousness is simply absorbed by the streetcar and the task of catching it.[38] We will say more about absorption shortly.

Authenticity

Authenticity is a kind of genuineness, a taking responsibility for oneself and one's actions; it is being the real thing. But because there is no such thing as the real thing, authenticity is particularly difficult. To feel comfortable in one's genuineness or authenticity is almost certainly to lack it. Rather, it exists in a perpetually uneasy state. In fact, recognizing our own limitations and shortcomings with regard to self-knowledge is part of being authentic. Much of our decision making is unconscious and is just rationalized after the fact by consciousness. There is more to us beneath the surface than above, but we can make and tame the self. The self never becomes a fixed and stable entity, but it can become a creation, a useful subjective creation like values.

Authenticity is aided by having a good nose for the truth and for authenticity in others. Being authentic is no easy task. One can easily take it too far and use authenticity as an excuse for saying or doing whatever one wants. But that is not authenticity as much as it is ugly self-centeredness. Authenticity requires that you be yourself. For some people that may mean being vulgar, uncensored, and unrefined. But simply imitating such people because they are authentic in their vulgarity is not necessarily authentic in its own right; in fact it most likely is inauthentic. Authenticity involves being, and making yourself a person who is true to herself. In Nietzsche's terms, the authentic person makes herself a work of art, not by performing to meet some image of herself but by becoming who she is and giving style to her character.[39] In that sense, authenticity is a matter of dignity and integrity in facing the facts about life and the world and resolving to take responsibility and make the best of the situation. It is about resisting the constant temptation to deceive ourselves and hide the truth.

Absorption

In his famous retelling of the myth of Sisyphus, Camus concludes by instructing us to imagine Sisyphus happy. This perplexes many readers. After all, Camus has just described Sisyphus as being subject to the gods' pointless punishment of rolling a rock up a hill every day only to have it roll back down again. There is no greater purpose served by rolling the rock up the hill. Like the child's punishment of writing lines on the blackboard, part of the punishment is its pointlessness. And unlike the child's punishment, this one can never be completed. Nor is there any great satisfaction to take in a job well done. So how can Sisyphus be happy? Camus tells us that "the struggle itself toward the heights is enough to fill a man's heart."[40] That he has a task, that he has something to do, even if it is not profound or objectively purposeful, is all that Sisyphus needs to get started. Sisyphus has an activity to commit to and to re-conceive as meaningful. And if anything is characteristic of existentialism it is the importance of our ability to re-conceive our circumstances and make our situations meaningful. We imagine not that Sisyphus tricks himself into thinking that he is doing something grand or elevated in rolling the rock but rather that he finds the activity absorbing. The existentialist must find the proper balance of reflection and absorption.[41]

One must reflect on life because "the unexamined life is not worth living," but one cannot reflect on life all the time because the constantly examined life is unlivable. One must discover activities that one finds absorbing. Having a commitment to a God, political party, or basketball team can be helpful in becoming so focused on a certain activity that one becomes absorbed in the activity and loses sight of oneself. That kind of experience of flow, or "being in the zone," is not itself pleasurable but it is rewarding and gratifying. Indeed, it is a large part of what makes life worth living.

In a life without obstacles to overcome through struggle, we would become soft and unhappy. A test of skill focuses attention and produces absorption in the task at hand. While Nietzsche emphasizes this need for obstacles and struggle, he can be balanced by Camus' insight that we need to come to accept "the gentle indifference of the world."[42] In truth, the world is not out to get us, not trying to throw obstacles in our way. The world is not absurd; it only appears to be. Rather, our interaction with the world is absurd—and only when we make demands and place expectations upon it. So there is subjective value in the struggle, and Camus' Sisyphus testifies to this in his happy rolling of the rock. We do ourselves a disservice when we see the world as alien and hostile. Our struggles are often of our own making, but we need our struggles. Sisyphus cannot be happy through resignation, but only through engagement and absorption.

Conclusion

This chapter began with my definition of existentialism as a philosophy that reacts to an apparently absurd or meaningless world by urging the individual to overcome alienation, oppression, and despair through freedom and self-creation in order to become a genuine person. Individual responsibility was highlighted throughout the discussion that followed. This account of existentialism will serve as the basis for the arguments of subsequent chapters, beginning in chapter 2 with the argument that individualistic existentialism does not fit well with Marxism.

Notes

1. Blaise Pascal, *Pensées*, trans. W.F. Trotter (New York: Modern Library, 1941), section 199.
2. To her credit, Hazel E. Barnes considers Ayn Rand's objectivism at length and notes some of the parallels with existentialism in *An Existentialist Ethics* (New York: Vintage, 1967), pp. 124–49.
3. *Macbeth*, act 5, scene 5.
4. David Detmer rejects this gloomy and pessimistic view of existentialism in *Sartre Explained: From Bad Faith to Authenticity* (Chicago: Open Court, 2008), pp. 55–7.
5. I owe this line to Jeremy Wisnewski.
6. Albert Camus, *The Myth of Sisyphus and Other Essays*, trans. Justin O'Brien (New York: Vintage International, 1991), p. 21.
7. This is Sartre's position in some places but not in others. See Detmer, pp. 7–9.
8. Here and throughout this chapter I do not mean the technical sense in which the later Sartre uses "group" as opposed to "series," which we will discuss in chapter 2.
9. Hubert Dreyfus, "'What a Monster then Is Man': Pascal and Kierkegaard on Being a Contradictory Self and What to Do about It," in Steven Crowell, ed., *The Cambridge Companion to Existentialism* (Cambridge: Cambridge University Press, 2012), p. 102.
10. Jean-Paul Sartre, *Existentialism*, trans. Bernard Frechtman (New York: Philosophical Library, 1947), p. 15.
11. Sartre acknowledges that there are Christian existentialists and atheistic existentialists, but the definition he gives would not fit all Christian existentialists comfortably. Some Christian existentialists would believe that God gives human beings their essence—an essence that would include free will.
12. I borrow this phrase from Stephen Batchelor, *Alone with Others: An Existential Approach to Buddhism* (New York: Grove Press, 1983).
13. The account in this paragraph would be true for some existentialists but probably not for Sartre at all times. See Detmer, pp. 181–5.
14. Jean-Paul Sartre, *No Exit and Three Other Plays* (New York: Vintage International, 1989), p. 45. Strictly speaking, it is the character Garcin who says this, but on my interpretation the view fits pretty well with Sartre's view of interpersonal relationships. For a different interpretation see Detmer, pp. 149–53.
15. Sartre, *Existentialism*, p. 36.
16. George Cotkin, *Existential America* (Baltimore: Johns Hopkins University Press, 2003), p. 17.

17 Jonathan Haidt, *The Happiness Hypothesis: Finding Modern Truth in Ancient Wisdom* (New York: Basic Books, 2007), pp. 217–19. Actually, Haidt's terms are "purpose of life" and "purpose within life."

18 Simone de Beauvoir, "Pyrrhus and Cineas," in *Simone de Beauvoir: Philosophical Writings*, ed. and trans. Margaret A. Simons and Sylvie Le Bon de Beauvoir (Urbana: University of Illinois Press, 2004), p. 90.

19 Thus, on a Buddhist interpretation of existentialism, meaning in life is not a matter of getting a sudden revelation or epiphany but of working hard to discipline oneself so that one no longer craves or desires, and so no longer becomes attached, and so no longer suffers. And inasmuch as Nietzsche respects the achievements of saints and ascetics, perhaps this interpretation is appropriate.

20 Even though concepts of the will vary and Sartre avoided the term "free will."

21 David Kyle Johnson, "Do Souls Exist?" *Think* 35 (2013): 61–75.

22 Nietzsche is an important exception. See, among other places, *Beyond Good and Evil* (New York: Vintage, 1989), section 21.

23 For a different view, see Hazel E. Barnes, "Sartre as Materialist," in Paul Arthur Schilpp, ed., *The Philosophy of Jean-Paul Sartre* (La Salle, Illinois: Open Court, 1981), pp. 661–84.

24 William James, from an entry in his diary for April 30, 1870, quoted by Ralph Barton Perry, *The Thought and Character of William James*, "Briefer Version," (Cambridge: Harvard University Press, 1948), p. 121.

25 Sartre, *Existentialism*, p. 27.

26 Jean-Paul Sartre, *Being and Nothingness*, trans. Hazel Barnes (New York: Washington Square Press, 1956), p. 731 (hereafter BN).

27 Sartre, *Existentialism*, p. 40.

28 William James, *The Principles of Psychology* (New York: Henry Holt and Company, 1890), p. 402.

29 Epictetus, *Enchiridion*, chapter 20.

30 Sartre, *Existentialism*, p. 27.

31 Simone de Beauvoir, *The Second Sex*, trans. Constance Borde and Sheila Malovany-Chevallier (New York: Alfred A. Knopf, 2009), p. 283.

32 BN, p. 703.

33 Sartre, *Existentialism*, p. 39.

34 BN, p. 71.

35 BN, pp. 69–70.

36 Cf. BN, pp. 65–8.

37 Ivan Turgenev, *Fathers and Sons*, trans. Richard Freeborn (Oxford: Oxford University Press, 2008), p. 90.

38 Jean-Paul Sartre, *The Transcendence of the Ego*, trans. Forrest Williams and Robert Kirkpatrick (New York: Hill and Wang, 1957), pp. 48–9.

39   *The Gay Science,* trans. Walter Kaufmann (New York: Vintage, 1974), section 290.

40   Camus, *The Myth of Sisyphus and Other Essays,* p. 123.

41   This is roughly the theme of Robert C. Solomon's *Dark Feelings, Grim Thoughts: Experience and Reflection in Camus and Sartre* (Oxford: Oxford University Press, 2006).

42   *The Stranger,* trans. Matthew Ward (New York: Vintage, 1989), p. 120.

2

Like Cigarettes and Existentialism

Why There Is no Necessary Connection between Marxism and Sartre

Jean-Paul Sartre, the person most identified with existentialism, became a Marxist after the publication of his most famous work, *Being and Nothingness*. These days the connection between Sartrean existentialism and Marxism has come to be taken for granted. This chapter argues, though, that the Marxism of the later Sartre is not a good fit with the existentialism of *Being and Nothingness*. In particular, Sartre's adoption of Marxism required a shift in his view of freedom. The negative work of this chapter in showing that existentialism and Marxism do not necessarily go together is in preparation for making a positive connection between existentialism and capitalism in chapter 3. My point is not that Sartre really should have embraced the free market. That is an individual decision that only he could have made for himself. My point is rather that my interpretation of Sartre's early philosophy yields a distinctly existentialist position that does not sit comfortably with Marxism and that does, as we will see in the next chapter, fit well with the free market.

The Free Market Existentialist: Capitalism without Consumerism, First Edition. William Irwin.
© 2015 John Wiley & Sons, Ltd. Published 2015 by John Wiley & Sons, Ltd.

The Early Sartre on Freedom and Responsibility

For the early Sartre, by which I mean the Sartre up to *Being and Nothingness* and shortly thereafter, freedom and responsibility are absolute and individual. Just as he says I am "condemned to be free,"[1] Sartre also says "I am condemned to be wholly responsible for myself."[2] Circumstances do not determine my actions. Rather, "The environment can act on the subject only to the exact extent that he comprehends it; that is, transforms it into a situation."[3] For Sartre, responsibility means that I am "the incontestable author of an event or of an object."[4] I am an author—I give meaning in making choices. "For human reality, to exist is always to *assume* its being; that is, to be responsible for it instead of receiving it from outside like a stone."[5] I choose the meaning of my world even though I do not cause everything in my world to happen. Sartre thus says, "the peculiar character of human-reality is that it is without excuse."[6] Responsibility does not come in degrees.[7] I am always fully responsible for my actions and the meaning I give my world—I cannot blame society, economic forces, or circumstances. For Sartre, even the person who gave in under torture was free in his choice to do so, "He has *determined* the moment at which the pain became unbearable."[8]

For the early Sartre, the burden of responsibility cannot be lifted by joining with others. Speaking in response to Marxists, in "Existentialism Is a Humanism," Sartre says, "given that man is free and that there is no human nature for me to depend on, I can not count on men whom I do not know by relying on human goodness or man's concern for the good of society."[9] In *Being and Nothingness* Sartre criticizes Heidegger for taking *Mitsein*, being-with-others, as original, and individual existence as derivative.[10] Beyond that, Sartre says that "the essence of the relations between consciousnesses is not the *Mitsein*; it is conflict."[11] In *No Exit* the character Garcin renders this insight memorably and poetically, declaring that "Hell is other people."[12] Conflict is thus at the heart of human relations.[13]

Sartre's views of the "other" would suggest an opposition to socialism: If hell is other people, then how can heaven be socialism? For the early Sartre, it couldn't be. As he says, "I was never in favor of a socialist society before 1939."[14] *Nausea*, published in 1938, is not kind to socialism in its portrayal of the socialist self-taught man, who turns out to be a pedophile. To be sure, *Nausea* is not kind to the bourgeoisie either, but the novel is certainly not a critique of bourgeois society. Roquentin, Annie, and the self-taught man are all bohemians of a sort, and they come off badly. Their troubles are not caused by capitalism and bourgeois society but by the human condition and the ways they respond to it.

Although *Being and Nothingness* was published in 1943, Thomas Flynn says of Sartre that "if his experience in the army and in the prisoner-of-war camp taught him the importance of social solidarity, he was still in thrall to the individualist ontology he was formulating in *Being and Nothingness*."[15] Mark Poster explains that "during the 1930s, when *Being and Nothingness* was worked out, Sartre was an apolitical literateur: he did not vote; he attended demonstrations only infrequently and then never sang or shouted slogans; he considered the political tracts of others as 'pointless propaganda.'"[16]

As Poster says, "Even after the experience of the Resistance and the German POW camps Sartre was still the atomized bourgeois who regarded dependence on others as a loss of freedom."[17] Sartre's words of criticism for socialism and Marxism were mild. By contrast, contemporary Marxists were harsh in their critique of his existentialism. As Raymond Aron encapsulates it, "The party of the Revolution pours scorn on the descendants of Kierkegaard, Nietzsche or Kafka as the intellectual jeremiahs of a bourgeoisie which cannot console itself for the death of God because it is so conscious of its own death."[18] It is not the human condition that brings on angst, for the Marxists, but rather social conditions. Facing criticism that it was a bourgeois luxury to sit around cafés bemoaning the death of God and the loss of meaning when there were real people suffering as a result of social injustice, Sartre was eventually "converted" to Marxism by Maurice Merleau-Ponty.[19]

Sartre's conversion was not welcomed by Marxists, however, as he rejected dialectical materialism and preserved a place for individual freedom. Thomas Flynn tells us that "Roger Garaudy, then reigning philosopher of the French Communist party, dismissed Sartre's existentialism as 'voluntaristic idealism' because, in the present-past relationship, it gives priority to the present. The true Marxist perspective, according to Garaudy, requires 'that project be subordinated to situation as superstructure to base.'"[20] In general, Marxists saw Sartre's existentialism as articulated in *Being and Nothingness* as self-indulgent, bourgeois individualism, and they were not willing to reconcile and find a place for him. For example, the Marxist Georg Lukács says "Above all, one thing must be made clear: freedom does *not* mean freedom of the individual."[21] As Flynn says concerning Lukács, "Such a conception [Sartre's], in his [Lukács's] view, is bourgeois and egotistical."[22]

If there is anything that Sartre, as a French intellectual, would want to avoid being labeled, it is "bourgeois." And one can see why a Marxist like Lukács would potentially label Sartre's view of freedom in *Being and Nothingness* as bourgeois.[23] After all, it locates all freedom and responsibility in the individual. This is precisely what the bourgeois shopkeeper celebrates under capitalism, the right and responsibility of producers and consumers to freely make trades and take responsibility for those trades in the free market.

So in converting to Marxism one would expect Sartre to reject his earlier existentialism. Sartre's existentialist predecessors including Kierkegaard, Nietzsche, and Heidegger show no sympathy for socialism. And for that matter, the early Sartre shows no sympathy either. As he says,

> Before the war I considered myself simply as an individual. I was not aware of any ties between my individual existence and the society I was living in. At the time I graduated from the École Normale, I had based an entire theory on that feeling. I was the "solitary man" (*l'homme seul*), an individual who opposes society through the independence of his thinking but who owes nothing to society and whom society cannot affect, because he is free. That was the evidence on which I based all that I thought, all that I wrote and all that I lived before 1939.[24]

So why did Sartre turn to socialism? Later in this chapter, I shall argue that the association of existentialism and socialism is primarily a historico-cultural accident of post-war France. For now, though, we must note that the Marxist Sartre did not completely reject his earlier existentialism. Instead he attempted to reconcile the two views, and it is to that attempted reconciliation that we must turn.

A New View of Responsibility and Capitalism

Sartre did not accept Marxism in its totality. Rather, in producing the synthesis called Marxist existentialism, he preserved a place for individual freedom. Sartre's experience in the war seems to have shifted his attention in a communal direction. Flynn describes Sartre as "the lonely thinker, apostle of individual responsibility, for whom the Other's existence was man's original fall, gradually discovering in the contingencies of history the need and the joy of communal action."[25] Even in his Marxist period Sartre says, "it is men whom we judge not physical forces."[26] So, for Sartre, *we are responsible* does not mean that *I am not responsible.*[27]

Regarding colonialism and capitalism, Sartre concluded that "the meanness is in the system."[28] A particular person may not be mean in his own actions within the capitalist system, but to the extent that he supports capitalism, which encourages meanness, the particular person is complicit and blameworthy. As Sartre says, "to wish to better only oneself ... is indicative of bourgeois, atomistic thought, which is ready to sacrifice others to oneself."[29] Flynn describes Sartre's notion of collective responsibility, saying "we are condemned to a responsibility which surpasses our individual actions, yet each must bear the burden himself."[30] So even though we are not the sole cause of a bad effect, we are nonetheless on our own in shouldering responsibility for it.

Alienation is said to be all-pervasive under capitalism, and so Sartre believes liberating the exploited and oppressed will also liberate the exploiters and oppressors.[31] Aron says that for Sartre the human being is "at once the victim and prisoner of scarcity, which makes every individual his neighbor's enemy."[32] So for Sartre, under capitalism we are in a situation much like a Hobbesian state of nature. But whereas Hobbes's solution is the leviathan, Sartre's solution is Marxism.

The individual must recognize the conditioning effects that capitalism has upon him, and yet the individual must still take responsibility for who he is and resolve to work for change. As Sartre says of the individual, "totally conditioned by his class, his salary, the nature of his work, conditioned in his very feelings and thoughts, it is he who freely gives to the proletariat a future of relentless humiliation or [one] of conquest and victory, according as he chooses to be resigned or revolutionary. And it's for this choice that he is responsible."[33]

A New View of Freedom and Situation

Sartre's political turn led to a broader view of responsibility, which seems to have led to his new view of freedom. Flynn describes the development of Sartre's view of freedom as "'thickening' to require socioeconomic liberation and … broadening to include all people in its scope."[34] Indeed, Sartre was moved by Marx's claim that, "Men make their own history, but they do not make it as they please; they do not make it under circumstances chosen by themselves, but under circumstances directly encountered, given, and transmitted from the past."[35]

The stoicism of existentialism offers comfort in control over one's own mind, not in the belief that history will unfold in a certain way and that salvation will be achieved. But in blending existentialism and Marxism, Sartre finds his previous conception of freedom, as essentially an affair of consciousness, to be inadequate, and he attempts to find a place for this kind of freedom in a worldview that nonetheless recognizes the way that socioeconomic forces guide us. As Poster says, "the entire intellectual journey of Sartre between 1943 and 1968 concerned his desire to preserve the concept of freedom, and still account for the actual distortion of man in society."[36]

Concerning this new view of freedom, Sartre says, "we do not attack freedom, but bring it about that freedom decides on other bases, and in terms of other structures."[37] Circumstances condition a person, but the person remains free to choose. We may want to act to change the circumstances that condition a person in that way, but we cannot say that the person is not responsible under those conditions. Sartre thus says "I believe that a man can always make something out of what is made of him."[38] On the one hand, this seems to assert absolute freedom. But on the other hand it seems to recognize a greater role for circumstances, such that the circumstances can make something of a person, which the person must then make his own or remake.

Sartre moves from the absolute freedom of existentialism to the conditioned freedom of Marxist existentialism without seeing this as a complete rejection of the earlier view. Indeed, in an interview near the end of his life Sartre said, "I myself think that my contradictions mattered little, that despite everything I have always remained on a continuous line."[39] On the other hand, Sartre not only admits that his thought contains contradictions but also a turning point, "I abandoned my pre-war individualism and the idea of the pure individual and adopted the social individual and socialism. That was the turning point of my life: before and after."[40] Sensing a major break in Sartre's thought, Thomas Busch points out that "On just about every occasion given him since then to comment on his works, Sartre has informed the world that he *changed* since that time [pre-war], primarily because of his experiences during the war years."[41]

In *Being and Nothingness* Sartre had argued that "there is freedom only in a *situation*"[42] and that "there is no situation in which the for-itself would be *more free* than in others."[43] Thus freedom was a matter of consciousness choosing how to interpret facticity, and the facticity always played a limiting role. For example, given human physiology, a person would be free to flap her arms in an attempt to fly, but she would not be free to succeed. In his Marxist existentialism, Sartre appears to re-conceive facticity as circumstances that do not simply limit us but actually condition thought and action.[44] As Flynn says, "Sartre's growing sense of objective possibility thickens his understanding of 'freedom' from a quasi-stoic 'freedom to think otherwise' … to a full-fledged notion of 'positive' or 'concrete' freedom that requires the change of socio-economic conditions; that is, 'the bases and structures' of our choices."[45]

Flynn characterizes Sartre as hearing the "'call,' to borrow from Heidegger, to become ontically what we are ontologically: free, to be sure, but free-in-society."[46] Flynn's distinction nicely illustrates that Sartre is concerned with two different senses of freedom. We are always absolutely free in the ontological sense, but the later Sartre becomes greatly concerned with freedom in the sense of practical opportunity as well, that is, freedom in the ontical sense.[47] In Heidegger's usage, the ontic is what there is; we deal with the ontic in terms of descriptive characteristics and plain facts. By contrast, the ontological deals in meaningful structures or the nature of the thing in question. So in this way, as Flynn sees it, Sartre's concern develops from being purely ontological to being more concerned with the ontical as well. We are ontologically free, but we need to say more about the ontical to do justice to human experience. Despite our absolute ontological freedom, that freedom is not always easy to exercise.

We consider our ontical circumstances in making choices, and often we choose what is easier or more pleasant rather than what is more difficult but more in line with our ideals or long-term goals. The reason for such choices is not simply a failure of ontological freedom, which remains absolute. Rather, our choices are understandable in terms of our circumstances. Sartre thus becomes more concerned with circumstances, because simply telling people that they have absolute freedom and responsibility will not necessarily motivate them to choose what is more difficult, or nearly impossible, though more in line with their ideals or long-term goals. By contrast, changing circumstances will likely have an effect on choices. Let's say, for example, that it is consistent with a person's ideals or long-term goals to get from A to B, but there is a mountain between A and B. It will be helpful to remind that person that she has absolute freedom and responsibility, but it will be even more helpful to remove the mountain or provide easy transport over it. Focusing on circumstances in this way seems to have led Sartre to Marxism.

Even before his conversion to Marxism, we see Sartre giving ground to the Marxists in "Existentialism Is a Humanism," saying, "in wanting freedom we discover that it depends entirely on the freedom of others, and that the freedom of others depends on ours ... I can take freedom as my goal only if I take that of others as my goal as well."[48] This begins to move him away from the individualism of *Being and Nothingness*, but, as Flynn says, "no clear link is forged in this lecture between the ontological freedom that defines the individual in abstracto and the socioeconomic freedom of concrete, historical agents."[49] Thus in "Existentialism Is a Humanism" we see Sartre struggling, not quite rejecting his view of freedom in *Being and Nothingness* but also not supplying the connection with his new view of the importance of socioeconomic circumstances and the freedom of others.[50]

So how can the link be made between Sartre's individualist conception of freedom and Sartre's later view in which freedom depends on others? Flynn says,

"No one can be free unless all are free." This statement must remain enigmatic until we realize that concrete freedom and the ideal of common effort converge in the concept of group praxis: we are free together and only as long as we remain in practical union. This is the message of the *Critique*. And it is a message of collective responsibility as well: we are responsible for each other's freedom, because the latter depends on our mutual, practical recognition. In this way, Sartre continues to respect the twin values of "socialism and freedom [*liberté*]" that have set the parameters of his political existentialism from the start.[51]

So we turn now to a very brief consideration of Sartre's *Critique of Dialectical Reason* in which he articulates the ontology that supports the conception of freedom integral to Marxist existentialism.

The Critique of Dialectical Reason

In *Being and Nothingness* Sartre saw freedom as situated within facticity, the sum of all facts that are true of an individual, "the realm of the given."[52] In the *Critique of Dialectical Reason* Sartre introduces the practico-inert, "the thing-iness of the social organization, to which everyone is subject as if it were a form of physical necessity."[53] Structures characterized by the practico-inert resist our attempts to "assign new meanings to things, because we find their meaning to be already present in them, having been put there through previous acts of freedom."[54] Under capitalism, then, we must act in situations limited by scarcity and the practico-inert. As David Detmer says,

> In order to understand Sartre's point it is necessary to add that scarcity is no longer imposed on us by nature. There is enough to go around, and there are no technological barriers to an equitable distribution of the world's resources. The problem, then, is that we persist in patterns left over from the interiorization of past physical scarcity. The rich continue to hoard the goods of the world, and the poor continue to die because of it.[55]

Thus, Sartre's conception of freedom is no longer one of consciousness, albeit situated in circumstances. Rather, freedom is now a matter of purposeful human action (i.e., praxis) that is very clearly

41

limited by circumstances. As Flynn describes Sartre's view, "Alienation is real; the bases and structures of choice are truly limiting; the practico-inert actually distorting. Scarcity must be overcome for permanent brotherhood (*fraternité*) to be achieved."[56]

Scarcity results in alienation; we relate to one another in a *series* as opposed to a *group*. As Detmer explains, "a series is a somewhat unstructured and uncoordinated social collective. It is a collection of people who each have the same individual purpose, but who do not share a common purpose."[57] Sartre famously illustrates the concept of the series with the example of people lining up for a bus.[58] They all want a seat on the next bus, a scarce resource. As a result, there is not a feeling of brotherhood (*fraternité*) among them. The only thing these people have in common is their need for a seat on the bus; there is no greater connection among them. Flynn observes that "Sartrean sociality at base consists of serial relations among atomic individuals gathered into collectives by material objects and operating in a practico-inert field."[59] The alienation that results needs to be overcome, and of course, the matter is concerned with much more than seats on buses. As Sartre sees it, capitalism results in scarcity and seriality, "on the ontological plane ... class-being is practico-inert."[60] Members of the working class exist as part of a series; they have the same individual purpose but do not act with a common purpose.

Alienation is overcome when people act in concert with one another as part of a *group*, which Detmer explains as a "collection of people who, unlike those in a series, *do* share a collective purpose. Thus, in a group, the individual members actively band together in a common cause. They self-consciously adopt each other's goals as their own, and engage each other in a complex coordination of efforts to achieve the ends that they mutually desire, as is the case with a soccer team or a revolutionary political organization."[61] So the people waiting for the bus form a series, whereas the people storming the Bastille form a group.[62] A person experiences alienation in the series and freedom in the group. As Aron describes it, for Sartre, "the life of men in society oscillates inevitably between the series and the group, between alienation and freedom; according to circumstances, the humanization of the relationships between individuals—the impulse towards reciprocity between the praxeis—calls for violence or can be reconciled with reformism."[63] We find ourselves as part of a series as a matter of circumstances or by default, but being part of a group is a matter of free choice. And it is, in transforming from a series to a group that the proletariat can unite in common cause to overthrow the capitalist system and eliminate scarcity.

Problems with Sartre's Shift in Freedom

Existentialism and Marxism may appear incompatible, but Sartre was an unorthodox Marxist. Clearly Sartre did not remain an existentialist in the individualist sense of *Being and Nothingness*, but did he remain an existentialist in another sense? Flynn believes he did,[64] but Aron disagrees, saying, "It is fundamentally impossible to call oneself an existentialist and a Marxist at the same time ... these two philosophies are incompatible in their intentions, their origins, and their ultimate ends."[65]

Sartre himself always maintained that he was an existentialist, but he recognized that his view of freedom changed or developed. Concerning his changing view, Sartre said, "Life taught me *la force* des choses—the power of circumstances."[66] As a result of his experience in the war and in his engagement in politics after the war, Sartre changed his view concerning how much freedom an individual has in her choices and actions. Tellingly, Sartre says,

> The other day, I re-read a prefatory note of mine to a collection of these plays—*Les Mouches, Huis Clos* and others—and was truly scandalized. I had written: 'Whatever the circumstances, and whereever the site, a man is always free to choose to be a traitor or not ... ' When I read this, I said to myself: I actually believed that![67]

Clearly, this indicates Sartre recognized that he had a significant change in his view of freedom. The question, then, is whether his later view of freedom is still existentialist. In *Sharing Responsibility*, Larry May argues that the later Sartre embraces a different kind of existentialism, *social* existentialism, which "stresses the way that our choices are generally affected by the groups of which we are members. Self-control is to be understood as partial control over the self by the self's use of social factors that shape who the self is."[68] So if we recognize social existentialism as a kind of existentialism, and not a contradiction in terms, then Sartre remains an existentialist.

In *Being and Nothingness* Sartre acknowledged that facts of the world can limit freedom. For the early Sartre, we are free to choose, though not necessarily free to accomplish. We are free to turn the knob on a locked door, flap our arms, and run for president, but we are not necessarily free to open the door, fly, or be eligible for the presidency. Still, even in these cases we are free to take other actions that could possibly change the circumstances, such as supporting legislation that would permit someone under 35 or born outside the United States to become president. There is never a lack of freedom, just an increase in the difficulties or circumstances. Having fewer options does not make you less free ontologically. Only two options are needed for ontological freedom, and there are always at least two options.

Rational-belief probability allows us to describe the chances of a person making a certain choice in terms of percentages. One sixteen-year-old boy may have a 95% chance of applying to college based on his demographic, and another sixteen-year-old boy may have a 15% chance of applying to college based on his demographic. They differ in the resources available to them and the roads smoothed in front of them. They differ in their ontical freedom, but they are both 100% ontologically free. Sartre's ontological freedom is untouched by epistemology. If we reject determinism,[69] the likelihood that a person will take one action rather than another is always a matter of rational-belief probability, not *a priori* probability. A person always remains 100% free to choose one way or another, but circumstances affect our beliefs about the likelihood of the action he or she will take. It is possible to be 100% free ontologically and yet less than 100% free ontically. Rational-belief probability may give me a less-than-100% chance of making a difficult choice that fits with my ideals and long-term goals, and yet I would remain 100% free ontologically.

To see how, consider an example. Let's say that the best assessment of the situation comes up with a rational-belief probability that gives me a 60% chance of declining chocolate cake when it is offered for dessert tonight. This does not mean that I am only 60% free ontologically. The epistemology does not touch the underlying ontology. I still remain 100% free. It is just that I may decide to pursue short-term pleasure instead of long-term goals. And my own physiology and brain chemistry form part of the circumstances in which the choice will have to be made.

I cannot deny my freedom even if the cake is put on a plate and served to me. Putting the dessert in front of me may decrease the rational-belief probability of my declining dessert to 40%, but we need to remember that rational-belief probability is just an epistemological tool, not a metaphysical fact. It is not like the *a priori* probability of drawing a red marble from a bag in which there are four red marbles and six blue marbles. Rather, rational-belief probabilities are based on what other people have done or, better, what I have done, in the past. But they do not mean that I am somehow less free to resist dessert when the dessert has been brought to the table—just less likely. Individual circumstances are always completely unique, and there is no algorithm that I am following or that can be used to say with certainty what I will do. The probability involved is like that of predicting the winner of a horse race; it is a rational-belief probability—an epistemological tool—and that is all.

For the early Sartre, the self is not caused to do anything because the self is a no-thing and only things are within the causal chain. While we might want to take issue with Sartre's ontology and reasoning, his insight provides a convincing phenomenology of freedom. We generally do not experience our "selves" as caused; we experience our selves as radically free. We find our selves in circumstances in which facticity provides reasons for acting one way or another, but we remain completely free to act in another way. So, accepting the phenomenology and rejecting determinism, I remain 100% ontologically free to decline the cake, and it will be somewhat helpful to remind myself of that. But it would be even more helpful if the host was told in advance that I was on a diet and would prefer not to be offered dessert. It is that kind of practical solution that the later Sartre became concerned with.

Sartre could have turned his attention to practical solutions for political problems and still maintained the existentialist view that we are 100% ontologically free under all circumstances. Indeed, David Detmer believes that Sartre did precisely this. But Sartre's own examples suggest that in embracing Marxism he came to think that we are not 100% ontologically free under all conditions. Rather, some conditions dictate our choices and actions. The proletarian, as Sartre comes to see it, faces "a limit to his practical comprehension."[70] In a famous example, Sartre discusses a woman working in a shampoo factory who is "wholly reduced to her work, her fatigue, her wages, and the material impossibilities that these wages assign to her: the impossibility of eating properly, of buying shoes, of sending her child to the country, of satisfying her most modest wishes."[71] As Thomas Anderson says, "This woman may be able to choose one brand of toothpaste or one breakfast cereal from others, or to do her job more or less quickly, but she has no freedom to leave or change her class and its oppressed state. She is *forced*, Sartre says, 'to live a prefabricated destiny as *her reality.*'"[72] Again Anderson captures the change in Sartre's view: "Explicitly rejecting positions adopted in *Being and Nothingness*, he asserts, 'it would be quite wrong to interpret me as saying that man is free in all situations as the stoics claimed. I mean the exact opposite: all men are slaves insofar as their life unfolds in the practico-inert field. ... The practico-inert field is the field of our servitude, which means *not* ideal servitude, but real subservience to 'natural' forces, to 'mechanical' forces and to 'anti-social apparatuses'. We see again the severe restrictions on freedom the Sartre of the *Critique* is willing to admit."[73]

It may be true that a person of limited education who is subject to certain social conditions may be unlikely to see or understand things from a broad perspective and thus may likely make certain decisions on that basis. However, the Sartre of *Being and Nothingness* would not have depicted this as constituting a lack of freedom but rather as a narrow perspective that could be overcome through free choices and actions. As Sartre says in *Being and Nothingness*, "to be free is not to choose the historic world in which one arises ... but to choose oneself in the world whatever this may be."[74]

Flynn says of Sartre that "By appeal to the exigencies of the practico-inert, he hopes to wed freedom to necessity in a union that will render history intelligible without depriving it of its moral character."[75] But freedom and necessity cannot be wed unless one accepts the compatibilist view that we can be free and determined at the same time, which the Sartre of *Being and Nothingness* rejected. The existentialist view of *Being and Nothingness* is that there is freedom in a situation, not freedom with determinism.[76]

Sartre gives ground to circumstances in the *Critique* saying, "man is 'mediated' by things to the same extent as things are 'mediated' by men."[77] This talk of "mediating" gives a causal power to things in shaping human choices and actions. In *Being and Nothingness* Sartre had instead spoken of things as providing a background against which free choices are made. Of course circumstances may be difficult, but circumstances do not determine a choice or absolve a person from responsibility in the choice made. Circumstances may provide an explanation but not a justification for one's choice. The circumstances-as-explanation may incline others to understand or forgive a choice, but it will not justify a choice. Only the individual can justify his or her choice in a situation.

→ Auth's View

In the *Critique* Sartre speaks of "exigency" as limiting freedom. Flynn thus says "the factory worker who procures an abortion because she cannot financially support a child is, in Sartre's words, 'carrying out the sentence which has already been passed on her' by her 'objective situation'."[78] Elaborating on the notion of exigency, Flynn says, "it is with the concept of exigency that Sartre translates Marx's dictum: man is the product of his own product."[79] Summing it up, Flynn says, "To the extent that concrete freedom is the expansion of the field of objective possibility, it will consist in liberation from these exigencies."[80]

This example of the pregnant woman illustrates well the extent to which Sartre's views changed from *Being and Nothingness* to the *Critique*. In *Being and Nothingness* Sartre would have said of the woman that she is responsible for her own choices. Assuming that she was not raped, she made the choice to have sex, knowing the risk of pregnancy and knowing that she would not be able to support a child. Now she has the free choice to have an abortion or carry the pregnancy to term and give up the child for adoption. Additionally, she could try to find other work, find someone to marry, or make some other arrangements to care for the child. None of these possibilities is very appealing, but it is not as if her circumstances have forced her to get an abortion. To claim that would be to deny her ontological freedom.

Of course, a wealthy woman would have more desirable options, which would make it easier for her to choose. But the individualist existentialist would say that both women are equally free ontologically. This does not mean that kind-hearted people like Sartre might not want to work to change things to help provide more appealing options for women. What they would be providing such women, though, is not more ontological freedom but more appealing options. Freedom in the individualist existentialist, ontological, sense remains absolute.

The only way that freedom could increase or decrease is in an altogether different, ontical, sense of the word in which freedom is equated with opportunity. This ontical sense of freedom as opportunity cannot determine a choice or action, however. We remain absolutely free in the ontological sense. Confusion arises when there is equivocation involving these two senses of freedom. For this reason, it is better not even to speak of opportunity as freedom; it just invites confusion and obscures the issue.

Speaking of "opportunity" also invites confusion in itself. Some people have more opportunity in the sense of having more resources available to them, but this kind of opportunity does not give a person more freedom in the ontological sense. Rather, consider that all native-born American citizens have the opportunity to become president. This does not mean, of course, that all such people have an equal likelihood of becoming president. It just means that they have the right to run for the office and be sworn in if they are elected. Citizens under the age of 35 and citizens born outside the United States do not have that right and thus do not have the opportunity, in the present, to be president.

Where does this leave us in terms of responsibility? Even with 100% ontological freedom in all situations, we could make a place for diminished responsibility. Responsibility can be decoupled from freedom. For example, compatibilists continue to speak of responsibility even though they do not believe in libertarian freedom of the will. Responsibility can be ontological rather than axiological. In fact, for a moral anti-realist, responsibility can only be ontological. Any values placed on responsibility are subjective projections. In the ontological sense, responsibility is just a matter of attributing a cause to an effect. For the moral anti-realist, there can be no moral responsibility, though there can be legal responsibility.

Legal responsibility would not necessarily be an all-or-nothing affair the way ontological responsibility would be. So we could decide to be lenient with the legal penalty even though someone is 100% ontologically responsible. For example, the person who commits a crime of passion is just as ontologically responsible as is the person who plots a cold-blooded murder, but the law could still decide to be more lenient in the punishment of the crime of passion. The person who is in an emotionally heightened state as a result of unfortunate circumstances still has 100% ontological freedom, but we find it understandable why his reason did not prevail over his emotions. We do not excuse his killing, as we would in a case of legitimate self defense, but we understand it—and so we may lessen the penalty.

Why Sartre Embraced Marxism

It makes practical sense to improve conditions, but we can disagree with Sartre concerning whether Marxism is the most effective way of doing this and whether Marxism can fit comfortably with existentialism. As Aron says, "The Marxism of Sartre was 'ontic,' not 'ontological.' It was difficult to understand how the quest for the classless society (on the ontic level) tallied with the ontological thesis of man as a 'useless passion.'"[81] And Aron is emphatic in saying, "When you begin with the *no* of Kierkegaard, you may arrive at Sartre, but never at Marxism. One cannot be at the same time the heir of Hegel-Marx and the heir of Kierkegaard."[82] Indeed, Kierkegaard rejected Hegel and most previous philosophers for forgetting about the existing individual in favor of the collective or in favor of some abstract conception of the person. Aron says,

> What will always prevent an existentialist from being a Marxist is that revolution will not solve his philosophical problem, that of the dialogue of the individual with the absence of God in atheist existentialism, and with God in the existentialism of the believer. Outside of this dialogue one may take an interest in the lot of the unfortunate and join the revolutionary party for some perfectly valid reason, but one will never arrive at the equivalent of a Marxist philosophy.[83]

So, Sartre's philosophy in *Being and Nothingness* may in some ways be consistent with Marxism, but it is at the very least in tension with it. Additionally, the philosophy of *Being and Nothingness* does not necessarily imply support of free market capitalism, but, as I shall argue in the next chapter, it is consistent with it and perhaps even expected from it.

49

Sartre's views on ethics changed significantly over the course of his career. *Being and Nothingness* concludes with the promise for a work on ethics that never fully materialized. Given the ontology of *Being and Nothingness*, this is not surprising. In that work Sartre rejects the objectivity of values, saying, "My freedom is the unique foundation of values .... *nothing,* absolutely nothing, justifies me in adopting this or that particular value, this or that particular scale of values."[84] And in characteristic hyperbole toward the end of the book, he adds that "all human activities are equivalent .... Thus it amounts to the same thing whether one gets drunk alone or is a leader of nations."[85]

Not only Sartre's ethics but his ontology changed significantly over the course of his career. Anderson says, "Just as his ontology progressed from a partial, one-sided, individualistic understanding of human beings in the world to a more complete, concrete, dialectical, and social conception so did his ethical thought."[86] Again, Anderson says, "Totally gone is any suggestion that salvation is an individual matter of pure reflection or a radical conversion to authenticity. In fact, the term *authenticity* is never used in the *Critique*."[87] So Sartre changed his mind. This would be easier to handle if he simply admitted as much and repudiated *Being and Nothingness*. But Sartre made no such admissions. He wanted to be both an existentialist and a Marxist. One can always redefine terms to make that so. Indeed Sartre was never an orthodox Marxist, and he ceased being an individualist existentialist in favor of being what Larry May calls a social existentialist.

Sartre needed to stretch his existentialist view of freedom from *Being and Nothingness* to the breaking point in order to accommodate his Marxism. So why did he do it? This question is not often asked these days because the link between Sartrean existentialism and Marxism is taken for granted. A friend of mine was "horrified," as he put it, when I told him about what I had planned in connecting existentialism and capitalism. He warned me that any other self-identifying existentialist would be horrified as well. What he could not tell me was why. What necessary connection is there between existentialism and Marxism?

The rest of this chapter indulges in sociological and psychological speculation. This speculation arises from my genuine puzzlement concerning Sartre's conversion to Marxism, and it issues from my

50

own biased perspective. Some readers may thus find the rest of this chapter unhelpful, naive, or distasteful. It may even elicit disdain in some readers, especially those sympathetic to Sartre's Marxism. I apologize in advance for any shortcomings of my presentation that bother readers who continue with this chapter. Those who do not wish to continue should feel free to skip ahead to the next chapter in which the positive connection between existentialism and the free market is made.

Both Marxism and existentialism are concerned with overcoming alienation and oppression, but individualist existentialism and Marxism have as much in common as existentialism and cigarettes or existentialism and wine or existentialism and cheese. That is, their connection is a cultural, historical accident.

Among other reasons for his conversion to Marxism, Sartre seems to have latched on to the fact that economic conditions are highly relevant to the choices people make. Without giving capitalism a full and fair hearing in print at least, Sartre accepted the most readily available and socially acceptable explanation for such choices, Marxism.

In "A Plea for Intellectuals," Sartre says,

> Thus, the true intellectual, in his struggle against himself, will come to see society as the arena of a struggle between particular groups (particularized by virtue of their structure, their position and their destiny) for the statute of universality. In contradiction to the tenets of bourgeois thought, he will perceive that *man does not exist.* But by the same token, once he knows he is not yet a man, he will grasp—within himself and then outside himself, and vice versa—man as a *task.*[88]

Here Sartre diagnoses the problem of being pushed and pulled and shaped by the struggles of groups within society. The challenge is to overcome the tendency and prejudice to simply identify with one's own group. Sartre thinks he has met this challenge himself by rejecting the bourgeoisie and identifying with the struggle of the proletariat.

Concerning the intellectual, Sartre says,

> He must strive to remain aware of the fact he is a petty-bourgeois breaking out of his mould, constantly tempted to renourish the

51

thoughts of his class. He must remind himself that he is never secure from the danger of lapsing into universalism ... into racism, nationalism, or imperialism.[89]

This is an intriguing claim but it seems wholly out of place from the author of *Being and Nothingness,* who would say that one can no more be a petty-bourgeois than one can be a waiter. For the early Sartre, the waiter is in bad faith if he simply thinks of himself as a waiter the way the dish is a dish. But the waiter is also in bad faith if, while wearing a waiter's uniform and carrying a serving tray, he denies that he is a waiter. In his facticity he is a waiter, though in his transcendence he is not a waiter. The same ontology and account could have and should have been used for social classes. A person may be a bourgeois in her facticity, but she is not a bourgeois in her transcendence. This means she is in bad faith if she appeals to her status as bourgeois to justify or excuse an action. In her transcendence she is not a bourgeois, and thus she is free to act in a way that would not be expected of a bourgeois. And, of course, if the bourgeois comes to find some action associated with her class repugnant to her, she should exercise her freedom to act otherwise. One can always cease to be a waiter by quitting that line of work. Quitting one's social class may be more difficult, but it is nonetheless possible. Of course, one can never change the fact that one was born into a particular class and raised that way, but one can reject its values and *weltanschauung.* As Sartre says, "I used to say one never is a coward or a thief. Accordingly, should I not now say that one *makes oneself* a bourgeois or a proletarian?" But "in order to make oneself bourgeois, one must be bourgeois."[90]

Aron says that "existentialism presents itself as a revolutionary doctrine, but it leaves the particular content, the nature of this revolution in a limbo."[91] When Sartre became politically engaged he would have been truer to his existentialism if he recognized that the content of his political engagement had nothing necessarily to do with his existentialism. It is tough to be an existentialist, and so it is not completely surprising that much as Kierkegaard advocated faith in the absurd, Sartre embraced Marxism. Sartre sought comfort in his political views much as Kierkegaard sought comfort in his religious views. As the title of Aron's famous book suggests, Marxism is "the opium of the intellectuals." Nietzsche predicted that many would not be able to deal with the death of God and would seek a substitute to worship, and he was correct. For many intellectuals, that new object of worship was political ideology. Indeed, Sartre described his turn to Marxism as a conversion.

Sartre and the existentialists are not unique, but rather are part of a tradition of European intellectuals who despise the bourgeoisie and associate them with the free market. Of course, there is no clear line from Plato to Sartre, and European intellectuals do not form a completely homogenous group. Nonetheless, a brief historical overview can help in understanding Sartre's move to Marxism.

European intellectuals have a tendency to think of themselves as a kind of new aristocracy, clearly above the bourgeoisie. In *Mind vs. Money*, Alan Kahan notes that intellectuals don't like the invisible hand; they like the visible hand.[92] And ideally they would like to *be* the visible hand or at least a counsel to the hand, directing the way society is formed and run. It is an insult to the intellect of the intellectual that no planning by intellectuals can do a better job of running society than can the unplanned spontaneous order shaped by the invisible hand.

Kahan says that "intellectuals look down on people who work for money."[93] By this he means that they look down on people who are chiefly motivated by profit, rather than the exercise of autonomy or the pursuit of personal fulfillment. I can identify with this to the extent that I think it is a crass and un-worthwhile way of living. For all that, though, I do not think there is anything morally wrong with pursuing profit inasmuch as I am a moral anti-realist. My distaste is subjective and informed by the prudential wisdom that such a life, working for someone else just to make money, is unlikely to be fulfilling for me. Then again, I recognize that there is enough human variety that some people may find this fulfilling.

Kahan shows that the intellectual's distaste for the bourgeois pursuit of profit is ancient in its roots and mired in ignorance. For Plato, money itself is suspicious. Consider that Plato forbids his guardians to possess gold or silver—or even to touch them. Plato's guardians set the template for the Western intellectual in being unconcerned with money and preferring to pursue the life of the mind. Aristotle wasn't as disdainful of money as Plato was: "One needs money, but earning it is either vile or too time-consuming."[94] The chief worry for Aristotle was that the pursuit of money could lead to pursuit of money for its own sake, an unworthy way of living a human life. This concern is genuine, but Aristotle was perhaps overly worried. Notably, both Plato and Aristotle had family money, and this was to become the intellectual's ideal—to have money and be able to live a life of leisure in pursuit of learning and civic virtue.

Curiously, the Greek philosophers express contempt for merchants because merchants buy a product at one price and sell it for another, higher price. Merchants were thus seen as ripping off the people they sold the product to. This, of course, reflects a profound lack of appreciation for the work that merchants do and the way they improve society by making goods available. Lending money and charging interest was seen as even worse than selling goods, because there wasn't an actual product that changed hands. Money was suspect as a means of exchange, but to use money to make money seemed perverse. Aquinas is known for his prohibition of usury, but he actually adopted it from Aristotle. The distrust arises partly because of mystery: How can you make money trading and loaning? There can't be any real work involved, and so bankers must be doing something wrong, something sneaky and unjust.

As Kahan explains, "Aristotle was telling his students that the pursuit of excessive wealth was chrematistic, an unnatural art, harmful to the community and unworthy of a free man. The life of a merchant was 'vile and contrary to virtue.'"[95] In the Middle Ages, Pope Leo the Great said, "a merchant is rarely or never pleasing to God."[96] Today's villains are not merchants but stock brokers and investment bankers, whose work most intellectuals do not understand but nonetheless often feel entitled to condemn and despise. There was a honeymoon period when intellectuals embraced capitalism in the Enlightenment, exemplified by Hume, Smith, and Montesquieu.[97] I would like to think that particular embrace had to do with a desire for individual freedom, but Kahan does not note freedom among the reasons. Instead, his interpretation is largely sociological, with the intelligentsia opposing the nobility and temporarily siding with the bourgeoisie. In any event, the honeymoon was brief, and by the late nineteenth century, intellectuals had mostly reverted to hostility to the bourgeoisie and to capitalism.

Sartre despised the bourgeoisie, understandably so in some ways, but he seems to have lumped capitalism in with the bourgeoisie for no necessary reason. Aron asks, "why do the intellectuals not admit to themselves that they are less interested in the standard of living of the working class than in the refinements of art and life? Why do they cling to democratic jargon when in fact they are trying to defend authentically aristocratic values against the invasion of mass-produced human beings and mass-produced commodities?"[98] Aron's insight fits with what Kahan says about intellectuals conceiving of themselves as a kind of aristocracy but being embarrassed by that label and seeking instead to identify with an oppressed group, the proletariat. As a result, Marxist intellectuals call for policies that suit the aesthetic standards of intellectuals but do not gain much traction among the proletariat.

Kahan also describes intellectuals as a "pseudo-aristocracy."[99] They cannot in good conscience consider themselves an aristocracy, and they clearly are not part of the proletariat. But by joining together with the proletariat in a revolution they can overcome their alienation. Speaking of the intellectual, Sartre says,

> If he were to try to place himself theoretically outside society in order to judge the ideology of the dominant class, *at best* he would take his contradictions with him; at worst he would identify with the big bourgeoisie which is economically situated *above* the middle classes and overlooks them, and he would then accept its ideology without demur. It follows that if he wishes to understand the society in which he lives, he has only one course open to him and that is to adopt the point of view of its most underprivileged members.[100]

Here Sartre proposes an intriguing and compassionate idea: identifying with the lowest members of society. Indeed it is rather Christlike. But, as we shall see in chapter 6, it does not adequately consider the possibility that capitalism may be the best way of improving the standard of living for all.

In "A Plea for Intellectuals," Sartre paints a picture of romantic struggle and alienation for the intellectual, saying,

> It remains true that, even so defined, the intellectual has a mandate from no one; suspect to the working class, a traitor to the dominant class, a fugitive from his own class who can yet never wholly escape it ... Is he not rather *one man too many*, a *defective* product of the middle classes, compelled by his imperfections to live on the fringe of the under-privileged classes without ever becoming a part of them?[101]

Sartre assumes that the intellectual cannot stay happily within the bourgeoisie, that he must reject the bourgeoisie. There is no necessary reason for this, however, except that it would be anathema for an intellectual, and especially a French intellectual, to embrace the bourgeoisie.

After World War II when Sartre and the French existentialists became increasingly political, the bad guys (Nazis and fascists) were identified with the political right (although both Nazis and fascists were anti-capitalist). And so it was easy for the existentialists to think that the good guys were on the political left (the communists). Sartre and company could have looked to America and free market economics, but there was a great deal of resentment on the part of the French at American success. Aron says, "the European left has a grudge against the United States mainly because the latter has succeeded by means that were not laid down in the revolutionary code. Prosperity, power, the tendency toward uniformity of economic conditions—these results have been achieved by private initiative, by competition rather than State intervention, in other words by capitalism, which every well-brought-up intellectual has been taught to despise."[102] Such resentment is the kind of poison that Nietzsche repeatedly warned about, and yet it was swallowed by Sartre and other French existentialists.

The free market was strongly identified with America, and America was seen as philistine, culturally and intellectually impoverished. Intellectuals had an easier time being recognized and valued in Europe, which has a long tradition of aristocracy and nobility. By contrast, Americans do not readily recognize the aristocracy of the intellectuals—and this causes resentment among intellectuals.

Kahan says, "We know the themes on which hatred of America is nourished ... puritan idiocy, barbarian arrogance, unchained capitalism, and drive for hegemony."[103] This captures well the attitude that psychologically precluded Sartre and the French existentialists from embracing the free market. Capitalism is associated with America, the most capitalist country in the world, and America is a place of puritan idiocy. Bohemians like Sartre would find it unseemly to be linked with a country that perpetuates puritan values. America's "barbarian arrogance," as seen in its tendency to inject itself in the armed conflicts of other nations, makes America anathema. And while capitalism had a foothold in France, that capitalism was tempered. In America, capitalism was "unchained" and vulgar, producing people who were obsessed with profits to the exclusion of high art and culture. Lastly, America's "drive for hegemony" meant it was not to be trusted. Yes, America helped to liberate France and defeat the Nazis, but it did so largely in the interest of expanding its influence. Indeed, the expansion of American influence was not just military but commercial.

Conclusion

This chapter has focused largely on Sartre because he is emblematic of existentialism and because among the French existentialists who embraced Marxism, the tension is clearest for Sartre. Ultimately, the reader may disagree with my Sartre interpretation, but that interpretation nonetheless offers a recognizably existentialist philosophy. While we can speculate on the psychological and sociological (1) explanations for Sartre's turn to Marxism, we cannot find logically necessary explanations. Indeed, as the next chapter will argue, by my interpretation, the existentialism of *Being and Nothingness* would (2) have been a better fit with free market capitalism. Beyond that, existentialism can actually be used to deal with some of the problems (3) most readily associated with the free market.

Notes

1 Jean-Paul Sartre, *Existentialism*, trans. Bernard Frechtman (New York: Philosophical Library, 1947), p. 27 (hereafter *Existentialism*).
2 Jean-Paul Sartre, *Being and Nothingness*, trans. Hazel Barnes (New York: Washington Square Press, 1956), p. 711 (hereafter BN).
3 BN, p. 731.
4 BN, p. 707.
5 Jean-Paul Sartre, *The Emotions: Outline of a Theory*, trans. Bernard Frechtman (New York: Philosophical Library, 1948), p. 12. Sartre's stoicism is fully on display here.
6 BN, p. 709.
7 Thomas R. Flynn, *Sartre and Marxist Existentialism: The Test Case of Collective Responsibility* (Chicago: University of Chicago Press, 1984), p. 15; cf. BN, pp. 708–9.
8 BN, p. 523.

9   *Existentialism*, p. 36.
10 BN, pp. 534–7.
11 BN, p. 555.
12 Jean-Paul Sartre, *No Exit and Three Other Plays*, trans. Stuart Gilbert (New York: Vintage International, 1989), p. 45.
13 Sartre may have had some ambivalence about absolute ontological freedom, interdependence, and the role of the other in parts of *Being and Nothingness*.
14 Simone de Beauvoir, *La Cérémonie des adieux*, with *Entretiens avec Jean-Paul Sartre août-septembre, 1974* (Paris: Gallimard, 1981), pp. 479–80. See Thomas R. Flynn, "Political Existentialism: The Career of Sartre's Political Thought," in Steven Crowell, ed., *The Cambridge Companion to Existentialism* (Cambridge: Cambridge University Press, 2012), p. 230.
15 Flynn (2012), p. 230.
16 Mark Poster, *Existential Marxism in Postwar France: From Sartre to Althusser* (Princeton: Princeton University Press, 1975), p. 75.
17 Poster, p. 127.
18 Raymond Aron, *The Opium of the Intellectuals* (New Brunswick, NJ: Transaction Publishers, 2001), p. 49.
19 Martin Jay, *Marxism and Totality: The Adventures of a Concept from Lukács to Habermas* (Berkeley: University of California Press, 1986), p. 361.
20 Flynn (1984), p. 71.
21 Flynn (1984), p. 75.
22 Flynn (1984), p. 75.
23 See Poster, pp. 109–60, for extensive discussion of Marxist criticism and rejection of Sartre and his long struggle to find a place.
24 Jean-Paul Sartre, "Self-Portrait at Seventy," in *Life/Situations: Essays Written and Spoken*, trans. Paul Auster and Lydia Davis (New York: Pantheon, 1977), p. 45. See Thomas R. Flynn, *Sartre: A Philosophical Biography* (Cambridge: Cambridge University Press, 2014), pp. 45–6.
25 Flynn (1984), p. 204.
26 Jean-Paul Sartre, *Search for a Method*, trans. Hazel E. Barnes (New York: Random House, Vintage Books, 1968), p. 47.
27 Flynn (1984), p. 182.
28 Jean-Paul Sartre, *The Communists and Peace*, with *A Reply to Claude Lefort*, trans. Martha H. Fletcher and Phillip R. Berk (New York: George Braziller, 1968), p. 138.
29 Jean-Paul Sartre, *Situations* (Paris: Gallimard, 1949), Vol. 3, p. 187. See Flynn (1984), p. 44.
30 Flynn (1984), p. 71.
31 Flynn (1984), p. 62.

32   Raymond Aron, *Marxism and the Existentialists* (New York: Simon and Schuster, 1969), p. 169.

33   *Situations*, Vol. 2, pp. 27–8. Flynn (1984), p. 138.

34   Flynn (1984), p. 188.

35   Flynn (1984), p. 72; from *The Eighteenth Brumaire of Louis Bonaparte* in David McLellan, ed., *Karl Marx: Selected Writings* (Oxford: Oxford University Press, 1977), p. 300.

36   Poster, p. 89.

37   Jean-Paul Sartre, *Anti-Semite and Jew*, trans. George J. Becker (New York: Schocken Books, 1948), p. 148.

38   Jean-Paul Sartre, *Between Existentialism and Marxism: Sartre on Philosophy, Politics, Psychology, and the Arts*, trans. John Matthews (New York: Pantheon, 1974), p. 35 (hereafter BEM).

39   *Le Nouvel Observateur*, March 10, 1980, p. 92; *Dissent*, Fall 1980, p. 399. Along these lines, William L. McBride offers a kind of a changes-within-permanence account in *Sartre's Political Theory* (Bloomington: Indiana University Press, 1991).

40   "Self-Portrait at Seventy," in *Life/Situations*, p. 48.

41   Thomas W. Busch, *The Power of Consciousness and the Force of Circumstances in Sartre's Philosophy* (Bloomington: Indiana University Press, 1990), p. 41; see also pp. 42 and 67.

42   BN, p. 629.

43   BN, p. 702.

44   As Flynn says, "'situation' proves to be a major bridge concept between existentialism and Marxism" (Flynn (1984), p. 26).

45   Flynn (2012), p. 233.

46   Flynn (1984), p. 185.

47   Flynn (1984), pp. 184–5.

48   *Existentialism*, p. 54.

49   Flynn (1984), p. 42.

50   In *Sartre's Ethics of Engagement: Authenticity and Civic Virtue* (London: Continuum, 2006), T Storm Heter argues that Sartre moves away from the Kantian sounding language of "Existentialism Is a Humanism" to justify his new view on the freedom of others in Hegelian terms: "The post-war works also reveal a dramatic reversal of Sartre's initial pessimism. Not only is mutual recognition possible, mutual recognition is the single most important mechanism for promoting human freedom. Freedom is not best achieved alone, in isolation, through radical self-assertion and honesty. Being free requires that other humans recognize me as free" (p. 35). This Hegelian view is a rejection of the view expressed in *Being and Nothingness*, but, as Heter says, "Sartre does not bother to revisit the claims in BN; he simply changes his tune"

(p. 43). On the other hand, Peter Poellner argues that Sartre is follow-ing Scheler's theory of values in arguing for the importance of the free-dom of others. See his "Early Sartre on Freedom and Ethics," *European Journal of Philosophy* (2012): DOI: 10.1111/j.1468-0378.2012.00532.x, pp. 17–19.

51 Flynn (1984), p. 48.
52 David Detmer, *Freedom as a Value: A Critique of the Ethical Theory of Jean-Paul Sartre* (La Salle, IL: Open Court, 1988), p. 40.
53 Aron (1969), p. 170.
54 Detmer (1988), p. 51.
55 David Detmer, *Sartre Explained: From Bad Faith to Authenticity* (Chicago: Open Court, 2008), p. 200.
56 Flynn (1984), p. 185.
57 Detmer (2008), p. 201.
58 Jean-Paul Sartre, *Critique of Dialectical Reason*, trans. Alan Sheridan-Smith (London: New Left Books, 1976), pp. 256–69 (hereafter CDR).
59 Flynn (1984), p. 95.
60 CDR, p. 686.
61 Detmer (2008), pp. 201–2.
62 Aron (1969), p. 171.
63 Aron (1969), p. 175.
64 Flynn (1984), p. 196.
65 Aron (1969), p. 28.
66 BEM, p. 33.
67 BEM, pp. 33–4.
68 Larry May, *Sharing Responsibility* (Chicago: University of Chicago Press, 1992), pp. 16–17.
69 As I do on one level, as a free will fictionalist and someone willing to "wager" that we have free will, as discussed in chapter 1.
70 CDR, p. 699.
71 CDR, p. 232.
72 Thomas C. Anderson, *Sartre's Two Ethics: From Authenticity to Integral Humanity* (Chicago: Open Court, 1993), p. 94; CDR, p. 232.
73 Anderson, p. 94; CDR, pp. 331–2.
74 BN, p. 668.
75 Flynn (1984), p. 84.
76 In contrast to the traditional interpretation, Poellner argues that Sartre's view of freedom in *Being and Nothingness* is "in essence com-patibilist" (p. 15).
77 CDR, p. 79.
78 CDR, p. 235.
79 Flynn (1984), p. 83.

80   Flynn (1984), p. 83.
81   Aron (1969), p. 73.
82   Aron (1969), p. 37.
83   Aron (1969), p. 37.
84   BN, p. 76.
85   BN, p. 797.
86   Anderson, p. 147.
87   Anderson, p. 102.
88   BEM, p. 250.
89   BEM, pp. 260–1.
90   CDR, p. 231.
91   Aron (1969), p. 38.
92   Alan S. Kahan, *Mind vs. Money: The War between Intellectuals and Capitalism* (New Brunswick, NJ: Transaction Publishers, 2010), p. 135.
93   Kahan, p. 14.
94   Kahan, p. 38, see Aristotle, *Politics*, Book VII, 9:1328b; Book VI, 4:1310a; Book III 5:1278a.
95   Kahan, p. 269.
96   Kahan, p. 269.
97   Kahan, p. 78.
98   Aron (2001), p. 228.
99   Kahan, p. 14.
100   BEM, p. 255.
101   BEM, p. 264.
102   Aron (2001), p. 227.
103   Kahan, pp. 246–7.

3

To Consume or not to Consume?

How Existentialism Helps Capitalism

In chapter 1 I defined existentialism as a philosophy that reacts to an apparently absurd or meaningless world by urging the individual to overcome alienation, oppression, and despair through freedom and self-creation in order to become a genuine person. The aim of chapter 3 is to show that an existentialist philosophy, one in accord with my definition and akin to my interpretation of *Being and Nothingness* in chapter 2, fits with the free market.

It has always puzzled me that existentialism did not catch on more in America. After all, as Robert Solomon says, "existentialism defines an important stream of American life and thought, especially its individualism and insistence on self-reliance ... "[1] The entrepreneurial spirit of working for yourself and not being beholden to others fits well with the existentialist ethic of self-reliance. There is a message of personal empowerment in existentialism and free markets, and existentialism can help us avoid potential problems of capitalism such as alienation, inauthenticity, and consumerism. In making the free market existentialist case, this chapter

The Free Market Existentialist: Capitalism without Consumerism, First Edition. William Irwin.
© 2015 John Wiley & Sons, Ltd. Published 2015 by John Wiley & Sons, Ltd.

moves away from the scholarly debates and explorations of the previous chapter and adopts a more informal tone and approach.

Individualism

A common link between existentialism and socialism is rebellion. Sometimes, though, the most rebellious thing to do is to resist the rebellion *du jour*. Don't conform to uniform anti-conformism. Find your own way to rebel. There is, for example, a spirit of rebellion against tyranny and deception in both existentialism and free market libertarianism, which share the belief that "you're on your own" even though you are surrounded by others.

The initial link between existentialism and libertarian politics is individualism. The individual is primary and the individual is responsible. Individuals deserve privacy and must not be made to conform. Not only can individuals usually discover what is best for themselves, but they often discover better ways of living that many people will appreciate. Humans likely evolved in much smaller groups—ranging from 35–150—than we tend to live in today.[2] So it was much more natural and sensible earlier in human history to look to a wise leader for governance. After all, it's much easier and more possible for a wise leader to determine what is good for a group of 35–150 than for a group of 300 million. And in fact we likely evolved to trust such leaders, though nowadays such trust is misplaced. We should note too, that even in groups of 35–150, individuals will be radically individual and may know things that the ruler cannot, or just does not, know that affect what would be best for the individual or even the group.

The old saying has it that we can't see the forest for the trees, but the neglected problem when it comes to the individual and society is that we can't see the tree for the forest. We look at the whole, society, and lose sight of the individual—we do not see the uniqueness of each person. What is it like to be, to exist, to experience life as an individual? This is the concern that drives existentialism. Likewise the value of individual knowledge drives free market economics. The social sciences tend to deal with groups and in generalities; this is especially true of economics. In the relevant sense, though, groups don't act; individuals act—and individuals act freely and idiosyncratically. For both free market economics and existentialism, it is wrong to think of someone primarily as a member of a group rather than as a unique individual. For the existentialist, meaning is a highly individual affair. Likewise, for the free market economist choice is a highly individual affair.

Knowledge, as F.A. Hayek argues in "The Uses of Knowledge in Society," is widely dispersed.[3] Information in a market economy is not only local but immediate, requiring the kind of quick action that is impossible if a government is going to intervene in a timely fashion. Making a government planning committee that is as efficient as the free market of individual actors would require a complexity akin to making a map of a territory as big and detailed as the territory itself. In other words, what would be required would be absurd, if not impossible, and certainly counterproductive. A large economy has a complexity akin to the history of evolution. Just imagine planning and managing the evolution of all creatures from the beginning of life on this planet. Evolution, like an economy, is messy, but it gets things done without central management or planning in a way that central management or planning of the process could not hope for. As Hayek says,

> The curious task of economics is to demonstrate to men how little they really know about what they imagine they can design. To the naive mind that can conceive of order only as the product of deliberate arrangement, it may seem absurd that in complex conditions order, and adaptation to the unknown, can be achieved more effectively by decentralizing decisions and that a division of authority will actually extend the possibility of overall order. Yet that decentralization actually leads to more information being taken into account.[4]

But might socialism be better suited to the expression of freedom? No. Central planning limits individual freedom. As Raymond Aron says,

> Philosophies of history of the Marxist type bring order to the chaos of events by relating it to a few simple principles of interpretation, and postulating an irresistible movement towards the fulfillment of human destiny. Classes obey their interests, individuals their passions, but the forces and relations of production call forth

from this anarchic confusion the procession of régimes, inexorable but also beneficent since the classless society will be its inevitable outcome.[5]

The key words here are "chaos" and "simple." Marx is unmindful of chaos, and he oversimplifies economics, as do all central planners no matter how sophisticated the mathematical models they employ. The alternative is not to give up planning but to leave planning to individuals. As a caveat, let me note that I am not necessarily making predictions about what policies will work better in the short run. Because people act with free will, economic predictions are always fallible, and sometimes the wrong policy can work and vice versa. What I am advocating is negative rather than positive rights when it comes to economic freedom. In chapters 6 and 7 I present the reasons for this advocacy in greater detail. Of course, not all advocates of free markets will embrace existentialism, and certainly not all existentialists will embrace free markets. But free market existentialism is a genuine possibility.

Alienation

The term "alienation" (*Entfremdung*), which came into vogue with the rediscovery of Marx's *Manuscripts*, is one of those terms and concepts that means something a little different to almost everyone who uses it. Still, the gist of alienation is clear enough: it is a sense of being ill at ease and not at home in contexts (such as work) where someone should not feel that way.

When, over the long run, it turned out that capitalism did not produce alienation in quite the way Marx had predicted, theorists looked to the culture and claimed that people were alienated in their consumer abundance. People were alienated both in terms of goods consumed and as a result of the mass culture that indoctrinated them in capitalist ideology. In other words, consumer society is alienated society.[6] People today have more consumption but less satisfaction.[7] This is mostly an ad hoc attempt to hang on to the charge of alienation, but there is some truth to it. Capitalism does indeed make the temptation ever-present to try to find satisfaction and fulfillment in money and things that money can buy, distracting people from potentially more fulfilling, satisfying lives. This is where existentialism, with its call for each of us to self-define, can be a useful corrective. Capitalism may have alienating tendencies, but they can be minimized and overcome.

As discussed in chapter 1, Camus retells the Greek myth in which Sisyphus is condemned to roll a rock to the top of a hill every day, only to have it roll back down again. His labor is pointless and repetitive; in short, it is alienating. Yet Camus tells us that we must imagine Sisyphus happy, "the struggle itself toward the heights is enough to fill a man's heart."[8] Camus was no friend of capitalism, but his depiction of Sisyphus can be used to illustrate that conditions do not make miserable alienation inevitable; no matter how alienating conditions are, we can overcome them.

The existentialist must take the responsibility to choose work that she finds meaningful rather than aimlessly drifting into work that is alienating. And even when she is compelled to do work that is dull, repetitive, and potentially alienating, the existentialist, like Camus' Sisyphus, can make meaning and soar above her fate. For example, in *The Fountainhead* Ayn Rand portrays Howard Roark working in a quarry after he has been expelled from architecture school. Like Sisyphus, Roark rises above his fate and makes meaning in his repetitious work.[9] Of course Rand did not conceive of herself as an existentialist, but Roark is the ideal of what an existentialist hero—rather than an anti-hero—would be.

Indeed, there is no reason that the self-creation or artistic creation by which one becomes authentic could not take the form of entrepreneurial activity. Ayn Rand's heroic characters, notably Dagny Taggart and Hank Rearden, illustrate this ideal, as do real-life entrepreneurs such as Bill Gates and Steve Jobs. Entrepreneurial activity need not be crass and cynical; it can be noble and inspiring. There should be a natural alliance among existentialists, artists, and entrepreneurs because they all take risks in their creative production. The entrepreneur is often seen as crass for the pursuit of profit, whereas the artist is seen as noble in creating art for art's sake. But neither stereotype is accurate. Some entrepreneurs are motivated more by the process of creating than by the pursuit of profit. When a company or enterprise becomes successful some entrepreneurs become bored and move on to the next challenge. And, of course, many artists are motivated partly by profit and would not continue producing their art if it didn't sell. Artists, in fact, could and should identify with entrepreneurs to the extent that they usually are, in fact, entrepreneurs, working for themselves by producing something new and different. The existentialist shares in common with both the artist and the entrepreneur an emphasis on making or creating. For the existentialist, the purpose or meaning of life is itself created and can be manifested in art or commerce.

The Marxist, by contrast, sees the entrepreneur as an agent of exploitation and alienation. The Marxist would want a given restaurant or plumbing business to be publicly owned because under capitalism people working for those businesses are exploited and alienated. After all, the proprietors own the tools and other hardware necessary for operating the business, and the proprietors pay the workers less than the actual value of their labor. Of course, though, many people refuse to find such work alienating or exploitative. Rather, they make meaning in the work and consider it an opportunity. The history of capitalism is replete with examples of people who start off penniless working for a business and eventually end up owning the business or starting their own rival business. This is not to say it is easy or guaranteed but only that it is possible through hard work and frugality.

In *Shop Class as Soulcraft* Matthew Crawford discusses harmonizing work and play, offering as an example of the ideal, the Volkswagen "speed shop" he frequented as a young man. Work and play were inseparable there; the workers were car enthusiasts, as were the customers.[10] Hopefully, most doctors and teachers also fit the ideal since the doctor really cares about healing and is fascinated by the body. Likewise the teacher really loves children and is fascinated by the process of teaching and learning.[11] Crawford contrasts the ideal with the office in which the technical writers who produce car and motorcycle manuals do not care about cars and motorcycles and cannot adequately envision the circumstances or concerns of the people who will use the manuals.[12] This is work that is not play, and the results are not happy.

Crawford valorizes pleasurable absorption in a task; we tend to think of this kind of flow as associated with leisure, whereas, in fact, it can be part of work.[13] In contrast to the ideal of absorbing work, Crawford offers the fictional example of a mortgage broker who finds his work unfulfilling and who spends his vacations climbing mountains, getting his psychic fulfillment that way.[14]

Clearly, we must be our own advocates in finding and maintaining work that suits us and allows for pleasurable absorption. The free market, as Crawford sees it, tends to transform jobs that begin as engaging, absorbing, and meaningful into mechanical procedures managed from above. As an alternative, Crawford champions the value of the trades and other stochastic arts in which we can actually see the valuable results of our work, as opposed to jobs like corporate management, where results are nebulous. In particular, Crawford points out that much of the work done by white-collar workers in cubicles is more alienating and less intellectually stimulating than that done by blue-collar workers in the trades.[15]

Crawford, though, seems to presume that we are often pawns in a way that his own experience belies. Like Crawford himself, we remain free to reject jobs that we find alienating. Crawford left the academic world and quit a job at a think tank to work with his hands instead, and he rejected the prospect of higher paying work as an electrician in favor of lower paying, more satisfying work as a motorcycle mechanic. Because time has subjective value and not every hour is worth the same, exercising intellect and creativity at a task may make us willing to do it for much less than we would otherwise sell our labor for on the labor market. This, of course, varies across individuals.

We might wonder, though, about the value of work in which we find absorption and in which we act largely apart from reflective thought. Crawford points out that much knowledge that is valuable in work is knowing-how rather than knowing-that. The firefighter who knows to leave the building seconds before it crashes cannot necessarily articulate how she knew. She is aware of a pattern based on her experience.[16] Likewise, an experienced mechanic develops knowledge of patterns based on experience. And much knowing-how is in the hands rather than in the head. This is true of a surgeon as much as it is of a mechanic. Such work is clearly not alienated, but is it authentic?

Authenticity and Responsibility

Sartre wrote much more about inauthenticity than he did about authenticity, but he captured the concept nicely in saying that authenticity "consists in having a true and lucid consciousness of the situation, in assuming the responsibility and risks that it involves, in accepting it in pride or humiliation, sometimes in horror and hate."[17] Authenticity is thus a matter of facing reality, taking responsibility for one's free actions, and accepting the results.[18] We can apply this concept of authenticity to the job we decide to take and whether we continue to work at it. It is a matter of individual responsibility whether or not to take a job that is alienating or one that is conducive to absorbing flow.[19] Of course, in tough economic circumstances there may not be many options, but nonetheless there is always at least the option to shape the attitude one takes towards one's job. Choosing a job that is conducive to absorption can be authentic, just as choosing to play an absorbing game of basketball can be authentic. In fact, it may be a hallmark of an authentic choice of work that we find the activity absorbing and conducive of flow. Absorbing flow results when there is intrinsic motivation, a sense of purpose, and an appropriate degree of challenge.[20] What could be more authentic? Such flow can be found in surprising places, including the hill where Sisyphus rolls his rock.

Existentialism calls for an internalization, rather than an externalization, of responsibility. This is where Sartre's philosophy of freedom and the free market economics he rejected actually fit together. Capitalism is the economic system that most demands personal responsibility. Socialism, by contrast, does not require the same level of personal responsibility, but rather externalizes and diffuses responsibility. It makes sense then for an existentialist to want the social conditions that minimize restraints on personal freedom as found in free market capitalism.

Opponents of capitalism fear and warn that we can become trapped by consumer society. This is a legitimate concern. The proper response, though, is not to avoid capitalism, but rather to adopt the existentialist's stance of self-definition and thus resist consumer culture. Capitalism does not make you act or think any particular way. It just provides a context to be interpreted as a situation, and, as Sartre argued, all freedom is situated. Work under capitalism may be highly conducive to, and sometimes designed to, make us into consumers, such that we work simply to buy more of what other workers make, rather than because we enjoy work or because we want to have money for certain basic necessities. Things do not have to be that way, however. Capitalism allows us to vote freely in practically all consumer choices. Of course the temptation is to let our tastes and desires be shaped to a great extent by those around us, but there is nothing necessary about that. Indeed, the existentialist, who is keenly aware of, and engaged in, the task of self-definition, will find that capitalism affords her a wide variety of choices that can aid, rather than hinder, her in self-definition. This, alas, takes a level of self-awareness, and a desire to cultivate oneself, that is all too rare. There is no need for it to be so rare, however. With the freedom of choice that capitalism affords, the existentialist can look at capitalism as a great opportunity rather than as a terrible evil. Though dealing with consumer culture and overcoming it may be difficult, it is just the kind of challenge the existentialist can relish for its opportunity to grow through challenge.

Still, we might wonder, is it possible to be an authentic consumer? The answer is that yes, one can be an authentic consumer by freely choosing and endorsing one's desires. Here we can think of Frankfurt's distinction between the willing and the unwilling addict.[21] There is nothing necessarily inauthentic about having a passion for electronic gadgets, for example, so long as one chooses and endorses that passion and desire rather than simply taking it on accidentally as a byproduct of one's culture or environment.

Fear of capitalism and free markets is just fear that people can't be trusted to think and act for themselves. Circumstances—and the ways choices are framed—can make a significant difference in the percentage of people who make a wise choice. The default choice matters, and sometimes there is no neutral choice. Still, this does not provide a valid excuse for anyone who chooses poorly, such as the well-paid executive who fails to take advantage of her employer's matching contributions to a 401K plan. Though choice architecture can be improved to increase the percentage of people who make the wise choice, that does not mean that in a metaphysical sense the change increases the probability that I personally will make the wise choice. It simply increases the epistemological, rational-belief probability that I—considered as a member of a group—will make the wise choice.

Consumerism and Voluntary Simplicity

Consumerism characterizes life in capitalist society. It is not just that we must work to earn money for the basic necessities. To grow, capitalism aims to create desire for unnecessary goods and services. As Zygmunt Bauman says,

> Consumer society thrives so long as it manages to render dissatisfaction (and so, in its own terms, unhappiness) permanent. One way of achieving this effect is to denigrate and devalue consumer products shortly after they have been hyped into the universe of consumers' desires. But another way, yet more effective, tends by and large to be kept out of the limelight: the satisfying of every need/desire/want in such a fashion that cannot help giving birth to new needs/desires/wants. What starts as a need might end up as a compulsion or an addiction. And it does, as the urge to seek in shops, and in shops only, solutions to problems and relief from pain and anxiety turns into a behavior that is not just allowed but eagerly encouraged as a habit.[22]

Bauman paints consumerism as a kind of opium of the people. Rather than face existence and make meaning for themselves, people attempt to fill the internal void with the momentary high of their latest purchase. The desire becomes an addiction. Because the addiction is effective in filling the void, it continues, and because others fill their void the same way, it is condoned, even encouraged.

Things do not have to be that way, however. Existentialism calls us to face the reality of an objectively meaningless existence and respond by creating subjective meaning. Under consumerism we are what we buy: We are the jeans we wear, the cola we drink, and the car we drive. This is not, though, a necessary consequence of capitalism. Existentialism calls for us to define ourselves as individuals and to resist being defined by external forces. The self-defining existentialist will find consumer culture crass without necessarily rejecting the free market that makes it possible. With freedom comes responsibility, including the responsibility to be an authentic individual with the sense of personal style that self-definition makes possible. It is important, of course, to get self respect from sources other than material possessions, and again, this is where the existentialist response to capitalism is key. Not wanting to be dependent on material possessions for self-worth, the self-defined existentialist finds other sources of self-respect.

Consumerist capitalism "manufactures" desire through marketing and salesmanship, attempting to get people to buy what they don't need and previously didn't even want. This is not in itself a condemnation of capitalism. Hayek was correct that the source of one's desire does not automatically make it less worthy. After all, our desire for literature and the arts is not so much natural as it is manufactured by education, yet we deem the desire worthy.[23] In all cases, though, the free market existentialist takes personal responsibility for her desires. The free market generates wealth and opportunity, but it also brings with it ubiquitous advertising. Consumer culture may be in tension with one's ideals and long-term goals. If so, it is up to the individual to recognize this and take control of her own desires and spending. The answer is not to limit the legal freedom of others to advertise but rather to exercise one's own ontological freedom to resist advertising. The existentialist remains free to opt out of consumerist society, to be in it but not of it. As Pascal said in a different context, "The sole cause of man's unhappiness is that he does not know how to stay quietly in his room."[24] This exercise of staying quietly is precisely what the existentialist can do and what she can model for the world.

We may wonder, though, are we responsible for our desires? The answer is yes, to the extent that we can manage them. They may arise outside our voluntary control but we can work to manage them once they arise. And if we do that, they will arise less frequently. Yes, environment is largely beyond our control, but how we react to our reactions is potentially within our control. We are not victims of our environment. Living in a consumer culture does not doom us to being mindless consumers filled with envy and resentment for those who have more than we do. The answer to the problem of satisfying desire is not redistribution of wealth but reduction of desire.

Technology should allow us all to work fewer hours, but instead we tend to work more hours to buy more technology. We are already at the point where virtually no one in the developed world *needs* more possessions than they have. This is not to say that producers should stop making new products. Rather, it is to say that we are well advised to be selective consumers. The problem occurs when desire gets away from us. For Sartre, we are responsible for our emotions, and it would follow, then, that for Sartre we should also be responsible for our desires. We cannot blame our desires on the world, and even more so, we cannot blame the world for any actions we take based on our desires.

While it has been said that necessity is the mother of invention, it might also be said that invention is the mother of necessity. A few generations ago, refrigerators and air conditioners were unavailable to anyone at any price. But just a short time after they became available at high prices as luxuries for the rich, they became available at modest prices and were considered "necessities" for all. This is a disturbing tendency and one that we must guard against by asking ourselves if we are really served by our desires for certain consumer goods. Do I have the desires? Or do the desires have me? Do I own things? Or do they own me? Plenty of people are owned by their cars and houses that keep them in debt and working long hours at jobs they do not find fulfilling.[25] Seneca wrote, "A thatched roof once covered free men: under marble and gold dwells slavery."[26] This is well said to the extent that we can become slaves to status. It takes a lot of time, money, and effort to keep up appearances, and even then, we are subject to the whims of others' opinions as to whether the appearance we make is up to standards. Liberation is found in the attitude that disregards displays of wealth and fashion.

In a famous scene from *King Lear*, facing a situation in which he will be stripped of most of his possessions, Lear says,

> O reason not the need! Our basest beggars
> Are in the poorest thing superfluous.
> Allow not nature more than nature needs,
> Man's life is as cheap as beast's.[27]

Lear is right, of course, that even the poorest among us generally have more than they need for mere survival. Indeed, this is something that distinguishes us from the beasts. Still, it is hard to feel badly for Lear simply based on the material circumstances in which he is being compelled to dwell. Rather, he elicits our pity because of his daughters' (Goneril and Regan) ugly ingratitude.[28]

Mother Teresa is reported to have said of the United States, "this is the poorest place I've ever been in my life."[29] Whether the quote is genuine or apocryphal does not matter, because we can easily imagine it being genuine. Thus, many people are tempted to reorganize society to make it less commercial. That, however, puts the focus in the wrong place. A better reaction would be to take responsibility for one's own desires and consumption and to lead by example for others. We don't need to curtail the free market; we simply need to become more discerning users of the free market, not buying every bauble it makes available but instead demanding quality products that meet genuine needs. The free market is the solution, not the problem.

By advocating the free market I am not advocating greed. Greed is not good. We should not feel obliged to consume inordinately. To the extent that we can restrain ourselves, it is better *not* to spend on what is *not* needed, thereby encouraging producers to make what *is* needed at a lower price and higher quality than the competition. We should, in particular, avoid the trap of conspicuous consumption. Keeping up with the Joneses for the sake of letting the Joneses know we are keeping up serves no good. It may seem to benefit the producers we patronize and the larger economy, but such benefits lack real fecundity. They do not encourage producers to make better quality, more affordable products, but rather more expensive, more desirable, less necessary products. In the long run, this serves no one well. So the free market existentialist resists the car, clothes, and jewelry that tell friends and neighbors that she has money to burn when she doesn't. Such purchases only encourage people to burn money they don't have. Far better for individuals and the larger economy would be to save the money and invest part of it in companies that meet desires with quality products, thereby benefiting the individual investor, the company, and the larger economy.

Affluenza is "a painful, contagious, socially transmitted condition of overload, debt, anxiety, and waste resulting from the dogged pursuit of more."[30] It is socially transmitted to the extent that we mimic one another and try to keep up with the Joneses. We can cure ourselves, though, by practicing "voluntary simplicity." Rather than indulge in consumption for the sake of keeping up with the Joneses, we can simplify our possessions. I offer myself as a highly imperfect example. I have the cheapest possible cell phone and I keep it in the glove compartment of my car for use only in case of emergency. And I drive a simple, plain car, nothing fancy. My clothes are basic, not chosen to impress. Voluntary simplicity is a nice way of combating conspicuous consumption, the kind of spending and purchases that are meant to signal one's wealth and ability to consume. Clothes and cars are common objects of conspicuous consumption, so by voluntarily choosing simpler, less showy alternatives we push back against conspicuous consumption. Of course we need to be careful not be too self-congratulatory in our voluntary simplicity, as perhaps I am. In fact we can potentially engage in "conspicuous simplicity," which is no more authentic than conspicuous consumption. We need to each find the pattern of consumption that suits us as individuals.

In early capitalism, when many people did piecework in their homes, capitalists tried to increase production by offering more money per piece. They got the opposite result. People tended to produce less because they could make enough money to support themselves in less time at the higher pay rate.[31] The free market existentialist aims to recapture that mentality. People say that time is money, but they don't often put much money-value on having time for themselves to do what they would like to do. We would do well to identify our genuine needs and desires and then work just enough to meet them. The great role model in this regard is Henry David Thoreau, who discovered that he could meet all of his expenses by working about six weeks a year.[32] Thoreau said, "If I should sell both my forenoons and my afternoons to society as most appear to do, I am sure that for me there would be nothing left worth living for."[33] Thoreau knew himself well in this regard, but how many other people know themselves well enough to say what makes their lives worth living? Thoreau lived a life of voluntary simplicity, indeed radical simplicity that goes further than most of us would perhaps like. Still, the ideal of voluntary simplicity is one that makes sense and that has been largely lost as a cultural value. People are foolish to waste their time and energy in pursuit of what they don't need, only to lose out on what they would truly enjoy. We can reject the commercial world without rejecting the free market.

The phrase "simplicity as subversion" captures the heart of free market existentialism.[34] Aware of environment and desires as they arise, the free market existentialist chooses not to change society but to change herself and thereby indirectly influence society. Her subversion is individual simplicity, not societal overturn. Consider grunge fashion as an example of voluntary simplicity in which the flannel shirt, that staple of lumberjack couture, became a way of rejecting glitz and glamour. As with most anti-styles, however, grunge came to be stylized and sold to the mainstream at inflated prices. Thus people began to strike a pose in their grunge faux-thenticity. Still, most clothes that can be bought in an army surplus store remain good examples of anti-style and voluntary simplicity.

Voluntary simplicity can be practiced by producers in addition to consumers to the extent that one refrains from being a purveyor of junk and harm. Many Buddhists refrain from dealing in weapons and intoxicants. Likewise, practitioners of voluntary simplicity might choose to refrain from making or selling needless junk. Of course it is the consumer who is ultimately responsible for buying needless junk, just as it is the consumer who is ultimately responsible for buying weapons or intoxicants. But one may wish to make a small statement or simply remove oneself from the chain by deciding not to make or sell needless junk. We may worry that if everyone practiced voluntary simplicity the economy would collapse. There is not much need to worry, though, since to the extent that people practice voluntary simplicity it will just motivate producers to offer better products.

We have come to "need" many things that in truth we only want. But at least some of these things, like automobiles, have real practical value, whereas other things, like the latest bedazzler sold on QVC, have virtually no real practical value. Most Americans could live with far less than they have, but that is not to say that they should. Prudentially, what they should do is examine their lives and define themselves. Consumer products are like alcohol. Everyone should have the right to them, but each of us needs to monitor our own consumption and be mindful of whether we are consuming or being consumed.

Personally, I like the idea of living a life of the mind without great concern for money. I think the pursuit of money easily becomes addictive, and I have a distaste for a life that is lived purely in pursuit of money. However, I recognize that my reaction is aesthetic, and I do not believe my aesthetic judgment in this case or any other is objectively and universally correct. More troublesome are people who have a distaste for the life lived in pursuit of money and who frame their distaste as a universal, objective ethical judgment. This is common among the intelligentsia who, for example, tend to like small businesses from an aesthetic point of view while despising big chains from an aesthetic point of view, all the while framing their judgment in a universal, objective ethical form.

One size does not fit all when it comes to the quantity and quality of consuming. I happen to think it is ridiculous to drive a large SUV. I find repulsive the amount of money the vehicle costs and the ostentatious display it represents. And I suspect that most people driving large SUVs haven't given much thought to what would really make them happy. They are like children who just want the next big toy. However, I am sure that this is not true of all people driving big SUVs. Some of those people really enjoy the vehicles enough such that they are worth the cost.

Personally, I favor minimizing desire for consumer goods in order to buy myself time to spend as I see fit. My job as a professor suits me well in this regard. I am fortunate, and I chose wisely. I did not have the aptitude to repair motorcycles, or to play professional baseball, or to sing in a band, so I was wise not to pursue those careers. I did have the aptitudes for law and business and could have made a lot more money in those areas, but they likely would have left far less time at my disposal. Not everyone is fortunate to have the same range of aptitudes and opportunities as everyone else. So in choosing work, one needs to consider many things. What are my aptitudes and opportunities? How alienating is the work? Or how engrossing and rewarding is the work? How much does it pay? How many hours does it demand? One size does not fit all when it comes to determining the work one would be happiest overall in doing. It makes perfect sense for some people to do work they find alienating if it pays well and gives them time and money to do other things they truly enjoy or value.

Working as a professor is a good choice for me. I would not continue doing it full time if I won the lottery, but aside from being a full-time writer (which is much riskier financially) it is the best job for my personal preferences and aptitudes. Being a professor gives me a great deal of autonomy and a great deal of time to pursue my intellectual interests. I suspect that a lot of people have not chosen wisely in picking their line of work. Too many people choose based largely on salary, not paying enough attention to how alienating they find the work and how little time it leaves them to pursue other interests. Once in the environment of their job they also elevate their desires for consumer goods to keep step with their coworkers. Again, for me this is one of the nice things about being a professor. I am surrounded mostly by people who could have made more money in other lines of work but chose this line of work because (among other reasons) fancy cars, clothes, and gadgets don't have great appeal to them. So the company I keep at work reinforces my own preferences in this way. By contrast, if I were a stockbroker I would be surrounded by many people who greatly desire fancy cars, clothes, and gadgets. The situation would call for me to exercise a lot of willpower in staying true to my own preferences. In fact, even as a professor I have acquired tastes and preferences that I wish I had not. Alas, I could retire earlier if I simplified my desires.

Alan Kahan proposes that intellectuals re-conceive themselves as "loyal opposition" to capitalism, showing that that there is more to life than the culture of the market.[35] As Kahan says, "it should be possible to dislike capitalists without wanting to get rid of them."[36] The market is not all there is; there is also, more importantly, the way the individual defines herself and resists the culture of the market. As Kahan notes, intellectuals can help with finding or creating a meaning of life beyond the market. This is not to say that there is one meaning of life that all intellectuals would agree to and that they should enforce. Rather, this is to say that the kind of discourse that intellectuals engage in can help people formulate for themselves a meaning of life beyond the market. The goal, for example, of a liberal arts education, imparted by intellectuals, should be to teach students *how* to think not *what* to think.

As Kahan says, intellectuals ought to "encourage people to have different goals, not *instead* of those the market satisfies, but *alongside* them."[37] Intellectuals can have a salutary influence by exposing people not just to alternative ways of making a living but to alternative ways of spending their leisure time. As Kahan says, "Intellectuals can help people think about what they should want, rather than about how to get what they already want."[38] So, again, in the realm of leisure time and disposable income, intellectual discourse can help people examine their desires and choices. Do I really want to spend my time or money that way? Why am I inclined to spend my time or money that way?

Enlightened Self-interest and Prudence

Lord Acton said that power corrupts and absolute power corrupts absolutely. Of course, this is not a logical argument but rather a persuasive warning. Likewise, suspicion of money and commerce is based partly on the common-sense observation that they are tempting and corrupting. Like power, though, money and commerce are not necessarily corrupting. As Kahan remarks, intellectuals typically see business as a stupid choice of a stupid life.[39] I plead guilty on that count, but for me, at least, this judgment is prudential and aesthetic, not ethical—and I recognize that it is also individual. One size does not fit all. I do not think a life in business would fit me, and I am guilty of anti-bourgeois prejudice. Doing something simply for the sake of making money tends to rub me the wrong way, not that all business is done simply for the sake of making money. Aron says, "The contempt with which the intellectuals are inclined to regard everything connected with commerce and industry has always seemed to me itself contemptible."[40] Again, I am guilty to some extent. Curiously, there is something priestly in this intellectual snobbery and contempt. As the priest takes a position of power above the workaday concerns of average people, so too does the intellectual. It is easy to pass judgment from that perch, and the priest and intellectual usually don't even realize how facile their judgment is.

There is a lot that is ugly and unappealing about capitalism, as far as I am concerned, with hucksters and salesmen near the top of the list. But for an existentialist to dismiss capitalism because of such things is to throw the baby out with the bathwater. Part of the problem with the rejection of capitalism is the assumption that those who embrace capitalism are motivated only by profits. But Ayn Rand's characters and Rand herself show that is not necessarily the case inasmuch as they value their creative activities and expression above profit. As an architect in *The Fountainhead*, Howard Roark does not design any structure for the sake of money, and he is quick to reject a job if he can't do it on his own terms. In *Atlas Shrugged* the railroad magnate Dagny Taggart and the steel baron Hank Rearden certainly pursue profit, but they are not willing to do just anything for a buck. They clearly enjoy the creative acts of running their businesses more than they enjoy making profits, and neither of them cares much

79

for luxury. Rand's heroes don't do things primarily for money, but great things do earn them money. Rand herself took a reduced royalty rate on *Atlas Shrugged* rather than cut its page count. She would rather publish the book as she wanted it than make more money on its sales.

One prominent criticism of capitalism is that it lacks good intentions à la Kant. The merchant doesn't cheat his customers, but he is motivated by self-interest in having a good reputation rather than by a sense of what is morally right. This, of course, is Adam Smith's invisible hand. The merchant serves his customers well without having their well-being as his primary aim. This can be depicted as a kind of hypocrisy in which the merchant is really not concerned with living up to the moral values he may espouse.[41]

For Alexis de Tocqueville enlightened self-interest included the tendency of merchants and capitalists "to anticipate and fulfill the needs and desires of their customers, like good spouses do for each other."[42] This brand of enlightened self-interest is epitomized in the Rotary Club motto, "he who serves best profits most."[43] It sounds cynical, and sometimes it is. But it need not be. Notice the comparison of merchants and customers to good spouses. As Adam Grant has shown, in business, givers find themselves at the very pinnacle of success. Takers, who try to get more than they give in nearly every exchange, ultimately find themselves disliked and distrusted. They may succeed for a time, but the long run is not usually kind to them. Matchers, who play tit-for-tat, make the same basic mistake that takers make; they see commerce as a zero-sum game in which each exchange has a winner and a loser. Givers, by contrast, realize, at least on some level, that commerce is not necessarily a zero-sum game. To be sure, some givers become doormats and do not succeed, but other givers are able to give without thought of return yet confident that good will come back to them.[44] Such givers have an expanded sense of self in the way good spouses do. In fact, most people have an expanded sense of self that includes at least some family members and friends, such that what benefits or harms those people benefits or harms them.[45] In business, highly successful givers cultivate a sense of self that includes colleagues, clients, and even rivals. They do not thus become doormats or pushovers, but they are willing to take a chance on another person. If the other person proves unworthy of giving, the giver will withdraw. It is worth the cost of being burned by the occasional taker to expand one's sense of self in relationship with others.[46] So while the invisible hand works well when the merchant decides not to cheat his customer out of pure self-interest in preserving his good reputation, it works even better when out of enlightened self-interest the merchant does not cheat his customer because the merchant's expanded sense of self actually includes his customer in the way it might include a friend or family member. Successful givers give out of a sense of being abundant and overflowing, and they do not keep score. This is not to say they are foolish and indiscriminate, but rather that through practice they develop practical wisdom and good habits. Their giving is prudential, but not in a cold or calculating way. Indeed, this is enlightened self-interest at its best and most effective.

Lest We Forget Nietzsche

Talk of being abundant and overflowing calls to mind Nietzsche's *Übermensch*, or overman, and we should not leave this consideration of existentialism and capitalism without discussing Nietzsche.[47] Nietzsche said so many things, including so many contradictory things, that interpreters and followers often feel free to pick and choose what to focus on and what to ignore, creating their "own personal Nietzsche." In what follows I am guilty of the same, as perhaps I have been guilty of creating my "own personal Sartre," though at least consciously so.

The traditional interpretation of Nietzsche has been that he is apolitical. At most he could be thought of as harmonious with Western liberalism, given its emphasis on individualism.[48] Nietzsche's Zarathustra clearly has no use for political entities, seeing the modern state in which all melt into one as the ruin of mankind and calling the state "the new idol."[49] We bow down before the wishes of the state and lose our identity; the modern state is depicted as the great liar, the entity that seduces us and trains us for obedience. As Zarathustra says, "the state tells lies in all the tongues of good and evil; and whatever it says it lies—and whatever it has it has stolen."[50] Continuing, he says, "State I call it where all drink poison, the good and the wicked; state, where all lose themselves, the good and the wicked; state, where the slow suicide of all is called 'life.'"[51]

Lester Hunt argues that "the point is to turn our backs on issues of state policy altogether and take up the neglected task. In this quite literal sense of the word, Nietzsche is 'anti-political.'"[52] What is this neglected task? Zarathustra instructs us thus: "Where the state *ends*—look there, my brothers! Do you not see it, the rainbow and the bridges of the overman?"[53] Nietzsche thus champions an individualism that privileges the conditions under which the overman can arise.[54] This sounds, at first, like Nietzsche is a "minarchist" or an anarchist. Hunt says, though, that Nietzsche's "concerns are obviously incompatible with thinking that the state ought to have large amounts of power, but they do not otherwise clearly imply anything about what state policy ought to be."[55] Nietzsche emphasizes the individual rather than the societal, and he has no detailed plans for a political order or ideal society. Rather, Nietzsche's ideal seems to be an individual like himself, living as an itinerant bohemian intellectual, a cosmopolitan perhaps. The state may be a problem, it may be the new false god, but an ideal state is not offered as an answer.

Keith Ansell-Pearson says that "Nietzsche is adamant that it is only an aristocratic society which can justify terrible but noble sacrifices and experiments, for only this kind of society is geared towards not justice or compassion, but the continual self-overcoming of man—and of life."[56] Thus, in sharp contrast to Marx, Nietzsche favors the exploitation of the masses to benefit the aristocratic elite. Ansell-Pearson says, "it is difficult to see how Nietzsche's aristocrats could maintain their rule without recourse to highly oppressive instruments of political control and manipulation."[57] I believe, however, that though on Nietzsche's terms there would be nothing objectionable to such oppression and manipulation, it would thwart his larger goal of providing the conditions for the overman to rise. There is no reason to think that those who occupy the aristocracy at a given moment are capable of producing greatness unless they earned their spot in the aristocracy through greatness. So protecting those who belong to the aristocracy through heredity or any other means besides greatness itself would frustrate Nietzsche's ultimate goal. I don't think that he is right that we need a social aristocracy— at least not as traditionally conceived—to promote greatness and self-overcoming. Nietzsche himself was not a member of any kind of social aristocracy. Rather, he was a member of the aristocracy of talent and intelligence in the Jeffersonian sense, and I would argue that this aristocracy of talent and intelligence flourishes best under free market capitalism and without any need for oppression or manipulation. Nietzsche does not aim for agreement, and he does not aim to make servile followers. So we are very much in his spirit to reject him where we find him wrong, all the more so when we find him wrong on his own terms.

We can accept Nietzsche's aristocratism and elitism without accepting the form of government or economy he may have thought was required to bring about great individual human beings and great culture. In fact, I believe that it is the minimal state and the free market that are most likely to produce great human beings and great culture by placing the fewest possible restrictions on people and giving them the greatest possible motivation to be productive, not just for profit but for a sense of purpose. Nietzsche is concerned with allowing individual geniuses to arise and flourish, and freedom and free markets make that more likely. Capitalism has made possible more interesting work that can run on intrinsic motivation. The pursuit of profit can aid in this regard, but it is not strictly necessary, as editing Wikipedia and working on open-source software illustrate.

To be sure, though, Nietzsche did not agree concerning capitalism. He said even less about economics than he did about politics, but with his emphasis on power Nietzsche was not an advocate of the spontaneous order that characterizes the free market. As Hunt says, "Nietzsche could not trust the sort of order in social life which arises spontaneously and is not conceived and imposed by an individual mind or will."[58] For Nietzsche, culture is more important than politics. To the extent that politics matters, it matters as a means to the end of developing a culture that would promote human greatness. Nietzsche may have been skeptical of a free market economy, thinking it leads inexorably to philistinism, but he was mistaken.

Yes, the free market produces a lot of cultural junk, but it also produces great art. As Paul Cantor has remarked, the twenty-five greatest American films of the twentieth century are "comparable in artistic worth to a similar sampling from almost any other moment in cultural history, such as the twenty-five greatest Victorian novels or nineteenth-century Italian operas."[59] And this is not even to mention the television shows, novels, and plays produced by Americans in the twentieth century. So even if we accept Nietzsche's questionable view that politics is a means to an end of producing culture, we should not accept his view that the free market will produce only philistinism. Quite the opposite—it will also produce cultural greatness. Let us not forget that Shakespeare wrote his plays for money, not just for personal expression. The pursuit of financial rewards is not an impediment to great art even if the pursuit also leads to bad art.

The importance of having an arena of conflict cannot be overstated for Nietzsche. In this respect the free market, devoid of sentimentalism, seems an ideal proving ground and opportunity for self-overcoming. We may love the guy who makes buggy whips and who has devoted his life to perfecting his craft. But, thanks to what Schumpeter calls in rather Nietzschean terms "creative destruction," with the rise of the automobile there is practically no more need for buggy whips.[60] The artisan who made them will have to do something else. Every entrepreneur, no matter how successful, takes the chance that her product will become outmoded or obsolete. Like many people, I miss used bookstores, which were much more common years ago. I miss browsing in them and making chance discoveries. Used bookstores have largely disappeared, though, because it has become much more efficient to sell used books online. This new business model has the great benefit to the consumer of making nearly any book available used and at a good price—and this benefit greatly outweighs the loss of shopping in used bookstores. The browsing experience is an aesthetic experience and preference, one that some people may be tempted to confuse with an ethical experience.

Pace Nietzsche, capitalism is Nietzschean to the extent that it is the economic system that most favors the development of individual genius. The market recognizes and rewards the genius, and it also makes possible work that is more autonomous and intrinsically rewarding. Of course capitalism also produces a lot of crap that panders to the lowest tastes, but so what? In "Noble Markets" Edward Romar argues that Nietzsche's master-and-slave morality make sense as a justification for free market economics.[61] The overman can be an entrepreneur, a creative risk taker, and the envious masses often adopt a slave morality fed by resentment. Socialism is to politics what the slave revolt is to morality, a complete reversal of values. Indeed, for Nietzsche, "Socialism is only a degenerate form of Christianity."[62] La Rochefoucauld says that "the contempt for riches among the philosophers was a hidden desire to revenge themselves on the injustice of Fortune ... "[63] Nietzsche's account of the rise of slave morality out of resentment partly explains the demand for redistribution of wealth through taxation. Many people who despise capitalism despise it in much the same spirit and for much the same reason that they despised the quarterback and the cheerleader in high school. Their resentment is the revenge of the nerds. Ironically, Nietzsche unwittingly shares this resentment in his failure to support capitalism. He doesn't actually oppose capitalism, and he certainly opposes socialism. But he does look down on commercial society and does not recognize it as a domain, like art and war, that is worthy of the overman.

Both Nietzsche and the free market seek to maximize freedom of individual choice to maximize the creative output of individuals. Both Nietzsche and the free market privilege the individual self-interest that ultimately leads to benefits for all. Individual genius is valued under capitalism because it has a tremendous spillover effect. Capitalism thrives on free trade in which both sides of a trade value what they get more than what they give, as testified to by the "thank you" from both sides.

In conclusion, even though he doesn't realize it, "my own personal Nietzsche" loves the free market for its tendency to produce greatness.

Notes

1 Robert C. Solomon, "Pessimism vs. Existentialism," *The Chronicle Review* January 26, 2007. http://chronicle.com/article/Pessimism-vs-Existentialism/8935.
2 See Scott M. James, *An Introduction to Evolutionary Ethics* (Malden, MA: Wiley-Blackwell, 2011), p. 59.
3 F.A. Hayek, "The Uses of Knowledge in Society," *American Economic Review* 35 (1945): 519–30.
4 F.A. Hayek, *The Fatal Conceit: The Errors of Socialism* (Chicago: University of Chicago Press, 2011), p. 76.
5 Raymond Aron, *The Opium of the Intellectuals* (New Brunswick, NJ: Transaction Publishers, 2001), pp. 192–3.

6   Alan S. Kahan, *Mind vs. Money: The War between Intellectuals and Capitalism* (New Brunswick, NJ: Transaction Publishers, 2010), p. 221.
7   Kahan, p. 221.
8   Albert Camus, *The Myth of Sisyphus and Other Essays*, trans. Justin O'Brien (New York: Vintage International, 1991), p. 123.
9   Thanks to Shawn Klein for this example.
10 Matthew B. Crawford, *Shop Class as Soulcraft: An Inquiry into the Value of Work* (New York: Penguin Books, 2009), pp. 182–5.
11 Crawford, p. 182.
12 Crawford, p. 177.
13 Crawford, p. 181.
14 Crawford, p. 181.
15 Crawford, pp. 126–60.
16 Crawford, pp. 161–2.
17 Jean-Paul Sartre, *Anti-Semite and Jew*, trans. George J. Becker (New York: Schocken Books, 1948), p. 90.
18 In *Sartre's Ethics of Engagement: Authenticity and Civic Virtue* (London: Continuum, 2006), T Storm Heter adds that "to be authentic I must respect others because others make me who I am" (p. 75). I disagree, as does Thomas C. Anderson, *Sartre's Two Ethics: From Authenticity to Integral Humanity* (Chicago: Open Court, 1993), pp. 68 and 55; cf. Heter, pp. 76–7.
19 On flow see Mihály Csíkszentmihályi, *Flow: The Psychology of Optimal Experience* (New York: Harper & Row, 1990).
20 See Csíkszentmihályi.
21 Harry G. Frankfurt, "Freedom of the Will and the Concept of a Person," *Journal of Philosophy* 68 (1971): 5–20.
22 Zygmunt Bauman, *Does Ethics Have a Chance in a World of Consumers?* (Cambridge, MA: Harvard University Press, 2008), p. 170.
23 F.A. Hayek, "The Non Sequitur of the 'Dependence Effect,'" *Southern Economic Journal* 27 (1961): 346–7.
24 Blaise Pascal, *Pensées*, trans A.J. Kreilsheimer (Harmondsworth, UK: Penguin, 1966), section 67.
25 John de Graaf, David Waan, and Thomas H. Naylor, *Affluenza: The All-Consuming Epidemic* (San Francisco: Berrett-Koehler Publishers, 2001), pp. 28 and 39.
26 Lucius Annaeus Seneca, Letter XC, "On the Part Played by Philosophy in the Progress of Man." http://www.stoics.com/seneca_epistles_book_2.html.
27 *King Lear*, act 2, scene 4.
28 Thanks to Paul Cantor for this example, though he may not agree with my conclusion.

29 See de Graaf, Waan, and Naylor, p. 70.

30 de Graaf, Waan, and Naylor, p. 2.

31 de Graaf, Waan, and Naylor, p. 130.

32 Henry David Thoreau, *Walden* in Carl Bode, ed., *The Portable Thoreau* (New York: Penguin Viking, 1982), p. 323.

33 Henry David Thoreau, "Life without Principle." http://thoreau. eserver.org/life1.html.

34 de Graaf, Waan, and Naylor, p. 179.

35 Kahan, p. 283.

36 Kahan, p. 272.

37 Kahan, p. 276.

38 Kahan, p. 277.

39 Kahan, p. 114.

40 Aron (2001), p. 70.

41 Kahan, p. 105.

42 Kahan, p. 275.

43 Kahan, p. 275.

44 Adam Grant, *Give and Take: A Revolutionary Approach to Success* (New York: Viking, 2013), pp. 33–4 and 179–85.

45 Cf. Robert B. Cialdini, Stephanie L. Brown, Brian P. Lewis, Carol Luce, and Steven L. Neuberg, "Reinterpreting the Empathy-Altruism Relationship: When One into One Equals Oneness," *Journal of Personality and Social Psychology* 73 (1997): 481–94.

46 Grant, pp. 198–201.

47 Corey Robin attempted to smear Hayek and libertarianism by associating them with Nietzsche in "Nietzsche's Marginal Children: On Friedrich Hayek," *The Nation,* May 27, 2013, pp. 27–36.

48 But see Keith Ansell-Pearson, *An Introduction to Nietzsche as Political Thinker: The Perfect Nihilist* (Cambridge: Cambridge University Press, 1994). Ansell-Pearson draws on Nietzsche's early unpublished essays, "The Greek State" and "Homer's Contest," to suggest that he views politics as essential to bringing about the culture necessary to produce great individual human beings. This early unpublished Nietzsche actually has a kinship to Rousseau and Hegel. But of course Nietzsche likely had his reasons for not publishing those essays and his later views should be seen not so much as supplementing them or growing from them as contradicting them. The published Nietzsche is clearly anti-Hegelian.

49 Friedrich Nietzsche, *Thus Spoke Zarathustra*, trans. Walter Kaufmann (New York: Penguin, 1966), "On the New Idol," p. 48.

50 "On the New Idol," p. 49.

51 "On the New Idol," p. 50.

52 Lester H. Hunt, "Politics and Anti-Politics: Nietzsche's View of the State," *History of Philosophy Quarterly* 2 (1985): 463.

53 "On the New Idol," p. 51.

54 F.A. Hayek in *The Road to Serfdom* (Chicago: University of Chicago Press, 2007), cites Nietzsche as a collectivist for Zarathustra's lament that humanity is lacking a goal (p. 162n4). But for Nietzsche humanity has no goal, is not going anywhere. It is the highest specimens that matter, not humanity as a whole. Ansell-Pearson says that for Nietzsche, "The existing one thousand goals of various people are to be united and brought together in the positing and creation of a new *single* goal: the *Übermensch*" (Ansell-Pearson, p. 161). This is an interestingly different interpretation of this section of Zarathustra and seems about right. The point is not that we need to have a collective united by a common goal but that previous, disparate goals have been inferior.

55 Hunt (1985), p. 462.

56 Ansell-Pearson, p. 149.

57 Ansell-Pearson, p. 155.

58 Hunt (1985), p. 466.

59 Paul Cantor, *The Invisible Hand in Popular Culture: Liberty vs. Authority in American Film and TV* (Lexington: University Press of Kentucky, 2012), p. xxiv.

60 Joseph A. Schumpeter, *Capitalism, Socialism and Democracy*, 3rd edn (New York: Harper Perennial Modern Classics, 2008).

61 Edward J. Romar, "Noble Markets: The Noble/Slave Ethic in Hayek's Free Market Capitalism," *Journal of Business Ethics* 85 (2009): 57–66.

62 Albert Camus, *The Rebel: An Essay on Man in Revolt*, trans. Anthony Bower (New York: Vintage, 1992), p. 69.

63 Francois de la Rochefoucauld, *Maxims*, in *The Oxford Book of Money* (Oxford: Oxford University Press, 1996), p. 332.

4

Why Nothing Is Wrong

Moral Anti-realism

This chapter shifts ground to make another unexpected connection, that between existentialism and evolutionary theory. Existentialism is readily associated with the rejection of objective values, but the basis of that rejection can be obscure.[1] So this chapter offers an evolutionary argument for rejecting objective morality—a morality that exists independently of people's beliefs and desires. In chapter 6 the rejection of objective morality argued for in chapters 4 and 5 will provide another link between existentialism and the free market.

This chapter begins by making a case for the harmony of existentialism and evolutionary theory. It then considers why the feeling of morality and belief in objective morality persists in the wake of the death of God. The answer, it is averred, is that evolution has endowed us with a "core morality," a set of moral beliefs, concepts, or feelings that result from our evolutionary history. Core morality does not, however, establish the existence of moral facts. Rather, core morality has survival value that is explained more parsimoniously without the existence of moral facts.[2] This chapter, then, argues for

The Free Market Existentialist: Capitalism without Consumerism, First Edition. William Irwin.
© 2015 John Wiley & Sons, Ltd. Published 2015 by John Wiley & Sons, Ltd.

moral anti-realism, the metaphysical view that there are no moral facts.

Evolutionary Existentialism

Before we begin the examination of the evolutionary account of morality, we should note that the connection between existentialism and evolutionary theory may seem odd. Sartre argued that there is no human nature, that existence precedes essence. How can this be reconciled with what genetics and evolutionary theory tells us, that our essence is our genotype? In short, it cannot; existentialism must be changed. It must adapt.

Existentialism must recognize that there is a human nature, but it is fluid and variable rather than fixed and stable. As we will discuss in more detail in chapter 5, human nature has limits, but there is great freedom and variability within those limits. Existentialism must recognize that we have genetically determined inclinations, though of course these inclinations do not preclude ontological freedom any more than concrete circumstances preclude ontological freedom. As David Barash says, "There is very little in the human behavioral repertoire that is under genetic control, and very little that is not under genetic influence. At the same time, human beings are remarkably adroit at overcoming such influences."[3] In sum, "Within a remarkable range, our evolutionary bequeathal is wildly permissive."[4] So we need to resist the temptation to treat our own choices as genetically predetermined: "'Going with the flow' of our biologically generated inclinations is very close to what Sartre has called 'bad faith' wherein people pretend to themselves and others that they are not free when in fact they are."[5]

Evolutionary theory does not necessarily imply existentialism, but the two are compatible once existentialism softens its stance on human nature. And there are some perhaps-surprising points of coincidence, for example the absurdity and pointlessness of life. Evolution is not teleological. Changes do not occur as part of some grand design, nor for the good of the species, nor even for the good of the individual. Rather, evolution is largely driven by the replication of what Richard Dawkins calls selfish genes.[6] As Barash says, "although evolutionary biology makes no claim that it or what it produces is inherently good, it also teaches that life is absurd."[7] Of course, as we noted with Camus in chapter 1, strictly speaking life itself is not absurd; only our relationship to the world is absurd. Nature is red in tooth and claw, but that itself is not absurd. Only our hope or demand that nature should follow some benevolent plan to achieve higher order is absurd. We are left, then, with a picture of life lacking inherent meaning. But that does not mean we have to sink into despair. On the contrary. As Barash says,

> Some critics say that if evolutionary biology reveals that life is without intrinsic meaning, then biology is mistaken. Not at all. From the perspective of natural science generally, there is no inherent reason that anything—a rock, a waterfall, a halibut, a human being—is of itself meaningful. As existentialists have long pointed out, the key to life's meaning is not aliveness itself, but what we attach to it.[8]

Dealing with the Death of God

In *The Brothers Karamazov*, Dostoevsky has his character Ivan say that if God does not exist then everything is permitted. More accurately, nothing is forbidden. To most people at the time, including Dostoevsky, the reasoning seemed obvious and it provided good motivation to maintain that there must be a God. But in the twentieth century and beyond many philosophers have sought to deny that there is a link between God and morality. As Nietzsche predicted, the dead God casts a long shadow:

> The greatest recent event—that "God is dead," that the belief in the Christian god has become unbelievable—is already beginning to cast its first shadows over Europe ... But in the main one may say ... [not] many people know as yet *what* this event really means— and how much must collapse now ... because it was built upon this faith, propped up by it, grown into it; for example, the whole of European morality.[9]

It has taken and will continue to take a long time for people to come to terms with the death of God and its implications for morality. The tendency of atheistic philosophers in the twentieth and twenty-first centuries has been to find a way to justify morality as real and objective without God. This chapter argues for a contrary view, namely that without God there is no real or objective morality. There are no moral facts.[10]

Atheistic philosophers are generally aware of the evolutionary basis of moral experience, but many argue that evolution produced moral intuitions that track a set of moral facts. Before we consider this possibility, we need to spell out the evolutionary explanation for moral feelings and experience.

The Evolutionary Explanation of Moral Experience

I do not aim to reinvent the wheel here, but rather to bring news of the wheel to those who have not heard. The wheel in question is the evolutionary explanation of moral experience or feelings. Michael Ruse puts the conclusion succinctly in saying "morality is a collective illusion foisted upon us by our genes."[11] In other words, moral experience or feelings do not reflect some metaphysical reality, do not reflect moral facts. To grasp this, we simply need to imagine humans emerging from a different evolutionary history; we would have had a very different sense of morality. We can, in fact, imagine another evolutionary history that would have led us to value as natural and good "cannibalism, incest, the love of darkness and decay, parricide, and the mutual eating of feces."[12] Closer to this actual world, we can imagine very different moral feelings if we had evolved like lions, bonobos, or social insects.[13] So our moral experience and feelings are not the products of pre-existing moral facts. Rather our moral experience and feelings are the products of our evolutionary history. And just because we evolved to believe that something is morally true does not necessarily mean that it really is morally true.

There are varying moral standards across times and places, but there is remarkable commonality as well. For example, despite our differences in specifics, no culture exhibits a complete indifference to killing or harming others.[14] Indeed, human beings share a "core morality," a set of moral beliefs, concepts, and feelings that result from our evolutionary history. Sharon Street says that across times and cultures we find agreement to the following:

1 The fact that something would promote one's survival is a reason in favor of it.
2 The fact that something would promote the interests of a family member is a reason to do it.
3 We have greater obligations to help our own children than we do to help complete strangers.
4 The fact that someone has treated one well is a reason to treat that person well in return.
5 The fact that someone is altruistic is a reason to admire, praise, and reward him or her.
6 The fact that someone has done one deliberate harm is a reason to shun that person or seek his or her punishment.[15]

Street frames the matter in terms of specific beliefs, but these likely develop out of general concepts. Thus Alex Rosenberg argues that core morality includes norms of reciprocity, fairness, and equality.[16] And Richard Joyce explains that whereas moral concepts may be innate, specific moral beliefs are not.[17] So, for example, the concept of "forbidden" will not necessarily emerge under all conditions, but it is there waiting to be developed.[18] And the specific belief that pork is forbidden will only develop in certain cultures. Specific moral beliefs grow out of general concepts, and a core morality rooted in general concepts can be found despite the great variety of specific moral beliefs. Cultures play a major role in shaping and developing specific moral beliefs, but basic concepts and a sense of morality are the work of nature, not nurture. As Joyce says, "Morality exists in virtually every human individual. It develops without formal instruction, with no deliberate effort, and with no conscious awareness of its special features."[19] Of course what he means by "morality" here is moral beliefs, feelings, and experience, not a set of metaphysical facts.

So who does a sense of morality not exist in? Answer: Psychopaths, who know the difference between the "right" and "wrong" of core morality and their specific cultural morality but don't feel it—don't have the emotional accompaniment that evolution endows most of us with.[20] They lack empathy and the ability to feel guilt or remorse. Psychopathy is a phenotype that occurs in about 1 percent of the population,[21] and its relative scarcity is testimony to psychopaths' general lack of fitness throughout human evolutionary history.

Instead of psychopaths, evolutionary history has generally favored humans who feel guilty when they transgress core morality and who seek to avoid or punish others when others transgress. These basics of core morality are manifested in numerous ways across times and cultures. Cultures adapt them and extrapolate upon them such that differing and conflicting moralities are generated. But, thanks to core morality, reciprocity is foundational to all moralities. As Joyce says, "all human moral systems give a leading role to *reciprocal relations*; if the human moral sense is prepared for any particular subject matter, it is surely this. It therefore seems eminently reasonable to assume that reciprocal exchanges were a central evolutionary problem that morality was designed to solve."[22]

Humans evolved to live together in groups of approximately 35–150.[23] In order to survive and pass on their genes, individuals had to adapt to group norms, the most basic of which is reciprocity, helping those who help you and harming those who harm you. Judging that someone morally ought to do something is not like judging that someone aesthetically ought to like something. If someone doesn't like a piece of music we think they should like, we don't think they should be punished. But, as Joyce argues, from an evolutionary perspective, judging that someone hasn't done something they morally should have done commonly involves judging that the person deserves punishment.[24] This is not a logical necessity. After all, many philosophers today think punishment is cruel and futile, but to arrive at such an enlightened view they must override their natural, evolutionary response.

Punishment comes in two forms: punishment from others and self-punishment.[25] We evolved to have a sense of guilt and a desire to punish in order to keep ourselves and others in line so as to enhance the survival chances of our own genes. It is easy to see why evolution would incline us to punish others who harm us, but why would it incline us to punish ourselves? Why not just leave our punishment to others who catch us in our transgressions? For two reasons: 1) because we are not always caught in our transgressions and 2) because the punishment of others may be more severe.

So evolution selected for a moral conscience. Actions depend on habits, and we cannot completely count on others to help us develop our habits; we need to monitor ourselves. The emotion of guilt can be conceived as the punishment we inflict on ourselves when we transgress a moral norm. The unpleasant experience of guilt makes us less likely to transgress that way again. And that is a very helpful thing because although guilt is unpleasant, it is not lethal or physically disabling, as the punishment from another can be. In addition, feeling guilty signals to others that I am experiencing my punishment and often saves me from punishment by others.[26] As Joyce says, "Guilt—involving a self-directed judgment that punishment is deserved—may serve the individual by inhibiting his own usual defensive mechanisms, prompting him to submit to punishment or at least to apologize, and thus quickly get back on a good footing with his fellows."[27]

Evolution endowed us with more than just the prudential inclination to avoid punishment. We have, in addition, a conscience that judges actions as right or wrong regardless of who takes them or what consequences result. Joyce has theorized that this tendency to make moral judgments serves an important purpose. We are all tempted by short-term pleasure and subject to weakness of will, but prudence can step in to tell us that the short-term pleasure is not in our long-term interest. Still, prudence does not always win the argument. To be clear, by prudence I mean the non-moral virtue in choosing and acting well, especially in successfully fulfilling one's desires. Because non-moral prudence does not always prevail, moral judgment has evolved as well. As Joyce says, "moral judgment can step in on those occasions when prudence may falter (in particular when the prudential gain is a probabilistic long-term affair)."[28]

If I can tell myself that it will be not only imprudent but morally wrong to steal an apple, then I increase my chances of making the prudent decision. In some cases there may be virtually no chance of getting caught stealing the apple, and so prudence needs to rely on the argument that stealing once will make me more likely to steal again the next time when perhaps the chances of getting caught will not be so minimal. In such cases prudence may have a hard time getting the better of short-term pleasure. But if I am convinced that there is a moral fact of the matter, that stealing the apple is objectively morally wrong, then I can bolster the case. As Joyce says, "moral judgments can act as a kind of *personal commitment*, in that thinking of one's actions in moral terms eliminates certain practical possibilities."[29] If I believe that killing someone is a grave moral wrong, then I won't even consider the possibility. For lesser moral offenses, though, like stealing the apple, "moral beliefs ... are a bulwark against the temptations of short-term profit."[30]

Belief that an action is objectively morally wrong helps to discourage a person from taking that action, because the person will be punished with guilt even if not punished by anyone else. But this motivation is not strong enough in all cases. Thanks to evolution, the idea that something is morally wrong is intimately tied to the belief that it should be punished. Language-communication plays a crucial role here. If I steal Rob's apple, he may not be strong enough to punish me, but thanks to language he can tell others about me. Others will not trust me, and I will be punished by their distrust. Thus gossip and reputation help to keep people in line, people who might be inclined to game the system. Living in society is an ongoing series of prisoner's dilemma scenarios in which to succeed we need to establish a reputation for playing well with others. Thanks to language, information can be dispersed in a way that spares us from having to experience dealing with every other person directly. We don't just talk about one another for the sake of entertainment and *Schadenfreude*; gossip serves a very practical purpose in fostering reciprocity. As Joyce says, "A language of gossip is a language of reciprocity."[31]

So the fear of being seen doing something morally wrong motivates us. Even if the person who sees us is unable to punish us directly, that person can punish us indirectly by telling others. It doesn't even have to be the person we are wronging who sees us. If Stan sees me stealing Rob's apple, he may gossip and tell others, harming my reputation.

Not everything is spoken. In order to understand and anticipate one another we need to realize that others have minds quite like our own; further we need to realize that their spoken words are not always the best clues as to what they think and how they will act. Determining other people's motives calls for us to think about what they are thinking. Evolution accomplishes this scattershot, not with laser precision. As Rosenberg says, "The simplest way to create someone who is good at reading motives from other people's behavior is to overdo it: endow them with a penchant for seeing motives everywhere."[32] So as a result of our overactive theory of mind, we conceive of a god or gods with a mind or minds who know our mind directly. This same tendency to see motives everywhere manifests when we get mad at our malfunctioning car or computer, as if it had a mind of its own and was out to get us. Obviously, we know that cars and computers don't have minds or motives, but the temptation to think and feel that way is still strong. In that light, consider how the world must have appeared to primitive people in the early stages of human evolution. It would have seemed as if the natural world was filled with other minds sending messages and reading their minds in turn. As Jesse Bering says, "At every turn, we seem to think there are subtle messages scratched into the woodwork of nature, subtle signs or cues that God, or some other supernatural agent, is trying to communicate a lesson or idea to us—and often to us alone."[33]

God is the final piece of the motivational puzzle. If prudence and potential punishment by others are not enough to prevent us from stealing the apple, then maybe fear of punishment by God will do the job. Indeed, Bering says that God is an "adaptive illusion" that helped us to solve the problem of human gossip.[34] Gossip was not enough, because sometimes we could escape human detection and thus escape gossip and the punishment to follow. As Bering says, "a God who actively punished and rewarded our intentions and behaviors would have helped stomp out the frequency and intensity of our ancestors' immoral hiccups and would have been strongly favored by natural selection."[35] It is no wonder, then, that God and morality have so frequently been linked. And because wrongdoers are not always punished by God in this life, we are easily led to the belief that punishment will come in the next life—that it is inescapable.

More mysterious than the tendency to punish ourselves is the tendency to help others. If the survival of my individual genes is all that matters from an evolutionary standpoint, then it would seem to be a waste of time and energy to help others. But just as our conscience and our tendency to make moral judgments can help us to avoid hurting others, so too they can help us to help others. By judging certain actions as morally right or obligatory we increase our likelihood of performing those actions. As Joyce says, "Certain helpful behaviors advance fitness, and the 'moralization' of these behaviors bolsters motivation to perform them."[36]

The people we are most inclined to help are our children. This makes sense, considering that our children share half our genes. But of course, many animals don't care for their offspring, going for quantity rather than quality.[37] Because of our large brains, which must mature outside the womb, human development is very slow, requiring great care from others. Our efforts to pass on our genes would be in vain if we did not invest time in caring for those who carry those genes. Of course our children are not the only ones who share our genes; to lesser degrees so do siblings, nieces and nephews, cousins, and even more distant relatives. So it makes sense that evolution would incline us to help genetic relatives. Rather than endow us with a genetic-relation-detector, evolution opted, as it usually does, for the quick and dirty solution: inclining us to help those physically close around us. They, after all, were more likely to be genetic relatives.[38]

So, how does this work? The main mechanisms are kin selection, mutualism, and reciprocal exchanges (direct and indirect).[39] Kin selection, helping those who are likely to be genetically related to us, fosters the survival of our genes. The genetic advantages of helping one's children are obvious, but there is genetic advantage even in helping more distant relatives as long as the cost is not too high. It is not surprising, then, that humans are much more willing to make a sacrifice for their children than for their cousins. Mutualism involves members of a group acting together to achieve a common goal. So, for example, a group of hunters may cooperate to take down a water buffalo. Though they are doing something that helps others, they are thereby helping themselves, promoting their survival and improving their chances of passing on their genes.[40]

Direct reciprocity is also called reciprocal altruism. We see it commonly among animals, as when primates groom one another, removing parasites. Among humans, the saying "you scratch my back, I'll scratch yours" is more than just literal.[41] Indirect reciprocity is less obvious; it occurs when "an organism benefits from helping another by being paid back a benefit of greater value than the cost of her initial helping, but not necessarily by the recipient of the help."[42] So, for example, one may help others who cannot help much in return simply for the benefit of the good reputation one gains. In a related way, sometimes helping another demonstrates strength and fitness that will attract a mate. This is akin to the way in which a peacock's extravagant tail demonstrates its fitness and overabundance, despite seeming to otherwise be a bad attribute from a survival and evolutionary perspective.[43]

Nothing in the evolutionary explanation rules out God. It is possible that God has guided evolution such that conscience, feelings of guilt, inclinations to punish, and so forth help us to know what is good. Indeed, that seems the only reasonable explanation for the theist. But for the atheist, what are the implications of evolution for objectively real morality, for the existence of a set of moral facts? One possibility is that evolution has guided us to form true beliefs about moral facts. That sounds reasonable. After all, true belief would seem to have survival value. For example, natural selection has given us a faculty for basic arithmetic, "False mathematical beliefs just aren't going to be very useful."[44] But while false mathematical beliefs would hurt the chances of survival, other false beliefs might help survival. Joyce, for example, discusses a plant that is falsely believed to have magical properties. The belief is false, but since the plant has medicinal properties, the false belief has survival value.[45] So the mere fact that we have evolved the propensity to believe that certain actions are objectively right and wrong does not necessarily indicate that they are objectively right and wrong. The evolution of moral beliefs does not establish that there must be moral facts.

Moral Anti-realism

We know that the beliefs of core morality have survival value. But could they have survival value even if they were false? The answer is yes, our moral beliefs do not need to correspond to an objective reality to be beneficial. We just need to *think* they correspond to moral facts. As Rosenberg says, "Our core morality isn't true, right, correct, and neither is any other. Nature just seduced us into thinking it's right. It did that because that made core morality work better; our believing in its truth increases our individual genetic fitness."[46]

According to Joyce and Street, unlike vision, which tracks reality, our moral sense (so to speak) does not track reality; nor do we have a moral sense organ the way we have eyes for sight. Instead, the moral sense is just an adaptive link. Our sense of sight is far from perfect and certainly does not guarantee that we see the world the way it actually is. Nonetheless vision is highly reliable on a certain scale for telling us that an object exists apart from our perception. It is dubious that whatever sense or faculty is supposed to put us in touch with moral facts actually does so. Our moral beliefs are completely explicable without moral facts.[47] So which is the better explanation, that we have a moral sense that tracks objective moral facts, or that our moral experience was an adaptive development for our evolutionary ancestors? Joyce answers that "the latter is superior in that it explains everything that the former does, but is simpler, more intelligible, testable, and, most importantly, avoids any mysterious items."[48] I agree and endorse Ruse and Wilson's view that the argument from redundancy is essentially Occam's razor: "The evolutionary explanation makes the objective morality redundant, for even if external ethical premises did not exist, we would go on thinking about right and wrong in the way that we do."[49] Joyce is more cautious, recommending agnosticism, warning that "the evolutionary hypothesis ... will not *independently* serve to show that moral judgments are probably false. At best it shows them to be unjustified, which is, of course, undermining enough."[50]

Joyce is more cautious than necessary, though. He is right that it is impossible to disprove the existence of objective morality, but even Thomas Nagel says that "moral realism is incompatible with a Darwinian account of the evolutionary influence on our faculties of moral and evaluative judgment."[51] Unfortunately for him, Nagel adds that "since moral realism is true, a Darwinian account of the motives underlying moral judgment must be false, in spite of the scientific consensus in its favor."[52] Surely, it is unwarranted to dismiss scientific consensus just because we feel attached to moral realism. Nagel is in a position akin to a person denying the heliocentric view simply because it continues to seem like the earth is at the center.

We might nonetheless take comfort in the notion that morality is useful even if it is not true. But here we need to realize that morality as an evolved tendency would not necessarily be useful for individuals but rather for genes.[53] Beyond that, the usefulness that morality had for genes in the distant evolutionary past may not hold in the present. As Joyce says,

> It is possible that a tendency to make moral judgments is like the human sweet tooth, which was adaptive relative to ancient

environments where sweetness was a rare commodity and a safe bet for nutritional value but which has become a life threatening hindrance to many people when the temptations are abundantly present and easily accessible.[54]

In the next chapter we will consider the possibility that moral belief has indeed outlived its usefulness.

The view that the evolutionary account points to is variously called amoralism or moral anti-realism, the metaphysical view that there are no moral facts. This is not to be confused with moral relativism, which claims that moral truth is relative to groups or individuals. While it is clear that core morality gets developed and expanded in a great variety of conflicting ways, this is no reason to think that moral truth itself is relative. If anything, this is reason to think that there is no moral truth, just a variety of moral beliefs. Relativism is contradictory and self-refuting, but anti-realism is not. Anti-realism (or amoralism) is what J.L. Mackie called "error theory" in *Ethics: Inventing Right and Wrong*.[55] It is simply an error to believe there is such a thing as objectively existing morality—moral facts that exist independently of people's beliefs and desires.[56] Given the evidence of modern science, most people are error theorists about ghosts; others too are error theorists about angels, souls, and gods. Beliefs about such things vary, but without proof of their existence it is safe to conclude that such things do not exist. Likewise, we can conclude that without proof of their existence, moral facts do not exist.

Even in light of the forgoing explanation, belief in moral facts can be tenacious. This is understandable, considering how strongly and deeply we sometimes feel certain moral beliefs. Joel Marks, a leading amoralist, recounts his struggle in renouncing morality and embracing amoralism in his memoir *Bad Faith*. There he tells us "I conceived obligation as part of the fabric of the universe"[57] and adds that "The *metaphysics* of morals struck me as beside the point. I already knew that obligation was real."[58] Here Marks sounds like Nagel, who is willing to oppose Darwinian evolution in order to hold on to the belief that morality is real. Atheist philosophers such as Nagel and Marks often succeed in turning a blind eye and ignoring the related metaphysical issues; the title of Marks's memoir says it all. As Marks encapsulates, "At some level of my being there had

101

been the awareness, but I had brushed it aside. I had therefore lived in a semi-conscious state of self-delusion—what the existentialist Jean-Paul Sartre called *bad faith*."[59] Nagel has yet to reconcile with his own bad faith, but when he does perhaps he will quote Marks, who says,

> My delusion of morality was as absurd, as flagrantly in opposition to the facts of the world, as are the Biblical beliefs of any fundamentalist. In fact, the kind of morality I espoused was simply theism without God. It had all the trappings. There was the *command* quality of obligation. There was the *mystery* of its origin. There was an absence of *rationale* for its authority. There was the *lack of fit* with the spatiotemporal universe known to science. All that was missing was the old man with the beard himself. But he was in psychological and logical fact *there*. For otherwise the whole system made no sense.[60]

Despite all explanations and despite Marks's candid admission of bad faith, some actions may continue to seem wrong to us. For example, "Torturing children for fun is wrong."[61] What could be more obviously true? If the moral anti-realist responds that she no longer finds it obviously true, then the realist will likely respond with what Richard Garner calls

> "The McEnroe," in which one says loudly and emphatically, [like the eponymous tennis player arguing a call] "You can't be serious!!" ... In a "Full McEnroe," some such gut reaction is followed by a volley of moral judgments the critic thinks "no one in their right mind" could deny. How can there be nothing wrong with bear-baiting, torture, genocide, or hammering nails into a living baby, chopping it into a billion pieces, boiling the remains, and then forcing its mother to drink the concoction?[62]

Of course the moral realist misses the point with this kind of reaction since, as Garner says, "avowals of certainty and litanies of atrocities are wasted effort because no description of some act or event, however appalling, is going to cause an alert moral error theorist to return to believing in moral objectivity. No one's rejection of moral objectivity is based on a failure to realize how cruelly we are capable of behaving."[63]

It certainly is true that, aside from psychopaths, virtually all human beings will find the torture of children for fun to be abhorrent. But that feeling does not make it true that the action is morally wrong. The feeling is not proof of an objective moral fact; it is simply evidence for an evolved reaction of strong disapproval. As strange and awful as it sounds, if our evolutionary history had been different we could have developed the tendency to approve of the torture of children. The near universal reaction of moral disapproval establishes nothing about objective morality.

Here is one analogical way to think about it: The fact that nearly every human being with normal olfactory operation finds the smell of dog droppings to be disgusting does not mean that dog droppings objectively smell disgusting. Rather, what the evidence tells us is that, given the senses humans have evolved, dog droppings smell bad to nearly all humans. Does that mean they smell bad objectively? Not in any objectively real or supernatural sense. Consider the fact that dogs seem to love the smell of dog droppings. With just some small differences in our evolutionary history, we might have come to really enjoy the smell of dog droppings too. Nor should we take our current inclinations to be fully fixed. Scott James makes a related point using the example of a rotting corpse.[64] Nearly all biologically normal humans would find a rotting corpse to be disgusting. But once we have given an evolutionary explanation for why we find the corpse disgusting there is no need to justify the feelings of disgust. There is no metaphysical fact of the corpse's disgustingness. A different evolutionary history would have produced a different response, and some people, like coroners, may be able to overcome feelings of disgust for rotting corpses. This is an important point that we will take up in the next chapter concerning our evolved moral inclinations. We are not necessarily stuck with them; we can potentially override them.

Non-cognitivism

Non-cognitivists can be considered moral anti-realists of a kind, though they are more concerned with the meaning and use of moral language than with the underlying metaphysics of morality. Nor do they typically consider evolutionary evidence. As Garner explains,

> according to non-cognitivism (also called emotivism, expressivism, and non-descriptivism) it is a mistake to see moral judgments as

statements about the way the world is. Some non-cognitivists say that moral judgments are expressions of emotions or attitudes, and others identify them with some other kind of non-descriptive speech-act, like commending, or commanding, or inviting, or forbidding. They all insist that moral judgments, not being statements, are not the right kind of thing to be called true or false.[65]

So the non-cognitivist differs from the standard moral anti-realist, who does think that moral judgments are statements and thus are truth apt. Specifically, for the standard moral anti-realist, all moral statements are false.[66]

Perhaps the best-known non-cognitivist theory is A.J. Ayer's emotivism, according to which moral propositions just express emotions. Expressing emotions is certainly one thing that people usually do with moral propositions, but it is not the main thing. Most people making moral statements are realists; they think they are expressing propositions that correspond to reality the way that ancient Greeks praying to Apollo thought they were praying to a truly existing deity. If, as I have argued, moral judgments of good and evil do not correspond to any reality, then they certainly can still express emotional approval or disapproval. But the intention behind the statements is typically more than just the expression of emotion.

Philosophers after Ayer have offered more refined versions of non-cognitivism and expressivism, but they all face the same problem: they deny the obvious fact that most of the time most people are realists when they speak morally.[67] As Nolan, Restall, and West say, the non-cognitivist denies "that our moral talk is really as it seems: namely, realist talk. Non-cognitivists either have to deny very plausible things about what we take ourselves to mean when we speak morally or they are offering us a substitute for our current moral talk that merely changes the subject."[68]

Moral Realism

Whereas non-cognitivism would count as an anti-realist theory, there are any number of ingenious attempts to hold on to objective moral values and obligations that would count as realist theories.[69] These include tracking accounts (which claim that moral discourse can track moral facts the way vision tracks visible objects) such as intuitionism, response dependency, moral constructivism, and a teleologically revised virtue ethics.[70] At one time they all would have been reasonable explanations for why we so readily form moral judgments. But that time passed with the entrance of the theory of evolution. Now we have a perfectly good explanation of why we form moral judgments that does not call for any of the odd abilities or properties that those attempts to hold on to moral realism require. As Street says, the tracking explanation is scientifically unacceptable.[71] Contra tracking accounts, our evaluative tendencies evolved not because they tracked moral facts but because they led to us surviving and reproducing. This explanation is more parsimonious, clearer, and sheds more light on what is to be explained: widespread tendencies to make certain kinds of evaluative judgments.[72]

Erik Wielenberg argues for a non-natural, non-theistic moral realism in which there are ethical brute facts, such as "pain is bad" and "torturing innocents for fun is bad." Concerning these ethical brute facts, Wielenberg says, "They come from nowhere, and nothing external to themselves grounds their existence; rather, they are fundamental features of the universe that ground other truths."[73] But Wielenberg's theory is not parsimonious.[74] As Nagel admits, "from a Darwinian perspective, the hypothesis of value realism is superfluous—a wheel that spins without being attached to anything. From a Darwinian perspective our impressions of value, if construed realistically, are completely groundless."[75] Nagel is thus driven to reject the Darwinian perspective, appealing to teleology: "The teleological hypothesis is that these things may be determined not merely by value-free chemistry and physics but also by something else, namely a cosmic predisposition to the formation of life, consciousness, and the value that is inseparable from them."[76] Alas, Nagel does not offer evidence or details concerning his teleological hypothesis. He is "willing to bet," though, in the closing lines of *Mind and Cosmos*, "that the present right-thinking consensus will come to seem laughable in a generation or two."[77] I would be glad to take that bet.

Advocates of objective morality often fall back on a piece of subjective evidence: morality feels true. That may be, but we need to ask why. Does morality feel true because we evolved in such a way that it would feel true? Does it feel true because we were raised with

105

morality? Probably both. The fact that a thing feels true may provide subjective reason to look for an objective reason that validates the subjective feeling, but if no such reason is forthcoming, the feeling must be rejected as insufficient evidence. Ironically, many people who reject the existence of God because they see God as an unnecessary hypothesis continue to cling to the unnecessary hypothesis of objective morality. Of course there could be objective moral facts; it is impossible to disprove their existence. But that is just like the case of God, whose non-existence is unprovable. Defenders of objective morality commonly appeal to their moral experience as justification for their belief. But many of these same people would find laughable the appeal to religious experience as justification for belief in God. If feelings and vague experiences won't work to prove God's existence, then they cannot prove the existence of moral facts either.

The intuition is strong that morality, good and bad, right and wrong are objectively real properties of the world, and epistemological conservatism would favor maintaining that intuition/belief unless the burden of proof otherwise can be met. However, we should reject this epistemological conservatism. There are any number of beliefs that are naturally very strong and that turn out to be false: the earth is flat, the sun orbits the earth, and so forth.[78] When it comes to an existence belief, or existential claim, the burden of proof should, all other things being equal, be on the person making the existential claim. So when someone claims that non-physical entities or properties such as good and evil exist, the burden should be on them to prove it.

Still, in this case the intuition is so strong for many people (not including myself) that for the sake of making progress in the debate, the moral anti-realist might as well take on the burden of proof. In that case the anti-realist has the task of explaining what else, aside from the real existence of right and wrong, would cause the experience and intuition of right and wrong. And, as we have seen, the answer is simple: evolution. We evolved to have inclinations to punish, to have feelings of guilt, and to have beliefs in right and wrong.

If we accept moral anti-realism, does that mean nothing will restrain our actions? Would a world of moral anti-realists be a dark and dangerous world? As we will see in the next chapter, the answer to these questions is a resounding no.

Notes

1 As Jean-Paul Sartre says in *Being and Nothingness*, "My freedom is the unique foundation of values .... *nothing*, absolutely nothing, justifies me in adopting this or that particular value, this or that particular scale of values" (trans. Hazel Barnes (New York: Washington Square Press, 1956), p. 76).

2 I do not take parsimony to be the final word, but rather one guide among others. In the past, parsimonious explanations have, all other things being equal, more often than not turned out to be correct. I do not think there is any single reason why this is so. Rather, I think incorrect explanations, often hold on in ad hoc ways by multiplying entities, as for example the epicycles employed in geocentric theories. I thank Justin Morton and Eric Sampson for pushing me on this issue, though they ultimately disagree with me concerning the relevance of parsimony.

3 David P. Barash, "Evolutionary Existentialism, Sociobiology, and the Meaning of Life," *Bioscience* 50 (2000): 1015.

4 David P. Barash, "Evolution and Existentialism, an Intellectual Odd Couple," *The Chronicle of Higher Education*, March 11, 2013. http://chronicle.com/article/EvolutionExistentialism/137715/.

5 Barash (2000), p. 1015.

6 Richard Dawkins, *The Selfish Gene*, 2nd edn (Oxford: Oxford University Press, 1989).

7 Barash (2013).

8 Barash (2013).

9 Friedrich Nietzsche, *The Gay Science*, trans. Walter Kaufmann (New York: Vintage Books, 1974), section 343.

10 Unlike some philosophers, I do not take the Euthyphro dilemma to show that God is irrelevant to morality. For a recent defense of divine command theory see David Baggett and Jerry L. Walls, *Good God: The Theistic Foundations of Morality* (Oxford: Oxford University Press, 2011).

11 Michael Ruse, *Taking Darwin Seriously* (Oxford: Blackwell, 1986), p. 253.

12 Scott M. James, *An Introduction to Evolutionary Ethics* (Malden, MA: Wiley-Blackwell, 2011), p. 171. James is discussing Michael Ruse and E.O. Wilson, "Darwinism as Applied Science," in Elliott Sober ed., *Conceptual Issues in Evolutionary Biology*, 2nd edn (Cambridge: MIT Press, 1994), p. 431.

13 Sharon Street, "A Darwinian Dilemma for Realist Theories of Value," *Philosophical Studies* 127 (2006): 120.

14 James (2011), p. 108.

15 Street, p. 115.

16   Alex Rosenberg, *The Atheist's Guide to Reality: Enjoying Life without Illusions* (New York: Norton, 2011), p. 133. In *The Righteous Mind: Why Good People Are Divided by Politics and Religion* (New York: Pantheon, 2012), pp. 153–78 and 197–205, Jonathan Haidt discusses six core areas of evolved moral judgment: care/harm, fairness/cheating, loyalty/betrayal, authority/subversion, sanctity/degradation, and liberty/oppression.

17   Richard Joyce, *The Evolution of Morality* (Cambridge: MIT Press, 2007), p. 181.

18   Richard Joyce, *The Myth of Morality* (Cambridge: Cambridge University Press, 2001), p. 162.

19   Joyce (2007), p. 135.

20   James (2011), pp. 92–4; and Yu Gao, Andrea L. Glenn, Robert A. Schug, Yaling Yang, and Adrian Raine, "The Neurobiology of Psychopathy: A Neurodevelopmental Perspective," *Canadian Journal of Psychiatry* 54 (2009): 813–23.

21   Craig S. Neumann and Robert D. Hare, "Psychopathic Traits in a Large Community Sample: Links to Violence, Alcohol Use, and Intelligence," *Journal of Consulting and Clinical Psychology* 76 (2008): 893–9.

22   Joyce (2007), pp. 140–1.

23   James (2011), p. 59.

24   Joyce (2007), p. 69.

25   Admittedly, the concept of punishment is a bit hazy and metaphorical here. Alternatively, one might prefer to think of doing harm to another or feeling regret oneself. But I follow Joyce and Street in speaking of punishment.

26   James (2011), pp. 74–5.

27   Joyce (2007), pp. 117–18.

28   Joyce (2007), p. 113.

29   Joyce (2007), p. 111.

30   Joyce (2001), p. 213.

31   Joyce (2007), p. 90.

32   Rosenberg, p. 13.

33   Jesse Bering, *The Belief Instinct: The Psychology of Souls, Destiny, and the Meaning of Life* (New York: Norton, 2011), p. 77.

34   Bering, p. 7.

35   Bering, p. 7.

36   Joyce (2007), p. 215.

37   Joyce (2007), p. 20.

38   Joyce (2007), p. 21.

39   Joyce (2007), p. 40. Joyce adds group selection as well.

40   Joyce (2007), pp. 22–3.

41   Joyce (2007), pp. 24–6.

42   Joyce (2007), p. 31.

43   Joyce (2007), p. 32.

44   Joyce (2007), p. 182.

45   Joyce (2007), pp. 214–15; for other examples see Joyce (2007), p. 222 and Rosenberg, p. 112.

46   Rosenberg, p. 109.

47   I side with Harman in his debate with Sturgeon concerning the ability of moral facts to explain moral beliefs. See Gilbert Harman, "Moral Explanations of Natural Facts: Can Moral Claims Be Tested against Moral Reality?" *The Southern Journal of Philosophy* 24, Supplement (1986): 57–68, and Nicholas L. Sturgeon, "Harman on Moral Explanations of Natural Facts," *The Southern Journal of Philosophy* 24, Supplement (1986): 69–78.

48   Joyce (2001), p. 168.

49   Michel Ruse and E.O. Wilson, "Darwinism as Applied Science," in Elliott Sober, ed. *Conceptual Issues in Evolutionary Biology*, 2nd edn (Cambridge: MIT Press, 1994), p. 431; Cf. James (2011), p. 172.

50   Joyce (2001), p. 168.

51   Thomas Nagel, *Mind and Cosmos: Why the Materialist Neo-Darwinian Conception of Nature Is Almost Certainly False* (New York: Oxford University Press, 2012), p. 105.

52   Nagel (2012), p. 105.

53   Joyce (2001), p. 206.

54   Joyce (2007), p. 107.

55   J.L. Mackie, *Ethics: Inventing Right and Wrong* (New York: Penguin, 1977).

56   In *Moral Error Theory: History, Critique, Defence* (Oxford: Oxford University Press, 2014), pp. 117–25, Jonas Olson argues that the best defense of error theory is in terms of the queerness of moral facts understood in terms of irreducible normativity.

57   *Bad Faith: A Philosophical Memoir* (Lexington, KY: CreateSpace, 2013), p. 55.

58   *Bad Faith*, p. 57.

59   *Bad Faith*, pp. 74–5.

60   *Bad Faith*, p. 74.

61   In "An Ontological Proof of Moral Realism," *Social Philosophy and Policy* 30 (2013), Michael Huemer uses the example of torturing babies as his prime example in arguing for moral realism, saying that "Given that moral realism might be true, and given that we know some of the things we ought to do if it is true [we have some reason to abstain from torturing babies], we have a reason to do those things. Furthermore,

this reason is itself an objective moral reason. Thus, we have at least one objective moral reason" (p. 259). The problem with this argument is, according to the moral anti-realist, that we don't know what would be true if moral realism were true. To say that we know that torturing babies would be wrong under moral realism Huemer has to say that his moral intuition might be reliable (p. 270). But the evolutionary debunking argument gives us reason not to put any stock in moral intuitionism.

62 Richard Garner, "A Plea for Moral Abolitionism," unpublished manuscript.

63 Garner, Plea.

64 James (2011), p. 173.

65 Richard Garner, *Beyond Morality*, revised edition, unpublished manuscript.

66 Taking the position that all moral statements are false raises questions with regard to the law of excluded middle concerning moral statements and their negations. For ways to handle these concerns see Olson, pp. 11–15, and Charles Pidgen, "Nihilism, Nietzsche, and the Doppelganger Problem," *Ethical Theory and Moral Practice* 10 (2007): 441–56.

67 Allan Gibbard offers the most sophisticated contemporary version of expressivism in *Wise Choices, Apt Feelings: A Theory of Normative Judgment* (Cambridge, MA: Harvard University Press, 1990).

68 Daniel Nolan, Greg Restall, and Caroline West, "Moral Fictionalism versus the Rest," *Australasian Journal of Philosophy* 83 (2005): 307.

69 In *Taking Morality Seriously: A Defense of Robust Realism* (Oxford: Oxford University Press, 2011), pp. 72–9, David Enoch argues that deliberation presupposes irreducibly normative facts, the very thing that error theorists deny. Olson replies that deliberation typically requires only reflection on one's desires and their comparative strengths, pp. 172–7.

70 For discussion and criticism of these views see James (2011), pp. 187–208. The general problem with most of these views is that they redefine what is meant by moral realism such that it does not mean being completely independent of human beliefs and desires. This is akin to the move made by compatibilists in redefining freedom. Interesting and worthwhile things can be said about what most humans under most conditions will find good, right, or conducive to flourishing, but there will always be exceptions. And even if there were no exceptions these would not amount to being moral facts inasmuch as they would not generate obligations. They would not have the property of irreducible normativity.

71 Street, p. 153.

72 Street, p. 129.
73 Erik J. Wielenberg, "In Defense of Non-Natural, Non-Theistic Moral Realism," *Faith and Philosophy* 26 (2009): 26.
74 In a subsequent paper, Wielenberg argues that it is possible for evolutionary theory to fit with his moral realism. Wielenberg's view is that "cognitive faculties are responsible for both moral rights and beliefs about those rights, and so the cognitive faculties explain the correlation between moral rights and beliefs about those rights" (p. 450). It is logically possible that Wielenberg's account is correct, but he does not supply compelling reason to think so and it is not parsimonious. See Erik J. Wielenberg, "On the Evolutionary Debunking of Morality," *Ethics* 120 (2010): 441–64.
75 Nagel (2012), p. 109.
76 Nagel (2012), p. 123.
77 Nagel (2012), p. 128.
78 Don Loeb, "The Argument from Moral Experience," in Richard Joyce and Simon Kirchin, eds., *A World without Values: Essays on John Mackie's Moral Error Theory* (Dordrecht: Springer, 2010), pp. 109–10.

5

Not Going to Hell in a Handbasket

Existentialism and a World without Morality

If one accepts moral anti-realism, what then? One possibility is to practice moral fictionalism, acting as if morality were objectively true even though one does not believe it. For obvious reasons, this will be unacceptable to the existentialist concerned with authenticity and the perils of self-deception. As an alternative, existentialism can embrace a one-size-does-*not*-fit-all approach to non-moral, prudential decision making. By prudence I mean the non-moral virtue in choosing and acting to fulfill our desires, though not necessarily selfish desires.[1] The question of what a world of moral anti-realists would be like remains an open, empirical question, but, as we shall see, there are reasons to think it would not be very different from the world today and might even be better.

Moral Fictionalism

Moral anti-realism can be scary. How will people act when they realize that there is no objective morality? Earlier generations had

The Free Market Existentialist: Capitalism without Consumerism, First Edition. William Irwin.
© 2015 John Wiley & Sons, Ltd. Published 2015 by John Wiley & Sons, Ltd.

similar concerns about atheism. Ironically, many of those today who are most concerned about moral anti-realism are themselves atheists. Admittedly, it is harder to motivate oneself to take certain actions once one gives up belief in objective morality. As Richard Joyce sees it, the belief in objective morality evolved to provide a bulwark against weakness of will, and with that bulwark removed we are more likely to give in to weakness of will. Because we would like to avoid this consequence, Joyce makes an ingenious proposal: moral fictionalism. As Joyce explains it, "to make a fiction of p is to 'accept' p while disbelieving p."[2] In plainer terms, Nolan, Restall, and West explain that "The simplest fictionalist approach to a discourse takes certain claims in that discourse to be literally false, but nevertheless worth uttering in certain contexts."[3] This approach is inspired by the way we engage with artistic fictions, not believing in their reality but rather suspending disbelief. For example, for the sake of enjoying a science fiction movie, I may accept that time travel is possible even though I do not believe it.

Clearly, this approach can come in handy in everyday life. Joyce gives an example concerning exercise.[4] I may tell myself that I need to do 30 sit-ups every day; I accept this even though I do not believe it. If someone asked me "Do you *really* need to do 30 sit-ups every day?" I would upon reflection answer that "No, I could probably get away with 5 times a week, and 25 sit-ups some days would be fine." But in an effort to combat weakness of will, I accept the hard-and-fast rule that I must do 30 sit-ups every day (even though I don't really believe it). Joyce speculates that some people probably take a fictionalist approach to God; they accept the existence of God but they don't really believe God exists. They accept that God is love and that (the concept of) God has shaped human history and guides human lives, but when pinned down they admit that they don't really believe in the actual existence of such a God. Their considered judgment is that the existence of God is not literally true but rather metaphorically or mythologically true.

Joyce is concerned that to abolish morality "may bring anxiety and confusion," and so he recommends moral fictionalism, according to which we accept moral principles but do not believe they are true.[5] As he says, "The strength of the advice that recommends moral fictionalism is no more and no less than this: it will be in the long-term best interests of ordinarily situated persons with normal

113

human desires."[6] We might worry, though, about what will happen when a person becomes aware of the fictionalism in the midst of making a decision. This will not be the norm, since most actions will be taken without extended deliberation. But Joyce thinks that when a person enters the critical mode in the midst of a decision and recalls that morality is just a fiction, the person can still have the prudent decision bolstered by reflecting on the instrumental value of the prudent decision—it is in the person's long-term best interest.[7] So, Joyce believes, nothing is lost. Relying on the fiction will bring more consistent results, but even when the fiction is revealed as such, prudence remains to reinforce the decision. Joyce anticipates that the curtain will be drawn up on fictionalism only in exceptional circumstances. When we are in the philosophy classroom discussing moral anti-realism, we are aware of the fiction, but the moment we walk out of the classroom things change. We engage the fiction once again. This is akin to the way a mathematician may be an anti-realist concerning numbers when she is theorizing, though she engages the fiction of numbers when she is calculating.[8]

Joyce insists that fictionalism is not a matter of self-deception, giving the example of a Sherlock Holmes fan exploring London: "when the person is asked about what he *really* believes—then the maker of the judgment can, but the victim of self-deception cannot, move with the context."[9] The fan is not delusional; he knows that there was no such person as Sherlock and he therefore knows that Sherlock did not actually do anything at the places he is visiting. But the fan enjoys the fiction nonetheless. Joyce suggests that, in a similar manner, we can benefit from moral fictionalism. Since we have been raised with a belief in objective morality, it is easy for us to fall back into the habits and patterns that accompany it, only occasionally taking a reality check. As Joyce says, "the decision to adopt morality as a fiction is not an ongoing calculation that one makes over and over … the resolution to accept the moral point of view is something that occurred in the person's past, and is now an accustomed way of thinking."[10] So, if it is that easy to avail oneself of the benefits of fictionalism, then why not do it?

Engaging in fictionalism by watching movies and reading novels is understandable and in many cases even commendable. Not so with moral fictionalism. Joyce maintains that moral fictionalism does not necessarily involve self-deception, but I disagree.[11] Moral fictionalism is disingenuous in the sense that it involves turning a blind eye to what one really believes. It may not be the most pernicious kind of self-deception, but it is self-deception nonetheless. Fictionalism has the understandable goal of facilitating what one wants to do—acting as a kind of commitment strategy—but it would be preferable if one could do what one wanted to do without this disingenuous maneuver. Life is too short to live in a fantasy world. We find engaging with movies and novels commendable only if the person does not spend more time in those fictional worlds than outside them. But in the case of moral fictionalism the person is spending nearly all of his time in a fictionalized world—only coming out of it briefly when he considers the theoretical/philosophical question of the reality of morality.

Joyce wants to make the case that morality is mythological in the sense of conveying a deep truth despite being literally false. But the truth it conveys—that certain actions and attitudes are useful and prudential—can be had and maintained without the fiction, without the myth. It is a mark of mental or emotional weakness to rely on the myth. It may suit some people to rely on this myth in that way, but others, like the existentialist, will prefer reality and eschew the myth.

As Joyce acknowledges, whether fictionalism can work is an empirical question that we cannot answer by philosophical speculation, but it seems likely that it will work well for some people and poorly for others. I, for one, do not think it would work for me, and I am not alone in thinking that way. Considering the example of whether or not to lie in a certain circumstance, Oddie and Demetriou conclude that "when the consequences of acting as though I really believe that lying is wrong compete with rude self interest, then why wouldn't I have more reason to be guided by my actual beliefs about lying (i.e., that it is not wrong to lie)?"[12] Richard Garner questions Joyce's confidence that fictionalism can be easily maintained, saying that "Questions about meaning and justification will turn up as soon as we disagree about anything that really matters to us."[13] In other words, we are likely to recall that morality is a fiction whenever we are in a situation in which we would prefer not to follow what morality dictates. Joyce seems to be aware of this problem when discussing Daniel Dennett's confusion about moral conversation-stoppers, like "slavery is wrong."[14] As Joyce says, "seeing the conversation-stoppers for what they are threatens to deprive them of their ability to fulfill this role so effectively."[15]

But how is moral fictionalism any better than Dennett's conversation-stoppers? Once you become aware that your moral judgments have no objective basis in metaphysical reality, how can they function effectively? They would require a kind of self-deception or bad faith that would be possible but that would be hard to maintain and would raise the question: Why bother? We do not need morality to guide our actions if we have prudence, the non-moral virtue in choosing and acting to fulfill our desires. It is true that the bright lines and conversation-stopping powers of morality make it much easier to do the prudent thing. But, like all other virtues, prudence can be developed and cultivated. This involves great effort, but the effort might be worthwhile for the sake of appreciating the authenticity of the approach—and in the long run relying on prudence might not be as hard as relying on self-deception, which can be quite exhausting. Commenting on the problems with fictionalism, Garner says, "what we say is sure to conflict with reality at many points, and then we will need to resort to evasion, obfuscation, or sophistry just to maintain our fiction."[16]

The appeal of moral fictionalism is clear. There can be benefits from acting as if morality were objectively real. Fictionalism can take away the anxiety of choice, making decisions easier—as if there really is no choice in some situations. However, the existentialist does not condone this. Fictionalism about morality is no better than fictionalism about ghosts or gods. If something is not real, we are inauthentic when we deceive ourselves about its reality, especially when the thing in question has such a powerful impact on our choices. Here we should distinguish between voluntary and involuntary fictionalism. Joyce counsels us to voluntarily cultivate moral fictionalism, perhaps as Pascal might counsel cultivating belief in God.[17] Indeed, it seems likely that some people practice just such a voluntary fictionalism concerning God. By contrast, for me at least, free-will fictionalism is involuntary. No matter how much I convince myself, and no matter how often I remind myself, that free will (in the traditional libertarian sense) is probably an illusion, I cannot help but feel it is real.

Joyce's view is that moral fictionalism is advisable because it provides a defense against weakness of will. But another thing that provides a defense against weakness of will is strengthening the will, and this is what the existentialist advises. Rather than trick the will, strengthen the will.[18] After all, the trick may not always work. Certainly, as Joyce admits, moral fictionalism will not work as well as sincere moral belief. But Joyce's account too readily separates ordinary life from the philosophy classroom.[19] It may be that people who are not very self-reflective by natural disposition will be successful this way, but moral considerations come up frequently. So the reflective person may make use of a disposition to act as if morality were real, but in the cases in which she is given pause to consider what to do, the fact that morality is just a fiction will come to mind. And the fiction will do no good then, no more good than the self-conscious employment of Dennett's conversation stoppers. In fact, the person may react cynically and resent her own attempt at self-deception, perhaps inclining her to choose the act that both morality and prudence recommend against. Far better would simply be to have a stronger will, one that has been trained to come to the rescue of prudence in such situations.

One Size Does not Fit All

Some will worry about human behavior in response to the loss of objective morality. Nolan, Restall, and West point out that an advantage of moral fictionalism is "its capacity to salvage the important role moral discourse is widely thought to play in co-ordinating attitudes and regulating interpersonal conflict in cases where people disagree about what they are to do."[20] As I see it, though, a world of moral anti-realists would be much like a group of students who go away to college and live together free from parental supervision for the first time. Some will abuse their liberty for awhile, but the great majority will eventually curtail their actions in a way that is best and healthiest for themselves and others. Some anti-realists have even argued that people would actually treat each other more kindly and more tolerantly in a world without morality. Ian Hinckfuss was the first to make this case, arguing that the parade of horrors done in the name of morality rivals that done in the name of religion.[21] Following Hinckfuss, Garner explains that "morality inflames disputes and makes compromise difficult, it preserves unfair arrangements and facilitates the misuse of power, and it makes global war possible."[22] As an alternative, Garner advocates for non-moral virtues, saying "A blend of curiosity, compassion, and non-duplicity will almost always result in behavior more 'virtuous' than morality alone could ever hope to produce."[23]

In *The Moral Fool*, Hans-Georg Moeller argues that love and law are more-than-adequate replacements for morality. In a well-functioning family, the members care for one another not out of a sense of moral obligation but out of love. Indeed, love takes us further than morality. We can think here of Plato's *Euthyphro*, in which the title character is bringing his father to court because of a wrong the father has done to someone outside the family. Euthyphro's action strikes us as cold and legalistic. Love ordinarily makes us treat family members in ways beyond what morality would mandate for our treatment of others. As Moeller says, "Love within the family makes morality obsolete. Parents and children are, in most cultures, not expected to mutually condemn each other ethically. Parents are, on the contrary, expected to love their children despite potential moral shortcomings. And this holds true the other way around as well."[24] Then again, one might contend that love is itself a matter of morality. Moeller disagrees, though:

> One could say that what I have called one of the antidotes against morality, namely love, is in fact a moral value and the ethical corner-stone of Christianity. My view of love, however, is more Confucian than Christian. Confucians view love in terms of affection as the natural emotional bond within a family—and not as a virtue or a moral value. I do not agree with the Christian vision of universal love, and I do not think that there can or should be an ethical obligation to love others.[25]

So, though Christian love is bound up with morality, love in a more general sense need not necessarily be moral. It can instead simply be natural affection of the kind that is quite explicable in non-moral evolutionary terms.

Outside the family, law can restrain behavior that would harm others. As Moeller sees it, the function of law is not to brand actions as right and wrong, but to "stabilize expectations."[26] For example, many traffic laws do not have moral resonance. There is no moral reason for a society to mandate driving on the right-hand side of the road as opposed to the left or at a speed limit of precisely fifty-five miles per hour on the highway, but having such laws allows people to know what to expect.[27] Inasmuch as we want protection from harm in the form of safeguards for our life, liberty, and property, the law need not be conceived as moral. And with the increasing pluralism of contemporary societies, it has become troublesome to connect law and morality. Even the harmful actions most likely to elicit broad moral condemnation do not need to have their status as crimes justified on moral grounds. Moeller says, for example, that "A sexual predator is confined not primarily for moral reasons but to protect others (and, one could argue, even himself) from further harm."[28]

On a personal level, Joel Marks reports that he has been less angry and has had fewer problems resulting from anger since becoming an amoralist,[29] and he has even become a vegan out of concern for the abysmal treatment of animals.[30] Of course this is merely anecdotal evidence, and Moeller's views on the effectiveness of love and law are simply speculative. It remains an open empirical question to what extent human behavior would change in a world of moral anti-realists, but my guess is that it would not change very much one way or the other.

Anti-realism is not moral relativism. Moral relativism says that moral truth is relative to the group or to the individual. But anti-realism says that there is no moral truth. In fact it is asserted as universally true that there is no moral truth. I would say that what is relative is prudence. What it is prudent for me to do, depends on me and my circumstances and my desires. For example, Martin Luther King, Jr. displayed great prudence in determining the right times and places to protest. The decisions that were prudent for him to make would not necessarily have been prudent for others to make. Still, in general, prudential relativism wouldn't likely lead to wildly different recommendations for individuals and their actions any more than it leads to wildly different diets for different people. No one would find it healthful to eat large quantities of rocks, and no one would find it prudent to regularly harm people who have not harmed them. Many of our judgments are rooted in reason and our common evolutionary inheritance, but, still, one size does not fit all. As Moeller says in a different context, "The good way to London is the way that, for various reasons, we find good at a particular time: it may be quick, comfortable, cheap, or have the most pleasant scenery."[31] Likewise, in general, what is prudent will depend on the individual and the individual's circumstances and desires, and of course the individual may freely choose to disregard prudence.

Existential-biological Implications

For Sartre there is no human nature. That would seem to make existentialism and evolutionary theory incompatible. But, as we saw in the previous chapter, it does not; it just makes a strict Sartreanism and evolutionary theory incompatible. Sartre's view should be refined. There is a human nature but it is not fixed and stable; instead it is fluid and variable. It has limits, but there is great freedom and variability within those limits. In "Evolutionary Existentialism, Sociobiology, and the Meaning of Life," David Barash argues that "Human beings may not literally define their essence by their existence, as the mid-twentieth century existentialists proclaimed, but a deep understanding of sociobiology suggests that the existentialists were absolutely right: Our genes whisper within us, they do not shout. They make suggestions. They do not issue orders. It is our job, our responsibility, to choose whether to obey. We are terrifyingly free to make these decisions."[32] Indeed, we are free to test the limits, to see where and how they apply to us individually.

The existentialism that I put forward in chapter 1 blends elements of Kierkegaard, Nietzsche, Sartre, and Camus—none of whom share anything like complete agreement with one another. Thus my existentialism should not be expected to fully agree with any of them in particular all of the time. Sartre overstated the case when he said that existence precedes essence. Part of our essence is determined biologically, but no complete or fixed essence is given to us. Sartre is right to the extent that it is up to us to shape and create our selves.

The great majority of people are between five feet tall and six feet tall. Some rare individuals are two feet tall and some are eight feet tall. But even the range of two to eight feet is pretty limited; no one is one inch tall or one mile tall. A particular person's ultimate height may vary several inches depending on nutrition and other environmental factors, but again the range is pretty small. Not just with height but with nearly all things, human nature is variable yet biologically circumscribed. Right and wrong are not written clearly in stone but vaguely in DNA. Moral taste has been programmed and hemmed in by evolution, as our taste in food has been hemmed in. Biology sets parameters on moral behavior as it sets parameters on taste. When it comes to food, we're inclined to like the taste of things that are sweet and fatty. While there is room for individual variation, no one likes the taste of vomit. All in all, there is great homogeneity. Similarly, there is variation in the actions people can be at peace with taking, but there are "moral" violations that no one can live with. Some people cannot strike another person without feeling incredibly guilty; other people, depending on the circumstances, can strike another person without any guilt; but I would aver that no biologically normal person (i.e., no one with normal brain chemistry and function) can slam a healthy baby against a brick wall without feeling guilty.[33]

Conscience is both the gift and the curse of evolution. Guilt had survival value for individuals, keeping individuals in line with the expected behaviors of groups. But we have outgrown the need for the levels of guilt we are inclined to have. As environment has some impact on a person's height, so too it has an impact on a person's conscience. While at first glance, the environmental impact on conscience would seem to be greater than the impact on height, we need to realize that we can reverse the impact on conscience whereas we cannot reverse the impact on height (past a certain age). So we can fine-tune the conscience, but we probably cannot eliminate it. As Caroline West says, "As a matter of practical, biological, and psychological fact, it is extraordinarily unlikely that we would be able to banish moral thoughts and urges from our psyches."[34] We can existentially define ourselves by hijacking our genes and flipping the bird to our environment, but only so far.

Our moral temperaments are like rubber bands; they can be stretched.[35] Nurture interacts with nature to form moral personalities. Consider the guilt still felt by an ex-Catholic in eating meat on a Friday during Lent. The rational part of the person knows there is nothing wrong with eating meat, but the emotional part still feels guilt and can't be, or hasn't yet been, stretched beyond this. Likewise, the former believer-turned-atheist may still feel guilt about not believing, and the moral anti-realist will likely still feel guilt, or at least regret, in taking certain actions that she no longer believes are objectively morally wrong. And that is generally desirable. Guilt is an emotion, and the root difference between psychopaths and normal people is emotional. Most moral anti-realists do not want to be the kind of people who could punch a baby and not feel badly about it. Getting to that extreme point would break us off from the feeling of connection with other human beings that we prize. On the other hand, a moral anti-realist may desire to overcome any guilt she feels about not believing in God, not giving most of her time and money to helping the poor, and so forth.

Can You Live with It?

For the moral anti-realist existentialist, the only standard by which an action can ultimately be judged is: Can you live with it? The key is to know your own boundaries and limits. As we all have different physical limits, such as how much pain we can endure, so too we have different "moral" limits—the kinds of things we can do and "get away with"—that is, without having our conscience bite us. For example, some moral anti-realists, having thought about it, will feel guilty eating meat, whereas others, having thought about it in the same way, will feel no guilt eating meat. The standard of "Can you live with it?" might seem to give wide-ranging permission to act in any way at all. In theory it does, but in practice it is quite limited by the biological constraints of conscience. We may imagine that many people who habitually lie, cheat, and steal are perfectly at ease with themselves, but in fact most are not. As long as their brain chemistry and function are normal (i.e., they are not psychopaths), they live with guilt, regret, fear, and cognitive dissonance. Still, how far we can go beyond the good and evil of core morality varies among individuals. Accepting what suits us may have to come after testing our limits by rejecting much of core morality. Any boy or girl who dreams of becoming a professional athlete will likely pursue that dream, but at varying points nearly all of us have to abandon that dream. We just don't have the talent. Similarly, we may dream of living with no concern for "core morality." We may try so far as it suits us, but at varying points all of us will have to face the reality that we cannot live well that way—we do not have the "talent" to live in that realm. And that is perfectly fine because life is about living where you are with what you have. While it makes sense to rebel and to shake off what is forced on us, some of it will almost inevitably have to be reclaimed, albeit likely from a different perspective.

Consider the case of the Macbeths, who discover that they cannot "live with it." Macbeth and Lady Macbeth favor the older pagan morality in which might makes right; they reject the encroaching Christian morality in which "men" are "gospeled" into meekness.[36] After she has framed the sleeping guards for the murder of the King, Lady Macbeth mocks her husband, saying, "My hands are of your color, but I shame to wear a heart so white ... a little water clears us of this deed."[37] The Macbeths fail to factor in core morality according to which killing an innocent person is wrong. This core morality is part of our biological inheritance and is very difficult to override. The Macbeths are consumed by fear that they will be found out and dethroned, but they are also haunted by guilt. Macbeth sees the ghost of Banquo, and Lady Macbeth in her sleepwalking state tries repeatedly to wash the blood from her hands, saying, "What, will these hands ne'er be clean?"[38] As we know, the story does not end well for either of them.

There is a real balancing act in rejecting core morality and yet living in a way that is happy and fulfilling.[39] We do not want to be coerced into conforming to core morality, but it is often prudent to recognize the wisdom at the heart of much core morality, the way in which it suits our nature. After all, sympathy for others has survival value for primates living in groups, like us. Through the course of evolution, members of the group who did not sympathize and cooperate were ostracized and were thus less likely to survive to pass on their genes. We have in fact evolved to have sympathy for others, and core morality across cultures has reinforced that sympathy. So just because there is no God to punish us for our transgressions does not mean that others will not punish us for transgressing core morality. As Jesse Bering says, "the consequences for acting selfishly are as much a deterrent as they've always been: those who don't play by the rules will—by and large, more often than not—suffer the *human* consequences."[40] And from a moral anti-realist perspective, Garner reminds us that "not all criticism is moral criticism. There are plenty of non-moral things to say to the bear-baiters and baby-punchers, or about anyone who hurts or oppresses others."[41]

Aristotle said happiness consists in doing what is uniquely human, namely using reason to govern actions and feelings. The existentialist takes it further, adding that happiness involves making ourselves into unique individuals and giving expression to that uniqueness. Humanity has no *telos*, nor does an individual human have an individual *telos*, but we can each choose a purpose or goal for ourselves based on our prudential desires. As Barash says, "thanks to evolutionary insights, people are acquiring a new knowledge: what their genes are up to, i.e., their evolutionary 'purpose.' An important benefit of evolutionary wisdom is that ... it leaves us free to pursue our own, chosen purposes."[42] Our individual task then is to find a way of life that will help us in achieving our chosen purposes.

Rejecting morality, we are left with what Marks calls *desirism*, which advises that you "Figure out what you really want, that is, the hierarchy of your desires all things considered, and then figure out how to achieve or acquire it by means that are themselves consonant with that prioritized set of your considered desires."[43] I agree, even though we are often far from perfect in our ability to determine what we most truly desire and in our ability to take all things into consideration.

Enlightened Self-interest

Prudence is the key non-moral virtue in choosing and acting well, that is, in successfully fulfilling one's desires. How much self-harm comes from violating core morality depends on the person and to a significant extent can be managed by the person. In this way it is like how fast someone can run. There is great variability among people but also a pretty limited range. With training a person can improve within the range.

We cannot count on self-harm to be a good motivator for every person resisting every violation of core morality, but it is enough to keep most of us from doing the most "egregious" things most of the time. My desire and my recommendation is to practice "enlightened self-interest." Other desirists, notably Marks, may have different desires. In other words, desire cannot be strictly equated with the pursuit of enlightened self-interest. A difficulty for my desire and recommendation is that most people much of the time are wrong about what will actually fulfill their well-considered desires. Doing what is truly in the interest of fulfilling my desires often requires me to delay gratification. What might bring the most pleasure in the moment or the short run is not always what's in the interest of fulfilling my desires in the long run. Thus, people fail to choose what is in the long-term interest of fulfilling their desires for three reasons: 1) They do not fully realize what will be in the interest of fulfilling their desires in the long run, or 2) they know what will be in that interest in the long run, but they lack the willpower to delay gratification, or 3) they care more about short-term interest. So instead they go for the short-term interest or pleasure.

The recommendation for the pursuit of enlightened self-interest is not meant to encourage us egoistically and thoughtlessly do whatever we want. Quite the contrary, it encourages us to look closely at our own motivations and the likely consequences of our actions. Far from advocating a crass, unmitigated selfishness, I recognize concern for the self as a real burden. As Joyce points out, it is possible on the grounds of self-interest to develop the habits of thinking and acting in non-self-interested terms.[44] This is possible because, as he says, "correct moral thinking and clear-headed instrumental reasoning generally *do* lead to the same conclusion."[45] There is, technically speaking, no such thing as "correct moral" thinking for the moral anti-realist, but we can take Joyce's point by understanding that phrase to mean "standard moral thinking."

Ironically, overcoming selfish desire is a great gift to the self. By *selfish* desire I mean the kind of unenlightened pursuit of self-interest that harms others and that thereby causes others to react negatively. Selfish desire is a major source of *un*happiness; in my experience, focusing on the self makes the self *un*happy. Happiness is the greatest gift one can give to the self, and in my experience that happiness is best achieved by taking the focus off the self.

How rooted we are in core morality will vary among individuals. As Alex Rosenberg says, "there is a wide range of variation in the degree of individual attachment to core morality. ... But most of us are within two standard deviations of the mean."[46] So, each generation will produce some "saints" and some sociopaths, but most of us will be in between.[47] Some people might find that core morality suits them fine. After recognizing that core morality is not rooted in metaphysical reality, one is still free to live by core morality. That may be what is most natural and comfortable for some people. But others will find parts of core morality are a hindrance to them in living their fullest and happiest possible life. They are free then to reject that morality and move beyond it as far as possible. Inasmuch as some moral inclinations are biologically rooted (e.g., guilt for harming the innocent) and other inclinations will have been strongly indoctrinated (e.g., respecting elders), we will probably not go completely beyond core morality.

Morality did not evolve for our individual benefit but rather for the benefit of our genes. Core morality is not always what is good for the individual, and it may lead us to do things that are good for our genes even though they are not good for us. So even though *the ought of morality* and *the ought of prudential self-interest* often coincide, they do not always coincide. And since morality is a fiction, it makes more sense to go with prudential self-interest as far as we can determine it. Aware of this, Barash reminds us that "As descendants of both existential and evolutionary perspectives, we have the opportunity to assert ourselves as creative rebels."[48] Still, the worry that we may become monsters if we abolish morality is misguided. Our evolved tendencies for guilt and fellow-feelings are not easily extirpated. In fact it seems impossible to root them out. All we can do is override them in some cases.

Consider prudence in eating and prudence in acting. One of the reasons in favor of moral fictionalism is that we just cannot fully trust ourselves to follow through on rational deliberation. We think about whether to eat that donut, conclude that it would be in our best interest in fulfilling our long-term desires not to eat the donut, resolve not to eat the donut, and eat the donut anyway. Presumably what happens is that either: 1) our desire for the donut ambushes our rational resolution so that we conclude that our long-term desire does not matter as much as our short-term desire or 2) we act without thinking. Smokers often recount that they lit up a cigarette without even thinking about it, and it is a safe bet that donut eaters sometimes put a donut in their mouth without even thinking about it—at least not consciously. Fictionalism about diet can help us by drawing a bright line law such as "Only one donut for breakfast" or, if that line is not bright enough, then "No donuts at all." The first bright line law can be supported by having only one donut available—but that's hard to manage. "No donuts at all" is easier to manage—do not have any donuts available and do not go into donut shops. Of course the truth is that occasionally having one donut (or even two) would not be a terrible detriment in itself. But the problem is that crossing the bright line once makes it easier to cross it again. So it is helpful to pretend that one must never cross the bright line. This is meant to shut down deliberation and establish a habit that will make the unthinking action of putting a donut in your mouth much less likely. In effect, setting and respecting a bright line law can strengthen one's willpower. But at least for some people the bright line law will never be perceived as a real law. It is not like free will, where many people really do involuntarily forget that we probably do not have it (in the full libertarian sense). By contrast, we never forget that we can have the donut. It is just that we choose to structure our lives and habits such that we are likely not to have the donut. We have recognized what is prudent, and we have developed habit and willpower to increase the likelihood of prudent action.

For some people donut fictionalism may work; they may at least pre-reflectively believe that they cannot or must not have a donut. The existentialist chooses not to live this way, however, as it constitutes a self-deception that she rejects. So prudence in eating is like prudence in acting. One size does not fit all. While one person can eat a donut a day without negative consequences, another will find that he can eat three donuts a day and not put on weight or have any negative consequences. And some people will have to abstain altogether. On the other hand, some people may choose not to care about weight or health; that is their choice. It may seem an imprudent choice from another person's perspective, and it may in fact be imprudent from even the chooser's perspective—but not necessarily. Individual circumstances vary—again, one size does not fit all. As with diet, so with choices in general, prudence is the key. And what will be prudent for one person will not necessarily be prudent for another. Of course there will be a great deal of convergence for what is prudent among individuals, just not complete convergence. And it is even possible that someone may prudently reject prudence and choose to live a purely Dionysian existence—or someone may choose imprudently to live such an existence. Prudence can only be recommended, not morally legislated.

Watch Your Language?

A final consideration: What is the best thing to do about moral language if we reject morality? As with religious and theological language, moral language is so deeply embedded in culture that it would be silly to think it could be completely and immediately exterminated. Still, we can curtail it. As Garner says, "cutting back on moral pronouncements will be no more difficult than cutting back on swearing, and not nearly as difficult as getting rid of an accent."[49] Because we don't want to become like hyper-sensitive politically correct types who rail against anything that does not fit their worldview, it will largely be an individual choice. Thus there are prudential and practical reasons why we would not want to eliminate, for example, the word *should*. Likewise there are non-moral meanings for *good* and *bad*, and so we would not want to eliminate them. We might want to avoid speaking of *evil*, but even that word might be used to speak of something one strongly dislikes or disapproves of. I do not think that it is advisable to use the word in this way, but to prohibit the word would be to give it even more power. Speaking of *evil* is akin to speaking of a *soul*. There is no such thing, and so it is confusing and misleading to perpetuate the words with different meanings—but we don't want to prohibit them either. We need to let such words die a natural death. An atheist may still say things like "thank God," so we can expect that there will be moral phrases that moral anti-realists will still use. It would take generations for the phrases to become antiquated and drop out of use. So, to be clear, the reader "should" not expect that I will eliminate the word *should* and all other moral-sounding language in the remainder of this book. Rather, I ask the reader to interpret all moral-sounding language in the preceding and subsequent chapters in non-moral terms.

Notes

1 Here and throughout this chapter I do not mean to assume psychological egoism. By selfish desires I mean those that are narrowly and even foolishly focused on the self.

2 Richard Joyce, *The Myth of Morality* (Cambridge: Cambridge University Press, 2001), p. 189.

3   Daniel Nolan, Greg Restall, and Caroline West, "Moral Fictionalism versus the Rest," *Australasian Journal of Philosophy* 83 (2005): 308.
4   Joyce (2001), p. 215.
5   Joyce (2001), p. 228.
6   Joyce (2001), p. 222.
7   Joyce (2001), p. 227.
8   For fictionalism about mathematics, see Hartry Field, *Science without Numbers* (Oxford: Blackwell, 1980) and *Realism, Mathematics and Modality* (Oxford: Blackwell, 1991).
9   Joyce (2001), p. 196.
10 Joyce (2001), pp. 223–4.
11 Joyce (2001), p. 194.
12 Graham Oddie and Daniel Demetriou, "The Fictionalist's Attitude Problem," in Richard Joyce and Simon Kirchin, eds., *A World without Values: Essays on John Mackie's Moral Error Theory* (Dordrecht: Springer, 2010), p. 201.
13 Richard Garner, "Abolishing Morality," in Richard Joyce and Simon Kirchin, eds., *A World without Values: Essays on John Mackie's Moral Error Theory* (Dordrecht: Springer, 2010), p. 228.
14 Richard Joyce, *The Evolution of Morality* (Cambridge: MIT Press, 2007), pp. 165–7.
15 Joyce (2007), p. 168.
16 Garner (2010), p. 227.
17 In *Moral Error Theory: History, Critique, Defence* (Oxford: Oxford University Press, 2014), p. 191, Jonas Olson specifically ties his alternative to fictionalism, moral conservationism, to Pascal.
18 For practical insight concerning strengthening willpower see Roy F. Baumeister and John Tierney, *Willpower* (New York: Penguin, 2011). This book encapsulates Baumeister's psychological experiments in which he shows that willpower is like a muscle that can be strengthened through exercise.
19 Olson even more readily separates ordinary life and the classroom: "conservationism recommends moral belief in morally engaged and everyday contexts and reserves attendance to the belief that moral error theory is true to detached and critical contexts, such as the philosophy seminar room" (p. 192).
20 Nolan, Restall, and West, p. 312.
21 Ian Hinckfuss, *The Moral Society—Its Structure and Effects* (1987). http://www.philosophy.ru/phil/library/hinck/contents.html;   cf. Joyce (2001), p. 180.
22 Garner (2010), pp. 219–20.

23 Richard Garner, *Beyond Morality* (Philadelphia: Temple University Press, 1994), p. 383.

24 Hans-Georg Moeller, *The Moral Fool: A Case for Amorality* (New York: Columbia University Press, 2009), p. 44.

25 Moeller, p. 50.

26 Moeller, p. 12.

27 Moeller, p. 13.

28 Moeller, p. 48.

29 Joel Marks, *It's Just a Feeling: The Philosophy of Desirism* (Lexington, KY: CreateSpace, 2013), pp. 157–61.

30 Joel Marks, *Bad Faith: A Philosophical Memoir* (Lexington, KY: CreateSpace, 2013), p. 137.

31 Moeller, p. 186.

32 David P. Barash, "Evolutionary Existentialism, Sociobiology, and the Meaning of Life," *Bioscience* 50 (2000): 1016.

33 This example is adapted from David N. Stamos, *Evolution and the Big Questions: Sex, Race, Religion, and other Matters* (Malden, MA: Blackwell, 2008), p. 170.

34 Caroline West, "Business as Usual?: The Error Theory, Internalism, and the Function of Morality," in Richard Joyce and Simon Kirchin, eds., *A World without Values: Essays on John Mackie's Moral Error Theory* (Dordrecht: Springer, 2010), p. 185.

35 I owe this image to Susan Cain, *Quiet: The Power of Introverts in a World that Can't Stop Talking* (New York: Crown, 2012), p. 118.

36 *Macbeth,* act 3, scene 1.

37 *Macbeth,* act 2, scene 2.

38 *Macbeth,* act 5, scene 1.

39 This is not meant to imply that all moral anti-realists will choose happiness or fulfillment as their ultimate goal.

40 Jesse Bering, *The Belief Instinct: The Psychology of Souls, Destiny, and the Meaning of Life* (New York: Norton, 2011), pp. 201–2.

41 Richard Garner, "A Plea for Moral Abolitionism," unpublished manuscript.

42 David P. Barash, "Evolution and Existentialism, an Intellectual Odd Couple," *The Chronicle of Higher Education,* March 11, 2013. http://chronicle.com/article/EvolutionExistentialism/137715/.

43 Joel Marks, *Ethics without Morals: A Defense of Amorality* (New York: Routledge, 2013), p. 86.

44 Joyce (2001), p. 183.

45 Joyce (2001), p. 184.

46   Alex Rosenberg, *The Atheist's Guide to Reality: Enjoying Life without Illusions* (New York: Norton, 2011), pp. 286–7.
47   Rosenberg, p. 142.
48   Barash (2013).
49   Garner (2010), p. 231.

6

What's Mine Is Mine

Moral Anti-realism and Property Rights

Chapter 4 showed that existentialism is compatible with an evolution-based case for moral anti-realism, and chapter 5 argued in existentialist terms for a rejection of moral fictionalism because it is a form of self-deception. Chapters 6 and 7 will argue that moral anti-realism is compatible with a libertarian approach to property rights and a minimal state. The upshot is that moral anti-realist existentialism is compatible with a libertarian approach to property rights and a minimal state.

Key to the argument of chapter 5 was that in place of moral reasoning we can engage in prudential decision making. Prudence is not a value, but it may be a non-moral virtue.[1] Existentialists in general are not logically committed to prudence. I am simply recommending prudence as a guide that existentialists can adopt. Likewise in the remainder of this book I will not be arguing that all existentialists must be committed to strong property rights, a free market economy, and a minimal state. Rather, I will be arguing that this conjunction of commitments is possible. In short, I will be making the

The Free Market Existentialist: Capitalism without Consumerism, First Edition. William Irwin.
© 2015 John Wiley & Sons, Ltd. Published 2015 by John Wiley & Sons, Ltd.

case for free market existentialism as a view worthy of consideration in the marketplace of ideas.

In preparation for making the free-market-existentialist case for the minimal state in chapter 7, this chapter considers the implications of moral anti-realism for property rights. In short, without objective moral facts and without God, there are no Lockean natural rights. Natural rights are "nonsense upon stilts."[2] So we need to look elsewhere for the source of rights. A right generates an obligation on the part of another, but in the absence of real and objective moral facts, no human being can place obligations on another without a contract. Even with a contract, acting in accord with the obligation will be merely prudential, and the right will be a mere artifact. Of course there are natural, rational desires for self-ownership, property, and liberty, but these desires are not rights just because they are natural, rational, and perhaps even universal. Rejecting natural rights, we need to look elsewhere for the basis of property rights. For the moral anti-realist, justice can be nothing other than a word for upholding a contract, an agreement to live by certain rules. That is all that property rights are, the fruits of an agreement. And we are bound to honor such an agreement only by prudence, inasmuch as we seek to avoid the formal and informal penalties that may attend breaking the agreement and enjoy the fruits of keeping it. As we will see, it is possible to move from a state of nature in which there are only property claims to a scenario in which there are property rights. This move does not require the formation of a state, but a minimal state may be desirable for protecting those rights. The property rights that I will argue are most desirable from a moral anti-realist perspective are generally Nozickian.

Property Claims and Contracts

For the moral anti-realist, there are no property rights prior to contracts. There are only property claims. The most basic property claim is to property in one's own person (i.e., the claim that one is a slave to no one). Everything else follows from that. An individual's claim of property in her own person starts as just that, though, a claim. In the state of nature, everyone's property claim to herself is subject to non-recognition by others who may take her life or enslave her. It is this danger, among other dangers, in the state of nature that can make it worthwhile to enter civil society by contracting for the recognition of a property right in one's own person. The property claim to one's own person may be generally recognized by others in the state of nature, but it is without guarantee. Likewise, property claims to one's land or the clothes on one's back may be generally recognized by others in the state of nature, but they are without guarantee.

We can have contracts to recognize property in the state of nature, but such contracts lack the power of universal enforcement. Outside the state, nothing binds us to keep our contracts except the prudential desire to preserve a good reputation and perhaps a desire to maintain a certain conception of oneself. A sense of what is "mine" emerges before contracts, and so contracts would likely seek to codify the pre-contractual understanding. As Gerard Casey points out, there is an important connection between possession and ownership.[3] Possession is physical, whereas ownership is metaphysical. You can possess something without owning it, and you can own something without possessing it. Still, possession is often an important first step towards ownership. Taking possession of something is often simultaneous to, or precedent to, taking ownership of it. So in the state of nature, taking possession is an important step in claiming ownership. Property claims only become property rights when others agree to recognize those claims as legitimate. Thus property rights are a contractual recognition of the legitimacy of property claims. This would not typically involve a separate contract for each piece of property but rather a general contract concerning what kinds of things can be acquired as property and how they can be acquired. The details of the general contract would be worked out spontaneously through time as a result of trial and error.

There are no natural property rights; there are only the rights that result from contractual agreement. Such rights are artificial, that is, human-made. They are not transcendent nor do they in themselves compel recognition. Contractual agreements and the resulting rights do not necessarily require a state, and such rights are certainly not granted by the state—they are not the state's to grant. People living in a condition of anarchy can make contractual agreements regarding property and can agree to have a third party adjudicate if any disputes arise.

Property, like marriage, is a conventional contract, an agreement. Without the agreement there are no marriage rights; without the contract there are no property rights. In the state of nature, there are property claims that may or may not be recognized by others as property rights. Likewise, in the state of nature two people could contract to be married to one another, but in order to have others bound to recognize their contract those others must be parties to the contract. Typically this occurs in the state, though it could occur outside the state.[4]

Claim to Self-ownership

Without recognition, without a contract, there are no rights, but the desire for property is prior to the state. In the state of nature any property that is claimed for oneself is at risk of being taken by another who does not recognize one's claim, and this includes the claim of self-ownership. One may certainly be taken as another's slave in the state of nature and any cries of a natural right will not mean a thing. Likewise, one may be killed.

We should note that historically not all persons have made the property claim to self-ownership. Women in many times and places have not made the property claim, nor have slaves. Claiming self-ownership is an important first step on the road to contracting for self-ownership and for other property rights. Anarchist philosopher Crispin Sartwell believes that there is a natural right not to be enslaved, but he offers no argument for this natural right. He just feels it.[5] Granted, no one wants to be enslaved and nearly all people today find slavery abhorrent, but that does not rise to the level of a right not to be enslaved—just a natural desire. Rather, one's personal freedom and protection from slavery would be the most basic right that parties would contract for in the state of nature or in leaving the state of nature to form a state.

Protection of property rights in one's own person and in the fruits of one's labor are the first things people want. Other rights flow from these rights. Following Locke, we can ground property rights in self-ownership. I own my person and my labor, and I can sell my labor to others in exchange for goods and services. Whereas Robert Nozick roots self-ownership in a Kantian respect for persons, the moral

135

anti-realist simply recognizes self-ownership as the first property claim. There is no natural right to respect or to self-ownership. But to end or avoid the perils of war and enslavement, parties will be inclined to contract for self-ownership. And once individuals have self-ownership it is possible for them to establish other contracts whereby they sell or invest their labor to acquire other property. From there free trade can lead to greater wealth.

Development of Property Rights

Although self-ownership is basic, other property rights do not follow immediately from it, as Locke thought they did. Though mixing one's labor with raw material may give one a strong property claim, it does not automatically give one a property right—not in the state of nature, anyway. The only way such a property right would follow would be in accord with a contract. The labor theory of property is not correct; mixing one's labor with nature may not be enough for others to be willing to recognize a property claim. And in the other direction, one may claim property in much more than one mixes one's labor with, a whole valley for example. Such extravagant claims are likely to be challenged and lost, however. Generally speaking, initial property claims in the state of nature would be limited to what one could use and defend. Claiming what one cannot use may call for one to defend what it would be impractical to defend.

In the state of nature one can claim as much or as little as one wants as property. Such claims, however, are likely to be contested by others. Without real objective moral facts, there are no natural law limitations such as Locke specifies, for example, that one must leave as much and as good for others. But in many cases if one does not leave as much and as good for others, the property claim will be contested. Without a contract, no one is bound to recognize your property claim. Of course, even with a contract one is bound only by non-moral prudence to honor the contract and the rights and obligations it establishes. We can expect that through time a common-sense theory and practice of property claims would spontaneously develop: People claim ownership of themselves, their labor, and the fruits of their labor. The claim to own an entire valley would not endure without challenge and loss. One of the chief things we wish to avoid in the state of nature is the threat of loss, and so in contracting to leave the state of nature we would likely agree to limit our property to our own persons, our labor, and the fruits of our labor. Of course we may also choose to sell our labor for pay and give up claims to the direct fruits of our labor.

Because we would not want to spend our time and energy defending property claims, we would agree to recognize property rights to reasonable property claims. In short, it would be prudential to seek mutual advantage, though motivated by self-interest and guided by the invisible hand.[6] People would agree to what is to their mutual advantage, namely to take reasonable property claims and recognize them as property rights such that a person has a property right to her own person, her labor, and the fruits of her labor. Trying to claim more than this for oneself, even if ultimately agreed to by others, would result in an unstable situation in which the agreement would be insecure. More complex rules may tend to evolve, but simplicity would be the hallmark of the original mutual advantage contract. So, on this account it is not morality, or freedom, but mutual advantage that leads us to establish property rights and would likely lead us out of the state of nature to form a state that would protect those rights. This mutual advantage theory is all about motivation. It does not appeal to some higher moral purpose; it appeals instead to enlightened self-interest. Indeed, once property rights are established they can be transferred, trading goods and services.

Concerning the importance of rights, David Schmidtz says that they allow us to know what to expect from one another and to plan accordingly.[7] That is, rights give us stability and rule of law (as opposed to rule of the sovereign). This is not to say that any set of rights is as desirable as any other. Rather, it is to say that rights aim at stability. An undesirable set of rights may not be stable. For example, a set of rights that grants a property right over the ocean to the person who first mixes his labor with it by pouring in a can of tomato juice is unlikely to be stable.[8] People will eventually oppose it. Likewise, it is possible that a set of property rights that grants Joe a monopoly over the drinking water in an area may not be stable. Although there is a valid contract, people may decide that they will not honor the contract. Honoring contracts is a matter of prudence, nothing higher. The set of property rights that would be most stable would vary with time and location. For example, we already see the set of property rights concerning intellectual property changing before our eyes.

So, in the state of nature, a property claim is simply that: a claim. If another person chooses not to recognize the claim, then some resolution is called for, a compromise or perhaps a violent conflict. This is an undesirable state of affairs and makes contracting for rights, and probably leaving the state of nature, attractive. Of course one then opens oneself up to potential limitations on freedom by the legislature, but that is still potentially a better scenario than living in the state of nature. To limit the unsatisfactoriness of the legislature, it is best to let property law develop spontaneously. Along these lines, Murray Rothbard argues that just as government is inefficient at planning an economy, it is inefficient at planning a legal system.[9] Knowledge is dispersed, spread out among individuals. No central planning committee, no matter how intelligent and well informed its members may be, would know as much as individuals who spontaneously form an economy and a legal system.

We can expect variety among sets of property rights contingent upon the circumstances in which claims are made and codified as rights. For example, among some Eskimos at one time, land was not considered property, but game animals were so considered. These Eskimos had no use for land. No claims were made on it, and so no contractual rights were agreed to. But the lack of property rights for land does not mean that Eskimos had no property rights.[10] Eskimos prized game, and a game animal that an Eskimo killed was considered his property. No one else was considered to have a legitimate claim to it.

Casey gives an interesting example of how laws will develop spontaneously and differently depending on the environment: According to common law, in England, where animals grazed and crops were grown, the spontaneous agreement came to be that those who owned animals were responsible for fencing them in so as to prevent them from damaging someone else's crops. By contrast, in the early days of the American West, the spontaneous agreement was that those who grew crops were responsible for fencing them off to keep them safe from grazing animals.[11] In England, where land was pretty limited, animals could be somewhat easily fenced in, but in the American West huge tracts of land were owned such that it would be impractical to fence in animals. So, in a sense, a kind of "natural selection" picks out the property laws that best suit the people and the environment. And of course since the environment can change, the laws can change.

Property rights involve exclusion. That is, if something is mine then it is not yours. If I own something, then I may exclude you from using it. This raises the question of whether certain things can be owned. Is it proper for others to be excluded from them? Natural resources come up in this context. Does anyone own them? Can anyone own them? Who owns them initially? At the time of the first generation of humans does everyone own the natural resources? Or does no one? Some want to say that natural resources belong to everyone, and no individual can take ownership of them. This makes sense concerning the air. Everyone makes use of the air and we don't want anyone to pollute it, since they can't just pollute the part of the air that they use. A better way of conceiving of this, though, would be to say that no one owns the air but everyone uses it. The air cannot really be owned and it inevitably must be used, so it would be desirable if no one were given the right to pollute it in a way that harms others.

Regarding other natural resources, it makes sense to say that no one owns them initially, but that people can make property claims on them—and those property claims may, or may not, be recognized as property rights. So, for example, I may have a spring on a piece of land that I claim as property and that is recognized as property by common contractual agreement. The spring water, then, is as much my property as the dirt, trees, and rocks. Others may be envious of the spring because I may be able to sell the water for a good price, but that does not necessarily mean that the water should not be my property. It will all depend on the property rights that are agreed to contractually by the people. It is conceivable that the people will specify that natural springs will remain owned by no one and open to use by all, but it is just as conceivable that people will agree that whoever owns the land that surrounds the spring owns the spring. One reason in favor of recognizing individual ownership of the spring would be that, as Schmidtz says, "A rule of first possession lets people live in communities without having to view newcomers as a threat; a rule of equal shares does not."[12]

But even if we make this contract, what rule or law requires us to follow the rules or laws of the contracts that we make? In the state of nature, no law. It is simply a matter of prudence. A person who does not keep her contracts will find it difficult to get others to make contracts with her in the future, and inasmuch as contracts are often advantageous, it is to our advantage to make ourselves attractive contract partners.[13] In the state, by contrast, one is subject to legal punishment for breaking a contract. Of course, the law will not catch up with everyone who breaks a contract. It will be a matter of prudence then for a member of a state to decide whether it is worth the risk of legal prosecution and loss of reputation that comes with breaking a contract.

First Appropriation

Nozick accepts the Lockean proviso according to which we are required to leave "enough and as good" for others, but Nozick thinks this generates difficulty in dealing with first appropriations. Consider the case of Joe, who turns out to have the only water source in an area. Say, for the sake of the example, that previously there had been several water sources that have since dried up or become unusable. Now Joe has a monopoly on drinkable water in the area. If we assume that he originally acquired the property that has the water source in a just manner (i.e., in a contractually recognized manner), does the justice of his possession now change since it has become a monopoly? Nozick does not think the answer is clear.[14] I, however, do think the answer is clear: Joe's possession continues to be just unless there was some clause in the property rights contract that specifies that the right is terminated if it turns out to give a monopoly on drinking water. The people in the area are at Joe's mercy, and he will charge a high price for water. But if the price he charges is too high, then people will move and not pay the price or they may find a way to import water at a cheaper price. Or they may decide to violate the contract and seize the water.

As Schmidtz points out, Nozick mistakenly concedes the game in accepting that it is impossible to leave enough and as good and that first appropriations always leave the next to come less well off. Not only is this not the case, but, in fact, first appropriators often make things better for those who follow.[15] Schmidtz counsels us to think of the Jamestown settlers or the people who first crossed the Bering Strait. It is not the case, as we may be tempted to imagine, that first appropriators use up all the best and leave things worse. Quite the contrary, first appropriators more often lay the foundation on which we build. As Schmidtz says, "Original appropriation diminishes the stock of what can be *originally appropriated*, at least in the case of land, but that is not the same thing as diminishing the stock of what can be *owned*. ... The lesson is that appropriation is typically not a zero-sum game. It normally is a positive-sum game."[16]

We can think of this in terms of Thomas Edison, who grabbed up many patents and made lots of money. Despite his self-interest, Edison made many people better off thanks to the wealth they gained as a result of spillover.[17] Because of the wealth-increasing nature of trade, Edison grew wealthier and so did the people he sold to. As Schmidtz points out, Edison gave more in his products than he could ever "give back" in taxes.[18]

Intellectual Property

The status of intellectual property claims needs to be negotiated such that contractual rights are agreed to. There are no natural property rights, intellectual or otherwise, but intellectual property is a commonsense convention, with strong utilitarian justification. It can be a claim agreed to by convention as a right.

N. Stephan Kinsella argues that property rights arise only in cases of scarcity. If a resource is unlimited, then no one needs to claim it as property. Intellectual property is by its nature not scarce, since it consists of ideal objects that are not diminished in sharing. For example, if I write a poem and you make a copy of the poem for yourself and share it with others I still have the poem. The poem is an unlimited resource that does not exist in a state of scarcity. Kinsella argues further that in claiming a property right in the poem I am actually infringing on your property rights inasmuch as I am saying you cannot take your own paper and pencil or your own photocopy machine and make a copy of the poem.[19]

Kinsella is correct that there are no natural rights to intellectual property and that appeals to utility do not amount to moral

141

justification (because nothing does). However, the current American system of protecting intellectual property seems appropriate to me. Of course there was a previous time when there was no recognition of intellectual property, and there may be a time in the future when it will become futile to try to preserve certain forms of intellectual property, for example, copyrights for books and music. So there is no one-size-fits-all answer to the question of intellectual property. As an author who is motivated partly by profit, I am prejudiced in favor of copyrights and intellectual property. It seems to me that intellectual property and the financial rewards that potentially attach to it are powerful motivators for producing valuable products that create wealth for society as a whole. This is the utilitarian argument, except that I am not presuming that the principle of utility is morally valid. I am simply saying that it is quite conceivable that rational actors concerned with mutual advantage would decide that they want the state to protect intellectual property even if most of them as individuals are not likely to create or invent any lucrative intellectual property. The motivation would be the belief that if intellectual property is recognized, then better products and more wealth will be created. So it would be through self-interest and the invisible hand that mutual advantage is achieved.

Granted, it is likely that many writers would still write and many artists would still make art even if their products were not protected as intellectual property. And many inventors would still tinker and invent. But some products that require a great investment of time and capital would likely not be produced, for example medications.

If intellectual property is property, then it should be transferrable to subsequent generations. When it comes to copyrights on songs and novels it is difficult to justify time limits. Songs and novels are unique creations; no one else could have or would have written the exact same song or novel. The case for time limits on patents is easier to make because patents are generally granted for scientific discoveries rather than artistic creations, and given enough time the same discovery would likely be made by someone else.[20]

Ultimately, intellectual property depends on contractual rights that third parties cannot be coerced to recognize. In selling a book or other product to a purchaser there could be a contract not to copy or allow others to copy the product. Of course that would work only very imperfectly, but it would at least have the force of law

142

behind it. As Kinsella points out, preventing third parties from making copies would be highly difficult, as would enforcing a law that holds the purchasers responsible.[21] If people in general liked the idea of respecting and rewarding intellectual property, presumably because they liked the products that it produced, then they would not buy third-party copies. We see this already to an extent. It is surprising, for example, that so much music is purchased through iTunes when it is pirated and available free of charge elsewhere. At one point it looked like Napster and pirated music would wipe out any chance of recording artists making money directly from their recordings, but that has not happened. So it is at least conceivable that people in the future will consider it in their interest to buy books and music from artists or authors rather than pirate them for free.[22]

What Property Do We Deserve?

In *A Theory of Justice* John Rawls argues that we do not morally deserve our natural talents and abilities because they result from a natural lottery. Thus, behind the veil of ignorance we would not choose a system in which people benefit inordinately from talents and abilities that they do not morally deserve. Rawls's talk about moral desert is a non-issue for the moral anti-realist since there is no such thing as moral desert. The only kind of desert is the conventional desert that results from contracts. People only deserve or fail to deserve things based upon the rules agreed to. The upshot is that Rawls cannot provide a moral anti-realist with motivation for action.

Along these lines, Schmidtz points out that there are two senses of "arbitrary" and only one is troublesome when it comes to property. There is "arbitrary" in the sense of random, and there is "arbitrary" in the sense of capricious. The natural lottery of talents and abilities is arbitrary in the sense of being random, but not in the sense of being capricious. In this sense the natural lottery is like a card game. The hand you are dealt is arbitrary, random, but you have no cause for complaint unless the deck is stacked, unless the dealer is capriciously dealing you a bad hand.[23] And as the free market existentialist sees it, it is up to each of us to play the hand we are dealt.

The rules of the game have been agreed to before we were born, and we did not ask to play. Life is "unfair" in that sense. But certain possibilities remain open to us: we can choose not to play or we can attempt to change the rules of the game. Of course neither of those options makes for an easy life, but they are genuine options.

Rawls tries to justify his approach to justice by asserting that everyone has some claim to the totality of natural assets.[24] Because no one morally deserves their natural intelligence, beauty, athletic ability, musical talent, etcetera, the "social product" that results from the application of those natural assets should be shared in accord with the difference principle such that any inequalities benefit the least well off. The social product is like a cake. One group will cut the cake and the other group will divide it, thus ensuring "distributive justice." But questions need to be asked: Where did the ingredients for the cake come from? Who baked it? In other words, Nozick was correct to say that Rawls fails to fully consider our choice and responsibility to develop natural assets.[25]

As Nozick argued, wealth is not something that needs to be distributed like manna from heaven.[26] Wealth is earned and created; it does not fall from the sky. Thus the contract we would be most inclined to make would recognize wealth as belonging to those who earned and created it. The government has no reasonable claim to that wealth, and it has no reasonable basis for taking the wealth and dividing it among people who did not earn or create it, calling the result "distributive justice." As Nozick points out, people differ in the quantity and quality of their friends and sex partners. But we do not speak about the "distribution" of friends and sex partners, and we do not seek to redistribute friends and sex partners out of a sense of justice for socially awkward or physically ugly people.[27]

There is simply no such thing as "distributive justice" because things such as wealth and beauty don't need to be distributed. As Nozick argues, justice boils down to justice in acquisition, justice in transfer, and justice in rectification.[28] This is an account that a moral anti-realist can accept on verbal and pragmatic (though not metaphysical) grounds since there is no such thing as justice in the abstract. Essentially the account says that we need to come to possess property in accord with agreed-upon rules; we can then sell or give property to others, but others may not simply take it from us; and if justice in acquisition or transfer is violated we need to have rules for rectifying that injustice. As long as the rules are followed then we have justice, whatever the outcome is.

Justice in transfer extends back beyond the immediate transfer. For example, if I buy stolen goods I cannot keep them even though I did not steal them myself. This raises the problem of justice in transfer traced back through history. Here it makes sense to be practical and apply the principle of *innocent until proven guilty*. If I cannot be shown to have done anything wrong in terms of force, fraud, or theft in acquiring my current holdings, then the holdings are justly mine. Of course, it may be pointed out that in America we are all living on stolen land and many of us have benefitted indirectly from the institution of slavery. But to be practical there needs to be a statute of limitations on injustice of transfer. As a starting point for discussion, I would suggest 75 years as the statute of limitations for most cases.[29] That is roughly the span of an average lifetime, and so the implication would be that we cannot be liable for the consequences of a theft that occurred a lifetime ago.[30] In practice, of course, the statute of limitations on theft in most states is much shorter (two to six years).[31]

In *Free Market Fairness* John Tomasi attempts a rapprochement between Rawls and libertarianism by arguing that free market capitalism satisfies the difference principle. Because of economic growth, it is increasingly possible to live well near the bottom of the economic ladder in free market societies. Consider that the poverty problems of today in free market societies include obesity and difficulty affording college. Compare these to starvation and illiteracy just a few generations ago. As Tomasi points out, the real income (adjusted for inflation) of Americans is eight times greater than it was a hundred years ago. Even that impressive figure does not fully capture the increase though, because it is calculated in dollars and cents (adjusted for inflation) and does not account for the fact that today even the poor can buy things inexpensively that were not available to anyone at any price a hundred years ago.[32] For example, how much wealthier are we all, in terms of resources and opportunities, thanks to antibiotics, the internet, and cell phones?[33]

Perhaps not surprisingly, some Rawlsians have not been quick to concede to Tomasi. Unfortunately, this seems to be because they consider relative equality of wealth more important than increased wealth and welfare for the least well off. In particular they voice concern about growing disparity in income between rich and poor. What they do not see, however, is that consumption power, rather than income, is the proper measure to consider if one is truly concerned about increasing the standard of living of the least well off. Today's poor residents in America have greater consumption power than many kings of previous ages. It is true that the spillover from the rich to the poor does not increase the income of each group proportionally, but why should it? There is no reason that income should increase at an equal percentage across income levels across time. To the extent that people are less skilled and less productive at lower income levels, income should be expected to rise at a lower percentage rate even though in mathematical terms an increase in the rate of growth is easier to achieve from a lower starting point. Even when income levels do not increase (much or at all) for lower income-level groups, however, they gain in being able to buy better things that make their lives better and easier, thanks to the free market. That virtually every American has internet access makes even the poor wealthier than previous generations could imagine. Just to take one example, think of the set of encyclopedias that middle-class people used to scrimp and save to pay for on installment plans. That sacrifice has been made unnecessary by internet access. Remember the "digital divide" that was going to split society into the haves and the have-nots of computer technology? That did not happen to any significant or lasting degree. The free market spurred scientific progress such that computing technology got cheaper, better, and faster—and virtually universally available to Americans. Some have worried that under capitalism wealth would accrue in families across generations and form an insurmountable obstacle to fair competition in new generations.[34] The historical record shows, though, that families do not pass on their wealth forever, with 70 percent of inherited wealth gone by the end of the second generation and 90 percent gone by the end of the third generation.[35]

Rawls justifies "excusable general envy"[36] on the part of those who are unfairly less well off and who as a result experience a loss of self-esteem, saying "envious feelings are not irrational; the satisfaction of their rancor would make them better off."[37] Siblings are often like this as children, keeping track of their parents' favors and willing to have less simply so that things will be more equal—willing to cut off their nose to spite their face. While this reaction may serve some evolutionary purpose among siblings as children, it is foolhardy and counterproductive among adults. To the extent that envy persists into adulthood it may motivate and aid us in pursuing and attracting mates, but in that way it is more to the advantage of our genes than it is to ourselves as individuals. Ultimately, it is prudentially desirable to overcome envy and resentment even when they masquerade as a more noble desire for equality.

Rawls's "excusable general envy" would seem to be vindicated, though, by an experiment called "the ultimatum game," which seems to suggest that a demand to share the wealth is natural. The experiment shows that people will pay to punish someone who is perceived as not sharing appropriately. In the experiment a person is given $20 and told they can give any amount of it to another person. But if that other person does not like the amount they are given, the other person can reject the allocation, in which case both parties will get nothing.[38] In the experiment most people require that at least $7 be given to them in order for them not to vote $0 for both participants. From a non-emotional standpoint, they should be satisfied to get even $1. Indeed, in the context of a single iteration of the game they are being irrational if they reject any amount of money. But the demand for greater sharing has benefits over repeated iterations.[39] So while it would be rational to accept even one dollar if the game were only going to be played once, the participants seem to be acting on the natural inclination to assert themselves so as to benefit in repeated iterations. Thus the refusal to accept one dollar may be a good strategy when viewed as part of a bigger picture.

The ultimatum game would seem to support the concern for approximate equality of outcomes. But the game does not replicate the reality of the free market. The game is an artificial context in which the player has done nothing to earn the money, whereas in the free market the person will usually have done at least something, and often quite a lot, to earn the money. In the game, the person who gets the $20 to start has done nothing to earn it; it is pure luck and happenstance, manna from heaven. This naturally arouses the envy of the other player or players and moves them to believe that the windfall should be shared—though not exactly equally. In a free market economy where the rules of the game are explained clearly to all, such envy is unlikely to arise to such a great extent. Few people

147

begrudge Bill Gates or Michael Jordan the money they have made. Gates and Jordan have played by the rules of the game and earned their wealth through talent and hard work. It is true that they did not do anything to "earn" or "deserve" being born with certain talents and aptitudes or to be born into circumstances that would support the development of those talents and aptitudes, but they did not get or develop those talents and aptitudes illicitly. We recognize that a certain amount of randomness and luck is part of the free market game. So it is likely that very different amounts would be demanded if the ultimatum game were structured differently such that the person who got the $20 earned it through some skill, and the situation did not necessarily allow the other player to deny the "winner" any money if some amount were not shared. In fact, many players would probably not ask for any of that money.[40] Beyond that, the ultimatum game has none of the spillover effect whereby productive individuals benefit others through the jobs and wealth they create. By contrast, productive individuals in the free market do not take from society; they benefit society. Thus they have no obligation to "give back."

The demand for approximate equality of outcomes, to the extent that it is natural, is one of the most obnoxious things about us as humans, and it would be prudentially desirable to root it out as best we can. Life does not guarantee approximate equality of outcomes, and the demand for such equality in the name of fairness is grounded in envy and resentment. As a free market existentialist, I need to be concerned about having enough for myself, but what is enough for me has nothing to do with how much my neighbor has. Here we confront the distinction between needs and wants. It is fine to want things as long as we do not delude ourselves into thinking we need them, much less that we have a claim on someone else for them. Then again, we may wish to look at what we want. As argued in chapter 3, the free market existentialist may decide to reject consumer culture and practice voluntary simplicity.

Conclusion

This chapter has explained how property rights can be established on moral anti-realist terms, and it has argued that moral anti-realism can support Nozick's conception of justice in acquisition, transfer, and rectification. This is not to say that all moral anti-realists are logically bound to these views on property. The appeal, though, should be clear inasmuch as these views on property take a minimalist approach that dovetails with the minimalist ontology of moral anti-realism.

A fortiori moral anti-realist existentialists are not logically bound to these views on property. But again, the appeal should be clear inasmuch as these views on property take an individualist approach. Granted, the sense of individualism characteristic of existentialism is not exactly the same as the sense of individualism characteristic of libertarianism, but they are not foreign to one another either, inasmuch as both strive for genuine autonomy. Libertarians have long recognized the importance of strong property rights in securing autonomy, and existentialists have long recognized the importance of choosing meaning and subjective values for oneself in developing authenticity. This all points in the direction of free market existentialism, in which economic autonomy and personal authenticity come together.

Notes

1 In endorsing moral anti-realism I am endorsing a general anti-realism concerning values.

2 *The Collected Works of Jeremy Bentham. Rights, Representation, and Reform: Nonsense Upon Stilts and Other Writings on the French Revolution*, edited by Phillipp R. Schofield, Catherine Pease-Watkin, and Cyprian Blamires (Oxford: Oxford University Press, 2002), p. 330.

3 Gerard Casey, *Libertarian Anarchy: Against the State* (London: Continuum, 2012), p. 86.

4 Of course it is generally far less important that others recognize a marriage than it is that they recognize property. But then again in many places marriage likely began as a property contract, with the woman becoming the property of the man.

5 Crispin Sartwell, *Against the State: An Introduction to Anarchist Political Theory* (Albany: State University of New York Press, 2008), pp. 21–2 and 48.

6 Mutual advantage is a phrase associated in different ways with David Gauthier and Loren E. Lomasky.

7   David Schmidtz, "The Right to Distribute," in Ralf M. Bader and John Meadowcroft, eds., *The Cambridge Companion to Nozick's "Anarchy, State, and Utopia"* (Cambridge: Cambridge University Press, 2011), p. 212.

8   Nozick uses the example differently in *Anarchy, State, and Utopia* (New York: Basic Books, 1974), p. 175.

9   Murray N. Rothbard, *For a New Liberty*, 2nd edn (Auburn, AL: Ludwig von Mises Institute, 2006), pp. 282–3. Michael Huemer echoes this view in *The Problem of Political Authority: An Examination of the Right to Coerce and the Duty to Obey* (New York: Palgrave Macmillan, 2013), pp. 271–2.

10 Casey, p. 104.

11 Casey, p. 97.

12 David Schmidtz and Robert E. Goodin, *Social Welfare and Individual Responsibility: For and Against* (Cambridge: Cambridge University Press, 1998), p. 83.

13 Of course it is also possible in a state of nature for parties to a contract to have in advance agreed to have a third party act as arbitrator in the case of a dispute.

14 Cf. Nozick, pp. 179–80 and Schmidtz (2011), p. 209.

15 Schmidtz (2011), pp. 210–11.

16 Schmidtz and Goodin, p. 30.

17 Schmidtz (2011), p. 221.

18 Schmidtz (2011), p. 221. Of course that's one of the wrongheaded things about a company or an individual talking about "giving back" to the community. The company or individual has already given more than most by creating a product or service that people are willing to pay for, a product or service that leaves both sides wealthier.

19 N. Stephan Kinsella, *Against Intellectual Property* (Auburn, AL: Ludwig von Mises Institute, 2008), pp. 32–6.

20 Of course the distinction between creation and discovery can be hazy in places.

21 Kinsella, p. 47.

22 I think the days of publishers and recording companies are numbered though. No one feels a need to support or encourage them when their products can be made directly available from the artists and authors at a fraction of the cost.

23 Schmidtz (2011), p. 218.

24 John Rawls, *A Theory of Justice* (Cambridge, MA: Harvard University Press, 1971), p. 179; Cf. Nozick, p. 228.

25 Nozick, p. 214.

26 Nozick, pp. 198 and 219.

27 Nozick, p. 150.

28 Nozick, pp. 150–3. Let me take this space to head-off the objection that in *The Examined Life* Nozick disavowed his views in *Anarchy, State, and Utopia*. In a 2001 interview with Julian Sanchez, Nozick said, "What I was really saying in *The Examined Life* was that I was no longer as hardcore a libertarian as I had been before. But rumors of my deviation (or apostasy!) from libertarianism were much exaggerated. I think [*Invariances*] makes clear the extent to which I am still within the general framework of libertarianism, especially the ethics chapter and its section on the 'Core Principle of Ethics.'" http://www.juliansanchez.com/an-interview-with-robert-nozick-july-26-2001/.

29 "It would be extremely difficult to prove that the earnings of any one person in this country were illegally taken from others in the past due to structural injustice. The burden should be on the state to so prove and it should act with great caution." Jeffrey A. Schoenblum, "Tax Fairness or Unfairness?: A Consideration of the Philosophical Bases for Unequal Taxation of Individuals," *American Journal of Tax Policy* 12 (1995): 268.

30 I stress that this would just be a starting point for discussion, not a hard-and-fast rule. As Eric Bronson pointed out to me, it would not be desirable to protect property stolen by the Nazis and hidden in Swiss banks for more than 75 years.

31 Statutes of limitations can apply only to specific cases. To make a valid claim we need to identify and specify thieves and victims. So reparations for whole groups of people whose ancestors were victimized can have no claim. The hypothetical scenarios that such claims rely on are invalidated by the certainty that any particular person making the claim would not even have been born if the previous injustice had not been committed. The network of causes and effects is vast and chaotic.

32 John Tomasi, *Free Market Fairness* (Princeton: Princeton University Press, 2012), pp. 58–9.

33 On the great wealth of today's poor see Schmidtz and Goodin, p. 42.

34 For the worries about inequality see Thomas Piketty, *Capital in the Twenty-First Century*, trans. Arthur Goldhammer (Cambridge, MA: Harvard University Press, 2014); for the problems with Piketty's analysis see Deirdre Nansen McCloskey, "Measured, Unmeasured, Mismeasured, and Unjustified Pessimism: A Review Essay of Thomas Piketty's *Capital in the Twenty-First Century*," *Erasmus Journal of Philosophy and Economics* 7 (2014): 73–115.

35 Missy Sullivan, "Lost Inheritance," *The Wall Street Journal*, March 8, 2013. http://online.wsj.com/news/articles/SB10001424127887324 662404578334663271139552.

36 For the problems with Rawls's view see George V. Walsh, "Rawls and Envy," *Reason Papers* 17 (1992): 3–28. For a more general account of economic envy, see Christopher Morgan-Knapp, "Economic Envy," *Journal of Applied Philosophy* 31 (2014): 113–26.

37 Rawls, p. 534.

38 Werner Güth, Rolf Schmittberger, and Bernd Schwarze, "An Experimental Analysis of Ultimatum Bargaining," *Journal of Economic Behavior and Organization* 3 (1982): 367–88.

39 Scott M. James, *An Introduction to Evolutionary Ethics* (Malden, MA: Wiley-Blackwell, 2011), pp. 68–9. James also discusses a version of "the dictator game" in which a third party punishes unfair splits at a cost to the third party.

40 For discussion of problems with the experiments along these lines, see Steven D. Levitt, and John A. List, "What Do Laboratory Experiments Measuring Social Preferences Reveal about the Real World," *Journal of Economic Perspectives* 21 (2007): 153–74; and John A. List, "On the Interpretation of Giving in Dictator Games," *Journal of Political Economy* 115 (2007): 482–94.

7

Who's Afraid of the Free Market?

Moral Anti-realism and the Minimal State

The previous chapter argued that, for a moral anti-realist, property rights are contractual and there is no ground for the redistribution of property. In this chapter we consider the virtues of liberty and responsibility in the free market, and see why the free market existentialist calls for internalizing responsibility as much as possible. We also consider a moral anti-realist justification of the minimal state and the equal tax. The minimal state would be conceived as a club in which members pay equal dues for equal protection of life, liberty, and property. No one could be forced to pay the dues, and everyone would retain the right to exit to another state. No firm predictions are made. Rather, on the basis of speculation, an experiment is called for in which the minimal state would exist as a choice among states.

Opportunity and Outcome

A typical person might feel he has no right to take money directly from a neighbor. But that same person is often willing to take money

---

The Free Market Existentialist: Capitalism without Consumerism, First Edition. William Irwin.
© 2015 John Wiley & Sons, Ltd. Published 2015 by John Wiley & Sons, Ltd.

from his neighbor when the state redistributes it from the neighbor to him.[1] The action of the state makes it seem like the money is not being taken from a neighbor. Instead, it appears to be coming from the government. But the truth is that the government has no money of its own; it can only redistribute what it takes from its citizens.

The person who is honest and informed enough to recognize that the government must take the money from someone may be inclined to justify it the way some people justify stealing from big companies: those companies can afford it and they deserve to be looted. Likewise, some would say that people who have made money must have exploited others, and so they deserve to have their money taken away and redistributed. People who think this way often believe that the government should play Robin Hood by confiscating money from some rich person or company and giving it to a poor person.[2] The public administration of welfare has thus distanced recipients from their benefactors, making the recipients shameless in their demand in a way that they would not otherwise be. Adding to the problem, the government facilitates dependence on welfare by giving it the aura of an entitlement.

Every American schoolchild learns that "All men are created equal." But that is not correct. We are not all men. We were not created. And we are not equal. Some of us have traits that make us better adapted to the current environment than others. We contract for equality before the law. But in no other way are we equal. There are always differences that make one person better or worse than another depending on the scale of judgment. Certainly, we are not all entitled to equal wealth. The problem comes when the word "equal" is equivocated on, when on the basis of equality before the law some other kind of equality is assumed. Individuals are not equal in abilities, however. When it comes to abilities, the differences between human beings may be small, but nonetheless the differences—the inequalities—in abilities, whether based in nature, nurture, or both, have real impacts on what people can do and produce.

"Life is tough," says the free market existentialist in a folksy tone, "get over it." In many situations, the odds are against you. Things seem "unfair," whatever that means.[3] Certainly things are unequal. People are not equal. Our equality before the law is one of the benefits of a society in which it is contracted for. It is not natural. Equality of opportunity and equality of outcome are very different things.

154

And even equality of opportunity need not be pure. Everyone may get a shot, an opportunity, but because of nature and nurture some people are going to have a head start and some people will be faster runners—and some people will be faster runners who have a head start. So what? You can still compete. This is clear in the case of immigrants to America who succeed financially in large numbers despite very humble economic beginnings.[4] And in any case, the metaphor of the race is misleading. There can be only one winner (barring a tie) in a race, but there is no limit on the number of people who can excel in the free market.

Core morality may favor a certain degree of material equality, or perhaps better put, it will only tolerate material inequality up to a certain point. But since morality is an illusion there can be no moral argument in favor of material equality. In fact we may come to see ourselves as dupes of our evolutionary history to the extent that we feel badly for those who have less and to the extent that we seek to make them closer to equal. There is no moral reason we should feel that way. And while we can't shut off the feeling with the flip of a switch, we can override it to a degree.

Those who are less endowed in terms of their talents and abilities will naturally tolerate a certain degree of economic inequality. The question is: how much? They may become resentful and potentially dangerous at a certain point of inequality, and so prudence suggests that they should be bought off. This is in effect what the welfare state does—buys off the potential bad behavior of its less economically successful members. Crime would be excessive if the resentment of the less successful were to boil over. The welfare state is not the only way to handle this problem, though. Private charity can work as well, and we might prefer that option, as we will discuss later in this chapter.

We leave the state of nature and form a state for protection from one another. Rule of law and property rights provide the basis for free trade, which leads to economic growth and greater wealth for all. It is easy to think rule of law and property rights are found everywhere, but in fact they are not. In many places in the world property rights are not well-defined, making it inadvisable for someone to make the investments of time and capital necessary to start a business. And when governments are corrupt or unstable, rule of law cannot be counted on, again making it inadvisable for someone to make the investments of time and capital necessary to start a business.

There are times and places in life where people genuinely can be, or decide to be, "in it together," but those are the exceptions, not the rule. The opposite of "we're all in this together" is "you're on your own." The latter is more often true. Although most actions affect and involve others, they rarely do so in an equal way. Some people invest more and take greater risks and thus reap greater rewards or take greater losses. Thus the "social product" is too complex for any individual or committee to disentangle, nor can they efficiently allot different rewards to different actors, but the free market is very efficient at doing both.[5]

Unfortunately, a scarcity mentality characterizes the proponents of redistribution. They think and act as if there is only so much pie to go around, when the truth is we can make a bigger pie. They act as though wealth were a limited resource, like wives in a polygamous society. Mates are indeed a scarce commodity. Assuming that nothing is done to manipulate the number of males and females in a population, then if Alex takes ten wives that means nine other men will have none. Because men left with no mates are unlikely to tolerate the situation, laws against polygamy spontaneously develop in most times and places. Aside from the prohibition of polygamy, nearly everyone in Western liberal societies agrees that we should have a free mate market with adults allowed to trade their mating status as they see fit. A handsome man may have done nothing to morally deserve his looks, but he did nothing unjust to acquire them. His looks are his legitimately; he is entitled to them and whatever flows from them.

Thankfully, wealth is not limited the way mates are. Wealth is not some fixed, limited resource to which no one has a special claim. It is an unlimited resource to which those who create it have a claim. Land and natural resources are scarce and limited. Ideas and innovations are unlimited, though, and thus the things that are limited become trifling. We do not need to equally divide the limited things because in many cases we can increase their supply and we can make up for what we do not have by acquiring more of what is unlimited. Even those who do not create or earn wealth can benefit because wealth spills over in a capitalist society in the sense that today's luxury goods become tomorrow's everyday "necessities" had by all.

So, for example, just because Bill Gates has billions of dollars does not mean that other people have less as a result. Nor did Bill Gates do anything wrong when, in order to produce wealth, he used his natural talents and his willingness to work hard. He may not "morally deserve" his talents and abilities or even his willingness and ability to work hard, but he did nothing unjust (i.e., violated no contracts) in acquiring or possessing those things. Hence he is entitled to his talents and abilities and all that flows from them. People are entitled to the wealth and advantages given to them by family or by luck of the natural lottery. Even if they have not earned them, they still "deserve" them in a non-earned sense of desert, that is, they did nothing unjust (violated no contracts) in acquiring them. Thus, to avoid confusion we can use Nozick's language in speaking of what we are "entitled" to rather than what we "deserve."

Humans are unique in the extent to which they benefit one another while pursuing self-interest. By contrast, great lions do nothing to improve the lives of lesser lions in pursuing their desires; in fact they may just make the lives of other lions worse by depriving them of resources. But greatly talented humans who produce marvels of technology and innovation improve the lives of less talented humans. Such producers can never keep all of the benefits of their creations. Indeed, capitalism thrives on free trade in which both sides of a trade value what they get more than what they give. As a result of free trade, genius entrepreneurs like Bill Gates create wealth and jobs; what they give us is of far more value to us than what we pay for it. And of course Gates and his ilk are not simply altruistic in sharing their products. The products would be much less valuable to them if they kept them to themselves, and so they sell their products for as much as they can get.

By the invisible hand, the products of geniuses and producers spill over to benefit others. Some complain that the spillover does not increase wealth proportionally. But why should it? The remarkable thing is that it increases the wealth of others at all. The envy and resentment that drive people to cry "no fair" in response to the increasing inequality in wealth between the top earners and bottom earners is misplaced. The bottom earners owe a debt of gratitude to the top for the spillover, which they did not earn and without which they would be worse off. As Nozick argues in *Anarchy, State, and Utopia* and as Rand depicts in *Atlas Shrugged*, the poor and unskilled need the wealthy and skilled more than vice versa.[6]

No one gets rich on their own. That is true. Rather, a person gets rich with the help of others to whom she pays a wage as determined by the market and to whom she owes nothing after that.[7] The free market is the ultimate in democracy. Each decision to purchase or not purchase is a vote that tells what you want or don't want. This includes the decision to accept or not accept a job for the pay that is offered. It is not a matter of how hard someone works or how difficult their job is. It is not a matter of what people need, want, or think they deserve. Rather, it is how much the free market determines their labor is worth. As in school we do not grade for effort alone, so in capitalism effort alone is not rewarded. The market judges the value of the product or service. And to really earn big you need to either create something or take a risk or both. Short of that, one must develop a skill that is valued by the market. Consider the fact that more than 95 percent of American workers make more than the minimum wage.[8] What makes employers pay them so much? The answer is that because people are not forced to work one particular job they can change jobs if their skills are in demand. To keep workers, employers need to pay them what their labor is worth on the market (i.e., more than the minimum wage in more than 95% of cases).

There is a false sense of deserving social mobility in America, a sense that every generation should be better off in socioeconomic terms than their parents. Although economic growth makes it easy for each generation to be wealthier than the previous generation, there is no guarantee that each generation in a family will climb to a higher socioeconomic status than the previous generation. In fact it is very likely that some people will be worse off than their parents in terms of socioeconomic status despite the increase in wealth. There are no guarantees. You need to be smart, hard-working, and lucky— not just hard-working—to succeed in the free market. Even with all three there is no guarantee. Nor should there be if we prize liberty above all else.

Who's Afraid of the Free Market?

Capitalism allows us to vote and freely choose in practically all consumer choices. Of course the temptation is to let our tastes and desires be formed by those around us, but there is nothing necessary about that. And the existentialist, who is keenly aware of, and engaged in, the task of self-definition, will find that capitalism affords her a wide variety of choices that can aid, rather than hinder, her in self-definition. Of course, this takes a level of self-awareness and a desire to cultivate oneself that is all too rare. But there is no need for it to be so rare. With the great freedom of choice that capitalism affords, the existentialist can look at capitalism as an opportunity rather than as an evil. While dealing with consumer culture may be difficult, it is just the kind of challenge the existentialist can relish for its opportunity to exercise responsibility and grow through challenge.

Freedom is manifested beyond the free market in libertarianism. Gerard Casey says that libertarianism is "kids' stuff" to the extent that its basic principles are so simple: don't use force against anyone who is not using or threatening force against you, and respect other people's property—don't take it. It really is that simple. This is "kids' stuff" but it is "kids' stuff for grown ups." People assume that things must get more complicated on a larger scale, but must they? Not as far as Casey and I can see. Casey says that the burden of proof must be on the person who would restrict freedom.[9] I quite agree. In the name of bad consequences, which they fear but cannot prove, liberals and conservatives alike restrict freedom. In the economic realm[10] in particular, real harm comes from the restriction of freedom, not just because such restriction of freedom is harmful in itself but because it brings harmful consequences, as when the state imposes a minimum wage and actually hurts those they intend to help by leaving them unemployed.[11]

Fear of capitalism and free markets is just fear that people cannot be trusted to think and act for themselves. Some believe we need to restrict freedom to be most free. But who needs protection from freedom? Children. Not only can free adults usually discover what is best for themselves, but they often discover better ways of living that many other people will appreciate. This is the case because we are radically individual. If we were all alike, then it would be the case that a single wise ruler or a group of wise rulers could in all cases determine what is best for us and best for society. But given our radical individuality and the great complexity of society, this just is not the case. An all-knowing God could make such determinations for us, but no person or persons could ever know enough about individuals and the societies they form to make good top-down decisions for all. Knowledge, as F.A. Hayek argues in "The Uses of Knowledge in Society," is widely dispersed and localized.[12]

The libertarian principle is that freedom should be limited only when it causes harm to another. The free market existentialist prohibits harm not because it is immoral but because it is prudentially undesirable—and thus we agree to contract to prohibit harm. Consider the issue of fraud. Is it paternalistic for the government to protect us from fraud?[13] The buyer must beware, and we do not need or want the government to protect us from the routine exaggerations of sellers and advertisers in the marketplace. But fraud is not just a deception or a lie. Fraud is tantamount to theft. When a seller outright misrepresents what he is selling in a way that a reasonable person could not have been expected to detect, then we have fraud (i.e., theft). In most cases we hope that fraud will be prevented by the market itself in addition to non-governmental watchdog groups and ratings agencies whose own reputations drive their commercial success in the market. There is, however, a minor role for government to play, not in preventing fraud (except by deterrence), but in punishing fraud when it constitutes harm in the form of a violation of a contract.

With freedom comes responsibility. For the existentialist, life is yours to do with what you choose and to make of it what you will. Some people do not need to be told this, and some people will never act on it no matter how often they are told. Most people are somewhere in the middle, needing to hear the message repeatedly and only partially taking it to heart. That is a shame. But the extent to which people accept the truth does not change the truth. Free market existentialism calls for an internalization, rather than an externalization, of responsibility. For example, it is commonly presumed that before the modern welfare state people had no way of protecting themselves against the costs of illness, injury, or unemployment. But that is not so. There were ways to internalize that responsibility by joining "friendly societies" and "mutual aid societies" that provided social insurance against illness, injury, and unemployment.[14] Friendly societies were groups, often organized around ethnicity or occupation, which pooled risk. Members paid their dues and received benefits in the event of misfortune. By contrast, the welfare state externalizes responsibility and thereby reduces a sense of fraternity and community.[15] It also reduces the extent to which people are willing to take responsibility for themselves and not abuse the system. With friendly societies and mutual aid societies it was very clear to the recipient where the money was coming from: his friends and neighbors. But with government social insurance and welfare, the source of one's benefits is obscured. The money appears to come from the government rather than from one's friends and neighbors, which can lead to unnecessary and even fraudulent claims. As David Schmidtz says, "when people take responsibility, they are less likely to need help in the first place."[16]

Robert Goodin argues, though, that the state, with its access to general revenue through taxation, is the superior source of social insurance programs because it can run over budget in a way that a mutual aid society could not.[17] It is true that the state is in a better position to handle a large number of catastrophic cases because it can decide to draw from general tax revenue rather than restrict itself to the revenue collected to cover social insurance. Unfortunately though, this tendency of the state to cover more than it has collected for results in budget deficits and increased taxes.

The free market existentialist calls for internalizing responsibility as much as possible. Consider who is responsible for the bad decisions people make. For example, a significant number of people who are fortunate enough to have a 401K plan do not contribute even though their employers match contributions, essentially giving them free money.[18] In most cases such people simply cannot seem to overcome inertia and opt in to the plan. Consequently, they will be left with little in savings for retirement and will want more from social security. In the meantime they will take home more money in their weekly paycheck than someone else with the same salary and will likely spend the money to satiate short-term desires. If it is not their fault that they did not save properly for retirement, then whose fault is it? Certainly not mine or yours, and so why should we pay more to compensate for their foolishness? We are all "predictably irrational" in various ways, but it is incumbent upon us to become aware of this and counteract it.[19] Having a certain weakness or foolish inclination may not be totally my fault, but being aware of it is totally my responsibility and thus so too is acting to counteract it.

Choice architecture can make a significant difference in the percentage of people who make a prudent choice. The default choice matters, and sometimes there is no neutral choice. Still, this does not provide a valid excuse for anyone who chooses foolishly, such as the person who is fortunate enough to have a 401K plan and yet fails to take advantage of his employer's matching contributions. The free market existentialist realizes that she is not perfectly rational and so plans accordingly. She will not always want to choose what is best for herself in the long run, but she recognizes that it is more prudent to make those choices for herself than to have government make them for her. There is much wisdom in behavioral economics and the choice architecture discussed by Richard Thaler and Cass Sunstein in *Nudge*, but the idea of "libertarian paternalism" is simply an oxymoron.[20] The government has no valid libertarian role to play in nudging us.[21] Rather, prudence dictates that we nudge ourselves by becoming aware of our tendencies and doing things like enrolling in the "save more tomorrow" program in which we pre-commit to having a percentage of future pay raises channeled into our 401K plan. In fact, there is a growing industry of companies and websites offering help and support for people who want to nudge themselves into weight loss, away from procrastination, or into getting up early in the morning. This is the proper place for nudging. In fact, any area outside government can be the proper place for nudging.

Minimal Government

"Government is best which governs least."[22] For the libertarian this means that the state should be restricted to acting as a night watchman, protecting us against force, fraud, and theft. Our lives and liberty are in that sense our property, in need of protection.

She who has decided she can live without God must next decide if she can live without the nanny state. God is the original central planner. If there were an all-good, all-powerful God, then he would be the best planner possible. For millennia people thought a God was the best explanation for human anatomy, but science has shown us it is actually evolution. With the death of God, people have looked to make a god of the state, thinking that wise politicians can plan things better for us than we as individuals can plan for ourselves. While an all-knowing God could plan that way, no group of humans can. The systems involved are just too vast and chaotic. Evolution works better than human planning would in the biological realm, and the spontaneous order that arises as a result of individual actors who know their own situations is better than the imposed order that wise politicians would dictate in the economic realm.

For ages, people fell prey to the illusion that they needed a king to provide order and stability. That seems foolish in retrospect, but it is no more foolish than the current belief that we need a government to centrally plan the economy and provide many goods and services. The better informed people are, the more they realize that government is inefficient. We need to be careful not to assume that only government can perform a certain function just because in recent history only government has performed that function. There was a time, for example, when many people thought only the government could effectively deliver the mail, but as Federal Express and UPS have taught us, that is not so. In fact, rarely does government do something better than the private sector could and would if given the chance. The exceptions, I believe, are police, courts, and national defense. In each of these cases the people are best served by a government monopoly because competition among service providers would lead to unnecessary and distracting complications as well as inefficiency of service.[23]

Still, one might be concerned about so-called public goods that "cannot be provided to anybody unless they are provided to everybody."[24] As we will see later in this chapter, there are ways to handle the provision of police, courts, and national defense. And when it comes to so-called tragedy of the commons scenarios, privatization eliminates the concern that, for example, street lights will not be provided or levees will not be built.

Of course people are still tempted to think that the government must regulate the economy. In truth, regulation is fine and necessary as long as it comes from the private sector. Consider assessment in higher education. The government tells colleges via accrediting agencies that they need to implement assessment practices and policies in order to qualify for federal funding. So deans make department chairs implement assessment practices for professors. The farther away one gets from the professor and the student the less one understands what is really going on in the classroom and how to judge its quality. The underlying concern is that colleges are not delivering a quality product to students, so government decides to get involved.[25] But when one college really does a better job of giving students what they want, that college succeeds in the free market and attracts students. There is no need for the government to get involved. The free market is a much better arbiter of the worth of a degree from one college as opposed to another than a government agency could be. Of course, from the outside it may appear to lots of people that assessment practices and policies make sense—the more so the less someone knows about the way higher education works. Likewise, the less one knows in a practical and firsthand way about any industry, the more one will be inclined to think that it is in need of government regulation.

We move now to consider the taxes necessary for funding the minimal government of the night-watchman state. Casey argues that historically taxes were collected only in times of war to fund the war. Thus the state's way of expanding was to make war virtually constant. This may not be universally true, but it is insightful when considered in the American context.[26] Income taxes have not always been part of the American system. Rather, excise taxes and tariffs sufficed for most of our early history. Indeed, there was no income tax in the United States until 1862, when such a tax was instituted to pay for the Civil War despite the fact that an income tax was prohibited by the Constitution. With the war over and reconstruction underway, the income tax was repealed in 1872. In 1894 an income tax was instituted again, but it was found unconstitutional and prohibited in 1895. In 1913 the Sixteenth Amendment to the Constitution gave us an income tax, and we have had it ever since. Predictably, the income tax increased dramatically throughout the next one hundred years as more and more wars needed to be paid for. Of course, through taxation the government does not just fund the military, but, at approximately 20 percent, the military is one of the largest parts of the American budget.

In addition to funding the military, the government also redistributes from the rich to the poor who can vote for them. This use of public funds is, however, against the letter and the spirit of the Constitution. Consider that when Congress appropriated $15,000 to assist French refugees in 1794, James Madison objected, saying, "I cannot undertake to lay my finger on that article of the Constitution which granted a right to Congress of expending, on objects of benevolence, the money of their constituents."[27] Madison was not ignoring the general welfare clause of the Constitution. Rather, he said, "If Congress can do whatever in their discretion can be done by money, and will promote the General Welfare, the Government is no longer a limited one, possessing enumerated powers, but an indefinite one."[28]

Later in American history, President Franklin Pierce refused federal funding for the care of the insane, remarking that the Constitution makes no provision for such care and that if the indigent insane can make a claim on such care then the indigent in general would be next to make a claim.[29] Along these lines, David Kelley offers an apt comparison: welfare amounts to compulsory Good Samaritanism.[30] The biblical Good Samaritan did far more than others did and more than anyone could have expected.[31] We admire him for this, and he no doubt felt good about himself for it. But under the welfare state we are compelled to do far more than we could reasonably be expected to do for the poor, and we do not even get gratitude in return. Thomas Nagel attempts to justify this, saying "Sometimes it is proper to force people to do something even though it is not true that they should do it without being forced. It is acceptable to compel people to contribute to the support of the indigent by automatic taxation, but unreasonable to insist that in the absence of such a system they ought to contribute voluntarily."[32] What makes this "proper" or "acceptable" is unclear, especially when it involves "forcing" and "compelling" people who are doing no harm to others and might be willing to play the Good Samaritan voluntarily if given the chance. Confiscation of property in this manner insults the dignity of all involved.

Tax collecting has always been a difficult and unsavory business. But in 1942, motivated by the need for greater revenue to fund World War II, the American government started taking income taxes out of weekly paychecks to increase tax compliance. This practice was wildly successful in increasing tax compliance, and it has certainly made paying taxes less painful. No one likes to see how much is taken out of their pay in taxes in their weekly paystub, but people get used to it. It requires no activation energy to pay taxes in this way. People never get to hold all the money they earned; the government takes part of it before it reaches the hands of individuals. People would find it painful indeed if they had to write a weekly, monthly, or yearly check for the full amount due in taxes. Some people do get to feel this pain, though: the self-employed, who must pay quarterly estimated taxes. They hold on to the money they earned for nearly three months before paying part of it in the form of taxes.

Remarkably, in *The Myth of Ownership* Liam Murphy and Thomas Nagel claim that pre-tax income is a bookkeeping illusion,[33] saying that "We have to think of property as what is created by the tax system, rather than what is disturbed or encroached on by the tax system. Property rights are the rights people have in the resources they are entitled to control after taxes, not before."[34] This is an ingenious, Orwellian reversal of common sense and what everyone knows to be true. By way of justification, Murphy and Nagel say, "There is no market without government and no government without taxes."[35] But this is simply not true. Markets do not necessarily require governments, and governments certainly do not create markets. More often than not, they hamper markets. The government exists to serve the people, not to decide what is best for the people. And as we shall see, there is a much more sensible way to construe the nature of property and taxation than the view offered by Murphy and Nagel.

The Equal Tax

Any law that infringes *contractual* rights to life, liberty, and property is by definition an unjust law. In most nations, however, a tyranny of the majority infringes the right to property in the form of unequal taxation. In a tyranny of the majority, a democratic majority imposes its will on a minority in a way that violates the rights of the minority. In this case the minority is the wealthy. Imagine if a tyranny of the majority imposed a 99 percent tax rate on the top 1 percent of income earners. The difference between this hypothetical scenario and the current taxation system in most nations is only a difference in degree, not a difference in kind. The wealthy would never consent to pay so much more than everyone else in taxes, but the tyranny of the majority forces them to pay.

Currently the top 10 percent of income earners in America pay approximately 70 percent of federal income taxes.[36] To be clear, the wealthy not only pay more in dollar amounts in taxes, they pay a higher percentage of their income in taxes.[37] They are understood to tacitly consent to this system. In other words, by accepting the benefits of the system they are agreeing to the system, even though they have never formally given their agreement in speech or writing. But that is false and misleading. As Nozick says, tacit consent is not worth the paper it is not written on.[38] The wealthy no more tacitly consent to pay more in taxes than did gay Americans tacitly consent to forgo the right to marry in many American states.[39] Gay Americans were deprived of equal rights (liberty), and the wealthy are deprived of their right to do with their property as they see fit. Money is property, and the tyranny of the majority enacts a law that takes more of it from a minority group than from the majority group. This is nothing short of theft.[40]

It is often presumed that fairness calls for a progressive tax, that is, a tax under which the larger an income one has, the larger the percentage of that income is paid in taxes. But just because the wealthy *can* pay a greater percentage of their income does not mean that they *should*. Concerning "ability to pay" theories, Jeffrey Schoenblum says, "Underlying this notion seems to be the fallacious premise that those who are better able to pay must have received more benefit from the government."[41] This is a generous interpretation by Schoenblum. Historically, soak-the-rich taxes have been imposed because the majority *can* impose them. Only after the fact have they been rationalized if at all.

The free-market-existentialist solution is not a regressive tax, mandating that the larger an income one has, the lower the percentage of that income that is paid in taxes. Simply cutting the percentage of income that the wealthy pay in taxes would not necessarily result in the wealthy paying the same as everyone else. Karl Marx called for a society with the guiding principle "from each according to his ability, to each according to his needs."[42] By contrast, the guiding principle for the free market existentialist is "from each the same, to each the same."

Taxes are not redistributive by their very nature; they do not necessarily have to take from one group and give to another. It is possible to have a tax system in which all individuals pay the same amount. Such a tax has been called a "poll tax" or a "head tax," but let's follow Schoenblum in calling it what it is: an "equal tax." A family's tax bill would be based on the number of people in the family. Such a tax would be akin to dues: everyone pays the same and everyone gets the same. Taxes would be proportional to benefits, and individuals would all receive the same benefits. Taxes would thus be like an Automobile Association of America (AAA) membership. You pay for the benefits you get. In any given year you may not use the benefits of membership much, and in other years you may use them a lot. In general you hope not to use or need them much or at all. They simply provide a sense of security.

So the state would be like a club in which we pay dues for benefits.[43] As long as we receive the same benefits we should pay the same amount in dues. Consider this: Would you join an organization that wanted you to pay more for the same benefits as everyone else just because you have a higher income? Perhaps some people would. But would you be willing to pay a fixed percentage of your income to join? Of course some people tithe to their church, but few churches enforce this. On that note, consider that 1 Samuel 8: 10–18 warns the people of Israel against having a king because a king will want to take 10 percent of what they produce. If only our income were merely decimated by taxes in America!

There may be some suspicion that the wealthy benefit more from the state, but Schoenblum argues that "There is no proven correlation between how much income a person earns and how much benefit he receives from society."[44] Wealthy people may have more to lose than poor people and thus they may benefit more from police protection. Does that mean then that they should pay more in taxes? Possibly, but the most important things that the police protect are life and limb. And the value of those is essentially the same for all people. We could try some Byzantine calculation to determine what the protection is subjectively worth to each person or family, but the transaction costs of the calculation would not be worth it. Indeed, Walter Block argues that interpersonal utility comparisons are intellectually bankrupt.[45] I tend to agree to the extent that they cannot reasonably be calculated and factored in to taxes.

The fact that some people will derive more subjective benefit from services is just one more reason to minimize the services provided by government. The absolute equalization of benefits in terms of subjective value is not a worthwhile goal; the solution is to minimize benefits, not to try to calculate who is subjectively benefitting more. Government should provide benefits in terms of personal safety and protection. The fact that some people might put a different dollar value on that service, that some people value their lives and safety less in dollar amounts, is not worth accounting for. The calculation would be impractical and unreliable, and so we have to live with the minor imperfection in the system since it is still the best system possible.

Some people may object that this approach lacks nuance and foresight. Most importantly, they might object that the equal tax might not generate sufficient revenue to run the government. That is possible, but I believe it is unlikely, given the way the economy would likely flourish under such a system. Still, even if the economy did not grow dramatically, the solution would be to reduce state spending to fit the equal tax. As in a home so in a state, budget should dictate spending, not vice versa. Richard Epstein objects that the burden on those with low incomes would be too heavy.[46] Again, this would not necessarily be the case with a flourishing economy. In any event, however, the budget should be based on tax revenue, not the other way around. The ideal is to get to a place where very little tax revenue is required to run a government. We should only tax for as much as we truly need, rather than finding ways to spend the money that is collected in taxes.

In 2013 there were 314 million people in the United States, with a federal budget of $3.8 trillion, meaning that every man, woman, and child would need to pay $12,101 a year under the equal tax. That is too much under current economic circumstances.[47] But we could downsize the military by 50 percent and completely eliminate welfare, Medicare, Medicaid, social security, the IRS, the ATF, the Department of Education, and the Department of Agriculture. A quick, back-of-the-envelope calculation shows that would reduce the annual budget to $1 trillion, or $3,184 per person.[48] That would be a good start, but we could and should make even more cuts to lower the tax.

169

Epstein shuns the equal tax because it would be regressive, charging a lower percentage of income the higher one's income rose. But this is misleading since the equal tax would not be based on a percentage of income at all. Instead it would be a flat charge for government services. In this way it would be no different from a gallon of gas, the cost of which is regressive if you frame it in those terms.[49] In reality, this price structure is simply a basic tenet of the free market; people pay the same amount for a gallon of gas no matter what percentage of their income that amounts to. Why should minimal government services be any different?

The fact that the equal tax would potentially be a heavy burden on some would be a very good motivation to keep the equal tax very low and thus to keep government services very minimal. In addition, charitably inclined people could pay the equal tax for other citizens. Rather than punishing those who do not pay the equal tax, we could accommodate them with a tag system.[50] People who pay would be given a tag for their house, vehicle, business, wallet, etcetera. If you do not pay and are without a tag you would be making a target of yourself, as would be your prerogative. Of course, it may be impossible to deny the free rider some of the benefits of the state, but in a truly minimal state those benefits would be very few and limited. For example, if there were a public fire department, the free rider would be protected from fire spreading from a neighbor's house, but he would not be protected from having his own house burn down. If taxation were modeled on club dues, then most club benefits would be denied to the person who declined to pay dues.[51] Being a club member would be something that people would likely want to advertise and promote, and so there would potentially be adverse effects for those who were not club members. For example, others might be less likely to hire them or patronize their businesses.

The free market existentialist thus finds no reason for the state to support the welfare of its citizens. The state itself should not be the locus of compassion. Compassion is a virtue to be found in the private sphere, in the individual. In fact, compassion for the suffering of others can relieve an individual's own suffering by directing her attention from herself and her own problems and refocusing it on the problems of others. It thus becomes in the self-interest of the individual to have compassion for others.[52] This is not to say we should have pity, a vice that Nietzsche denounced. Pity is degrading both to the person who feels it and to the person towards whom it is directed. Pity is an uncomfortable emotion that one wants to get rid of as soon as possible. Compassion, by contrast, is ennobling.[53] Both the person who feels compassion and the person towards whom it is directed are lifted up by the compassion. None of this is to say, though, that there is a duty or obligation to feel compassion in general or in any particular instance. Rather, it is up to the individual when and if to indulge compassion. Compassion arises out of the recognition of the suffering of another and the fellow-feelings that result. Dispositionally, some people will be more inclined towards compassion than others, and some people may wish to curtail their compassion whereas others may wish to develop it. It simply depends on what the individual finds most suitable to her well-being and happiness.

What would happen, though, if the welfare state were eliminated? Would private philanthropy be sufficient to take care of those in need? This is an empirical question that could only be satisfactorily answered by trying the experiment. However, as Nozick argues, there is good reason to be optimistic that charitable giving would increase dramatically in the absence of compulsion.[54] Government codifies and mutes the magnanimous impulse to give and to help others. By telling me that I have to give, government actually diminishes my impulse to give spontaneously of my own accord. I have already "given at the office" in the form of the taxes deducted from my paycheck. Thus the realm of my individual action is diminished. We would not have to rely entirely on the magnanimity of the wealthy to fund private charities, though. Their self-interest would motivate them as well. It makes sense to help the poor, because if people are hungry and unoccupied they are less likely to respect property rights.

There is reason to think, though, that there would be much less poverty in the minimal state. Not only would eliminating welfare free up money that people could and would give to private charity, but even the money freed up that did not go to charity would go into the economy and generate wealth and jobs that would benefit the poor. So the free market existentialist says let the wealthy be patrons, giving largess at their pleasure and discretion. Some may wish to fund schools, others hospitals, etcetera. We can be confident that such private charity would be more efficient than government-run institutions and could do more with less. Of course there would still be irresponsible and vicious people who would game the charity system. It would, though, be worth dealing with those abuses, if we could be rid of the problems and issues we face under the welfare system.

What about free riders on charity? If we leave education and care of the poor and the elderly to charity, then some people will contribute a great deal to charity for these purposes and others will contribute nothing and yet will derive "neighborhood benefits" from having the poor taken care of and the children educated. There is nothing much that can be done about this except to promote the generosity of those who contribute and to shame those who do not. In any event, these free riders would be preferable to the free riders on the welfare state.

One concern about the minimal state is that society would be cold and uncaring. That too is an empirical issue that could only be satisfactorily answered by trying the experiment. However, a strong argument can be made that society in the minimal state would be at least as warm and caring as current Western democracies. In the minimal state we could not just tell ourselves that the government will take care of those in need. Rather, we would each be more likely to see ourselves as our brother's keeper. Indeed, as argued above, charity and philanthropy would likely increase dramatically. We would also likely see an increase in concern for the groups one is a part of, such as family, church, and community.

The communitarian view has it that "we're all in this together," as if society were a giant family rather than a conglomeration of strangers. However, as Loren Lomasky notes, "It is no small thing to agree to share one's fate with another." Family members, lovers, friends, or members of an army platoon may be willing to share their fate.[55] But forcing others to do so is a mistake.

Justifying the Minimal State

Having presented a vision of the minimal state, we must now ask: Can the minimal state be justified? Or must we remain in the anarchic state of nature? Certainly, as Locke notes, the inconveniences of the state of nature are enough to move most people to form some minimal state.[56] But if the protections against force, fraud, and theft are either more or less than what a person wants, does that mean the state is not justified? No, it means that the person who is discontent should be free to leave and form a new state or go to another state, including the state of nature. So the minimal state can be justified to the extent, and only to the extent, that people accept it.

Crispin Sartwell says that any limited state is a snowball that will grow larger as it rolls downhill.[57] So the state is to be opposed even in its minimal form. I share Sartwell's cynicism about the state; indeed it will inevitably grow and expand its own power. To give the state power is to give it power that it will abuse to expand. Despite all of that, I do not oppose the minimal state. Because states will tend to expand well beyond their original and intended limits, states must be dissolved, emigrated from, or seceded from on a regular basis by those who do not wish to live under anything more than a minimal state. Of course revolutions do not come easily because people are busy living their lives and cannot be bothered overthrowing a government until its abuses have become intolerable and until those abuses affect them personally. But if the alternative to the minimal state is anarchy I do not find that palatable. I prefer the minimal state.

In advocating anarchy, Sartwell is quick to remind his readers not to be elitist in believing they could be trusted in a world without government law but that other people could not. I do not find this persuasive. Even if I think that 90 percent of people could be trusted to live in a world without government law and protection, I could be justified in thinking that the state is unfortunately necessary to protect me from the other 10 percent.[58] Sartwell's response is to ask me to do the cost–benefit analysis. Yes, the state can protect me from the 10 percent, but who will protect me from the state? Doesn't the history of the twentieth century show that states can do far more harm to people than people would do to one another in anarchy?[59] My answer to this is yes, but that just means we need a *minimal* state, and we need to topple the state and start over whenever the state gets too powerful and over-reaching.

Sartwell insists that he does not have a utopian vision, but I think he does. Even though he does not envision specifics of how life would be under his desired anarchy, he does presume it would be relatively peaceful and stable. In the absence of a state I do not think we can reasonably hope that someone or some group would not seize power and establish a state anyway. Thus I think that ironically the state is the best defense against the state (i.e., a minimal state needs to be established to protect us against someone setting up a more expansive state).

Exeunt

The minimal state is not an historical inevitability, but it is a viable option—one that ideally would be offered as a choice among liberal states that share in common the right to exit.[60] Under this system people could shop for and find the state that suits them best. My view calls for a minimal state that would appeal to the free market existentialist. I am not claiming that the minimal state would or should appeal to all people or even all existentialists, only that it should exist as a choice among others. They key to success would be for the minimal state to steer clear of legislating morality in any way and to keep its laws minimal and simple so that they would be unlikely to be objectionable. Since there can be no tacit consent, each adult would need to give explicit consent.[61] Ideally there would be competing states in reasonable proximity so that if an adult does not want to consent to the state and its laws, she could exit to another state with minimal cost or hardship imposed on her.

Notes

1   Cf. David Kelley, *A Life of One's Own: Individual Rights and the Welfare State* (Washington: The CATO Institute, 1998), pp. 1–3.

2   With apologies to Robin Hood, who in most versions of the story is robbing from a tyrannical king and nobility who have robbed the common people.

3   See Stephen T. Asma, *Against Fairness* (Chicago: University of Chicago Press, 2013).

4   Amy Chua and Jed Rubenfeld, *The Triple Package: How Three Unlikely Traits Explain the Rise and Fall of Cultural Groups in America* (New York: The Penguin Press, 2014). See also Pew Research Center, *Second-Generation Americans: A Portrait of the Adult Children of Immigrants*

(Washington, DC: Pew Research Center, 2013), p. 7; Ron Haskins, "Immigration: Wages, Education, and Mobility," in Ron Haskins, Julia B. Isaacs, and Isabel W. Sawhill, eds., *Getting Ahead or Losing Ground* (Washington, DC: The Brookings Institution, 2008), pp. 81–8. http://www.brookings.edu/~/media/Research/Files/Reports/2008/2/economic%20mobility%20sawhill/02_economic_mobility_sawhil l_ch7.PDF; Lingxin Hao and Han S. Woo, "Distinct Trajectories in the Transition to Adulthood: Are Children of Immigrants Advantaged?" *Child Development* 83 (2012): 1623–39; Rubén G. Rumbaut, "The Coming of the Second Generation: Immigration and Ethnic Mobility in Southern California," *The Annals of the American Academy of Political and Social Science* 620 (2008): 196–236.

5 See John Meadowcroft, "Nozick's Critique of Rawls: Distribution, Entitlement, and the Assumptive World of *A Theory of Justice*," in Ralf M. Bader and John Meadowcroft, eds., *The Cambridge Companion to Nozick's Anarchy, State, and Utopia* (Cambridge: Cambridge University Press, 2011), pp. 168–96. Meadowcroft points out that even Rawls implicitly recognizes that it is possible to some extent to determine that some people should get more than others to the extent that the difference principle recognizes that some people will need to be paid more for them to provide certain services (p. 183).

6 Robert Nozick, *Anarchy, State, and Utopia* (New York: Basic Books, 1974), pp. 193–5; Ayn Rand, *Atlas Shrugged* (New York: Signet, 1957).

7 Nor does she owe more to society because the workers were publicly educated and the roads were built with tax dollars. Ideally the workers would be privately educated and the roads would be privately built. In paying workers the salaries they command on the free market and making jobs, products, and services available, business owners do more than their share. Issues of tacit consent are discussed later in this chapter.

8 The exact figure is that in 2013 4.3% of hourly wage employees made minimum wage. The percentage drops to 2.6% when all wage and salary workers are included. http://www.pewresearch.org/fact -tank/2014/09/08/who-makes-minimum-wage/.

9 Gerard Casey, *Libertarian Anarchy: Against the State* (London: Continuum, 2012), p. 45.

10 Casey does not discuss this in this context.

11 See standard textbook discussions of the subject such as James D. Gwartney, Richard L. Stroup, Russell S. Sobel, and David A. Macpherson, *Economics: Private and Public Choice*, 10th edn (Mason, OH: South-Western, 2003), pp. 57–100. For a study of the effects see David Neumark and William Wascher, "'Minimum Wages and Employment: A

Case Study of the Fast-Food Industry in New Jersey and Pennsylvania': A Comment," *American Economic Review* 90 (2000): 1362–96.
12 F.A. Hayek, "The Uses of Knowledge in Society," *American Economic Review* 35 (1945): 519–30.
13 Will Kymlicka raises this issue in *Contemporary Political Philosophy*, 2nd edn (Oxford: Oxford University Press, 2002), p. 161n3.
14 David Schmidtz and Robert E. Goodin, *Social Welfare and Individual Responsibility: For and Against* (Cambridge: Cambridge University Press, 1998), pp. 63–9.
15 Schmidtz and Goodin, pp. 76–7.
16 Schmidtz and Goodin, p. 7.
17 Schmidtz and Goodin, pp. 164–5.
18 Richard H. Thaler and Cass R. Sunstein, *Nudge: Improving Decisions about Health, Wealth, and Happiness*, revised and expanded edn (New York: Penguin, 2008), pp. 109–10.
19 Dan Ariely, *Predictably Irrational: The Hidden Forces that Shape Our Decisions*, revised and expanded edn (New York: Harper Perennial, 2008).
20 Thaler and Sunstein characterize their theory as "libertarian paternalism," *Nudge*, pp. 4–6. In defense of this characterization see Richard Thaler and Cass Sunstein, "Libertarian Paternalism," *American Economic Review Papers and Proceedings* 93 (2003): 175–9. Against this characterization see Gregory Mitchell, "Libertarian Paternalism Is an Oxymoron," *Northwestern University Law Review* 99 (2005): 1245–77.
21 See Mark D. White, *The Manipulation of Choice: Ethics and Libertarian Paternalism* (New York: Palgrave Macmillan, 2013).
22 Thoreau said this, but he endorses it as a motto. It may have been said originally by Thomas Jefferson or Thomas Paine.
23 Perhaps it is just a failure of imagination on my part to think that we need government for even these purposes, though. To consider the case for libertarian anarchy, see Murray N. Rothbard, *For a New Liberty*, 2nd edn (Auburn, AL: Ludwig von Mises Institute, 2006); Aeon J. Skoble, *Deleting the State: An Argument about Government* (Chicago: Open Court, 2008); Gerard Casey, *Libertarian Anarchy: Against the State* (London: Continuum, 2012); and Michael Huemer, *The Problem of Political Authority: An Examination of the Right to Coerce and the Duty to Obey* (New York: Palgrave Macmillan, 2013).
24 Liam Murphy and Thomas Nagel, *The Myth of Ownership: Taxes and Justice* (Oxford: Oxford University Press, 2002), p. 46.
25 Especially because the government is footing part of the bill in terms of grants and loans.
26 Casey does not bring up the American context.

27   *Annals of Congress,* House of Representatives, 3rd Congress, 1st Session, p. 170.
28   Letter to Edmund Pendleton, January 21, 1792, in *The Papers of James Madison Digital Edition,* J.C.A. Stagg (Charlottesville: University of Virginia Press, Rotunda, 2010).
29   Franklin Pierce, "Veto Message," May 3, 1854, in *A Compilation of the Messages and Papers of the Presidents* (New York: Bureau of National Literature, 1897), Vol. 7, pp. 2781, 2782. Cf. Kelley, p. 36.
30   Kelley, p. 97.
31   Luke 10: 25–37.
32   Thomas Nagel, "Libertarianism without Foundations," *The Yale Law Journal* 85 (1975): 145.
33   Murphy and Nagel, pp. 36, 63, 74, 99.
34   Murphy and Nagel, p. 175.
35   Murphy and Nagel, p. 32.
36   http://taxfoundation.org/article/summary-latest-federal-individual-income-tax-data-0.
37   Yes, there are loopholes that lead to exceptions in the current American system.
38   Nozick, p. 287.
39   Schoenblum compares singling out the rich to singling out racial, ethnic, religious groups, or by gender for harsher treatment under the law, in "Tax Fairness or Unfairness?: A Consideration of the Philosophical Bases for Unequal Taxation of Individuals," *American Journal of Tax Policy* 12 (1995): 257.
40   Of course it would be theft even if taken in equal or lesser amounts as long as there was no genuine consent. In "Libertarianism as if (the Other 99 Percent of) People Mattered" (*Social Philosophy and Policy* 15 (1998): 350–71), Loren E. Lomasky reflects on the phenomenological differences in experiencing this phenomenon. Because of these differences and for reasons of civility, he cautions libertarians against using the mantra "taxation is theft." Though I try hard, albeit imperfectly, to be civil, I do not find the phenomenological argument sufficiently compelling.
41   Schoenblum, p. 234.
42   Karl Marx and Friedrich Engels, *Marx/Engels: Selected Works in One Volume* (London: Lawrence and Wishart, 1968), pp. 320–1.
43   See Crispin Sartwell, *Against the State: An Introduction to Anarchist Political Theory* (Albany: State University of New York Press, 2008). In passing, Sartwell (pp. 50–1) uses an analogy that I like to use concerning taxes. The state, as he sees it, is not a voluntary organization. Citizens

do not consent but are coerced. By contrast, clubs are based on voluntary consent. No one has to be part of a club if they do not want to
be (p. 50). I take this further by suggesting that we think of the state
as like a club for which we pay dues. All members of a club pay dues
in the same amount, and if they do not want to pay the dues or do
not like what the dues are being used to fund they are free to leave
the club.

44 Schoenblum, p. 225.
45 Walter Block, "The Justification for Taxation in the Economics Literature," in Robert W. McGee, ed., *The Ethics of Tax Evasion* (Dumont, NJ:
Dumont Institute for Public Policy, 1998), p. 48.
46 Richard A. Epstein, "Can Anyone Beat the Flat Tax?" *Social Philosophy
and Policy* 19 (2002): 157.
47 Though it would not necessarily be too much in the future in a flourishing economy unburdened by high tax rates.
48 Thanks to Trip Johnson for figures and calculations.
49 Cf. Block, p. 78.
50 Cf. Block, p. 57.
51 Whether or not non-paying members could vote would have to be
worked out. As a solution, I might suggest that those who did not pay
the tax because they were below a certain income level would have the
right to vote, whereas those above that income level would not have
the right to vote.
52 In this way, compassion need not be conceived as a moral virtue but
rather as a kind of prudence.
53 Nietzsche himself does not make this distinction between pity and
compassion.
54 Nozick, pp. 265–8.
55 Loren Lomasky, "Libertarianism at Twin Harvard," *Social Philosophy
and Policy* 22 (2005): 186–7.
56 John Locke, *The Second Treatise of Government* and *A Letter Concerning
Toleration* (Mineola, NY: Dover Thrift Editions, 2002), p. 6, section 13.
57 Sartwell, p. 70.
58 Or even the 1% if that's all it is.
59 Sartwell, pp. 66–7.
60 An idea inspired by the title of Chandran Kukathas's book *The Liberal
Archipelago* (Oxford: Oxford University Press, 2003).
61 Though each person would retain the right to internal exit whereby
a person remains within the geographical boundaries of the state but
refuses to be governed by its laws.

Conclusion

Not Your Father's Existentialism

No, this has not been your father's existentialism, or your mother's. To make sense of the rejection of objective values we needed to take account of evolutionary biology. Human nature is not fixed and stable; it is fluid and dynamic. There is, though, a human nature, and it explains why we have moral feelings even though there are no moral facts.

In chapter 1, existentialism was defined as a philosophy that reacts to an apparently absurd or meaningless world by urging the individual to overcome alienation, oppression, and despair through freedom and self-creation in order to become a genuine person. Adding an atheistic worldview and an emphasis on freedom and responsibility, we have free market existentialism. Of course this is not to suggest that everyone who identifies with this conception of existentialism will necessarily support the free market. The point is simply that such a concept of existentialism is compatible with free market thinking.

Indeed, we saw that Sartre's early existentialism does not fit well with Marxism. Rather, Sartre's existentialist emphasis on

The Free Market Existentialist: Capitalism without Consumerism, First Edition. William Irwin.
© 2015 John Wiley & Sons, Ltd. Published 2015 by John Wiley & Sons, Ltd.

individual, ontological freedom and responsibility makes his early philosophy a better match with free market capitalism than with Marxism. Beyond that, a kind of Sartrean authenticity is a key asset in dealing with the alienation and consumerism that often accompany the free market. On a related note, we saw that creative risk taking and crafting of the self à la Nietzsche fit well with the productive activity of the entrepreneur. This is not to say that every entrepreneur is likely to rise to the level of the Übermensch, no more so than will every warrior or artist. The free market, though, is an apt arena for creativity and self-overcoming. Nietzsche himself should have favored it to the extent that it rewards genius and excellence; only his misguided prejudice against spontaneous order prevented his approval.

For the free market existentialist, a minimal state with an equal tax is a desirable environment. This book's introduction began with the recognition that I may be the only free market existentialist. Though you have now read the book, I still may be alone. I hope not, however. My goal in writing has not been to set up a new orthodoxy but instead to draw attention to an alternative. It would be gratifying indeed if more free market existentialists were to come out of the closet; others might realize for the first time that this philosophy fits them. Then the discussions and debates within free market existentialism can begin, for there are certain to be differences and disagreements. That is as it should be.

Select Bibliography

Anderson, Thomas C. *Sartre's Two Ethics: From Authenticity to Integral Humanity*. Chicago: Open Court, 1993.

Ansell-Pearson, Keith. *An Introduction to Nietzsche as Political Thinker: The Perfect Nihilist*. Cambridge: Cambridge University Press, 1994.

Ariely, Dan. *Predictably Irrational: The Hidden Forces that Shape Our Decisions*, revised and expanded edn. New York: Harper Perennial, 2008.

Aron, Raymond. *The Opium of the Intellectuals*. New Brunswick, NJ: Transaction Publishers, 2001.

Aron, Raymond. *Marxism and the Existentialists*. New York: Simon and Schuster, 1969.

Asma, Stephen T. *Against Fairness*. Chicago: University of Chicago Press, 2013.

Bader, Ralf M., and John Meadowcroft, eds. *The Cambridge Companion to Nozick's Anarchy, State, and Utopia*. Cambridge: Cambridge University Press, 2011.

Baggett, David, and Jerry L. Walls. *Good God: The Theistic Foundations of Morality*. Oxford: Oxford University Press, 2011.

Barash, David P. "Evolution and Existentialism, an Intellectual Odd Couple." *The Chronicle of Higher Education*, March 11, 2013. http://chronicle.com/article/EvolutionExistentialism/137715/.

Barash, David P. "Evolutionary Existentialism, Sociobiology, and the Meaning of Life." *Bioscience* 50 (2000): 1012–17.

Barnes, Hazel E. *An Existentialist Ethics*. New York: Vintage, 1967.

Barnes, Hazel E. "Sartre as Materialist," in Paul Arthur Schilpp, ed., *The Philosophy of Jean-Paul Sartre*, pp. 661–84. La Salle, Illinois: Open Court, 1981.

Batchelor, Stephen. *Alone with Others: An Existential Approach to Buddhism*. New York: Grove Press, 1983.

Bauman, Zygmunt. *Does Ethics Have a Chance in a World of Consumers?* Cambridge, MA: Harvard University Press, 2008.

Baumeister, Roy F., and John Tierney. *Willpower*. New York: Penguin, 2011.

Beauvoir, Simone de. *The Second Sex*. Constance Borde and Sheila Malovany-Chevallier trans. New York: Alfred A. Knopf, 2009.

Beauvoir, Simone de. "Pyrrhus and Cineas," in Margaret A. Simons and Sylvie Le Bon de Beauvoir, ed. and trans, *Simone de Beauvoir: Philosophical Writings*, pp. 89–149. Urbana: University of Illinois Press, 2004.

Beauvoir, Simone de. *La Cérémonie des adieux*, with *Entretiens avec Jean-Paul Sartre août-septembre, 1974*. Paris: Gallimard, 1981.

Beauvoir, Simone de. *The Ethics of Ambiguity*. Bernard Frechtman trans. New York: Citadel Press, 1976.

Bentham, Jeremy. *The Collected Works of Jeremy Bentham. Rights, Representation, and Reform: Nonsense Upon Stilts and Other Writings on the French Revolution*. Phillipp R. Schofield, Catherine Pease-Watkin, and Cyprian Blamires ed. Oxford: Oxford University Press, 2002.

Bering, Jesse. *The Belief Instinct: The Psychology of Souls, Destiny, and the Meaning of Life*. New York: Norton, 2011.

Block, Walter. "The Justification for Taxation in the Economics Literature," in Robert W. McGee, ed., *The Ethics of Tax Evasion*, pp. 36–88. Dumont, NJ: Dumont Institute for Public Policy, 1998.

Boaz, David. *The Libertarian Mind: A Manifesto for Freedom*. New York: Simon & Schuster, 2015.

Brennan, Jason. *Why Not Capitalism?* New York: Routledge, 2014.

Brennan, Jason. *Libertarianism: What Everyone Needs to Know*. Oxford: Oxford University Press, 2012.

Brownlee, W. Elliot. *Federal Taxation in America: A Short History*. Cambridge: Cambridge University Press, 2004.

Burgess, John P. "Against Ethics," in Richard Joyce and Simon Kirchin, eds., *A World without Values: Essays on John Mackie's Moral Error Theory*, pp. 1–15. Dordrecht: Springer, 2010.

Busch, Thomas W. *The Power of Consciousness and the Force of Circumstances in Sartre's Philosophy*. Bloomington: Indiana University Press, 1990.

Cain, Susan. *Quiet: The Power of Introverts in a World that Can't Stop Talking.* New York: Crown, 2012.

Camus, Albert. *The Rebel: An Essay on Man in Revolt.* Anthony Bower trans. New York: Vintage, 1992.

Camus, Albert. *The Myth of Sisyphus and Other Essays.* Justin O'Brien trans. New York: Vintage International, 1991.

Camus, Albert. *The Stranger.* Matthew Ward trans. New York: Vintage, 1989.

Cantor, Paul. *The Invisible Hand in Popular Culture: Liberty vs. Authority in American Film and TV.* Lexington: University Press of Kentucky, 2012.

Casey, Gerard. *Libertarian Anarchy: Against the State.* London: Continuum, 2012.

Chartier, Gary. *Anarchy and Legal Order: Law and Politics for a Stateless Society.* Cambridge: Cambridge University Press, 2013.

Chua, Amy, and Jed Rubenfeld. *The Triple Package: How Three Unlikely Traits Explain the Rise and Fall of Cultural Groups in America.* New York: The Penguin Press, 2014.

Cialdini, Robert B., Stephanie L. Brown, Brian P. Lewis, Carol Luce, and Steven L. Neuberg. "Reinterpreting the Empathy–Altruism Relationship: When One into One Equals Oneness." *Journal of Personality and Social Psychology* 73 (1997): 481–94.

Cohen, G.A. "Robert Nozick and Wilt Chamberlain: How Patterns Preserve Liberty." *Erkenntnis* 11 (1977): 5–23.

Conway, Daniel W. *Nietzsche & the Political.* London: Routledge, 1997.

Cotkin, George. *Existential America.* Baltimore: Johns Hopkins University Press, 2003.

Crawford, Matthew B. *Shop Class as Soulcraft: An Inquiry into the Value of Work.* New York: Penguin Books, 2009.

Csíkszentmihályi, Mihály. *Flow: The Psychology of Optimal Experience.* New York: Harper & Row, 1990.

Dawkins, Richard. *The Selfish Gene*, 2nd edn. Oxford: Oxford University Press, 1989.

Detmer, David. *Sartre Explained: From Bad Faith to Authenticity.* Chicago: Open Court, 2008.

Detmer, David. *Freedom as a Value: A Critique of the Ethical Theory of Jean-Paul Sartre.* La Salle, IL: Open Court, 1988.

Dreyfus, Hubert L. "'What a Monster then Is Man': Pascal and Kierkegaard on Being a Contradictory Self and What to Do about It," in Steven Crowell, ed., *The Cambridge Companion to Existentialism*, pp. 96–110. Cambridge: Cambridge University Press, 2012.

Enoch, David. *Taking Morality Seriously: A Defense of Robust Realism.* Oxford: Oxford University Press, 2011.

Epictetus. *Enchiridion*. George Long trans. Mineola, NY: Dover Publications, 2004.

Epstein, Richard A. "Can Anyone Beat the Flat Tax?" *Social Philosophy and Policy* 19 (2002): 140–71.

Field, Hartry. *Realism, Mathematics and Modality*. Oxford: Blackwell, 1991.

Field, Hartry. *Science without Numbers*. Oxford: Blackwell, 1980.

Flynn, Thomas R. *Sartre: A Philosophical Biography*. Cambridge: Cambridge University Press, 2014.

Flynn, Thomas R. "Political Existentialism: The Career of Sartre's Political Thought," in Steven Crowell, ed., *The Cambridge Companion to Existentialism*, pp. 227–51. Cambridge: Cambridge University Press, 2012.

Flynn, Thomas R. *Sartre and Marxist Existentialism: The Test Case of Collective Responsibility*. Chicago: University of Chicago Press, 1984.

Frankfurt, Harry G. "Freedom of the Will and the Concept of a Person." *Journal of Philosophy* 68 (1971): 5–20.

Franklin, Todd. "The Political Implications of Nietzsche's Aristocratic Radicalism." *The Southern Journal of Philosophy* 37 (1999): 143–9.

Gao, Yu, Andrea L. Glenn, Robert A. Schug, Yaling Yang, and Adrian Raine. "The Neurobiology of Psychopathy: A Neurodevelopmental Perspective." *Canadian Journal of Psychiatry* 54 (2009): 813–23.

Garner, Richard. "Abolishing Morality," in Richard Joyce and Simon Kirchin, eds., *A World without Values: Essays on John Mackie's Moral Error Theory*, pp. 217–33. Dordrecht: Springer, 2010.

Garner, Richard. *Beyond Morality*. Philadelphia: Temple University Press, 1994.

Garner, Richard. "Beyond Morality," revised edition. Unpublished manuscript.

Garner, Richard. "A Plea for Moral Abolitionism." Unpublished manuscript.

Gauthier, David. *Morals by Agreement*. Oxford: Clarendon Press, 1986.

Gibbard, Allan. *Wise Choices, Apt Feelings: A Theory of Normative Judgment*. Cambridge, MA: Harvard University Press, 1990.

Graaf, John de, David Waan, and Thomas H. Naylor. *Affluenza: The All-Consuming Epidemic*. San Francisco: Berrett-Koehler Publishers, 2001.

Grant, Adam. *Give and Take: A Revolutionary Approach to Success*. New York: Viking, 2013.

Güth, Werner, Rolf Schmittberger, and Bernd Schwarze. "An Experimental Analysis of Ultimatum Bargaining." *Journal of Economic Behavior and Organization* 3 (1982): 367–88.

Gwartney, James D., Richard L. Stroup, Russell S. Sobel, and David A. Macpherson. *Economics: Private and Public Choice*, 10th edn. Mason, OH: South-Western, 2003.

Haidt, Jonathan. *The Righteous Mind: Why Good People Are Divided by Politics and Religion.* New York: Pantheon, 2012.

Haidt, Jonathan. *The Happiness Hypothesis: Finding Modern Truth in Ancient Wisdom.* New York: Basic Books, 2007.

Hao, Lingxin, and Han S. Woo. "Distinct Trajectories in the Transition to Adulthood: Are Children of Immigrants Advantaged?" *Child Development* 83 (2012): 1623–39.

Harman, Gilbert. "Moral Explanations of Natural Facts: Can Moral Claims Be Tested against Moral Reality?" *The Southern Journal of Philosophy* 24, Supplement (1986): 57–68.

Haskins, Ron. "Immigration: Wages, Education, and Mobility," in Ron Haskins, Julia B. Isaacs, and Isabel W. Sawhill, eds., *Getting Ahead or Losing Ground.* Washington, DC: The Brookings Institution, 2008.

Hayek, F.A. *The Fatal Conceit: The Errors of Socialism.* Chicago: University of Chicago Press, 2011.

Hayek, F.A. *The Road to Serfdom: The Definitive Edition.* Bruce Caldwell ed. Chicago: University of Chicago Press, 2007.

Hayek, F.A. "The Non Sequitur of the 'Dependence Effect.'" *Southern Economic Journal* 27 (1961): 346–8.

Hayek, F.A. "The Uses of Knowledge in Society." *American Economic Review* 35 (1945): 519–30.

Heidegger, Martin. *Being and Time.* John Macquarrie and Edward Robinson trans. San Francisco: Harper Collins, 1962.

Heter, T Storm. *Sartre's Ethics of Engagement: Authenticity and Civic Virtue.* London: Continuum, 2006.

Hicks, Stephen R.C. "Egoism in Nietzsche and Rand." *The Journal of Ayn Rand Studies* 10 (2009): 249–91.

Hinckfuss, Ian. *The Moral Society—Its Structure and Effects* (1987). http://www.philosophy.ru/phil/library/hinck/contents.html.

Howells, Christina, ed. *The Cambridge Companion to Sartre.* Cambridge: Cambridge University Press, 1992.

Huemer, Michael. "An Ontological Proof of Moral Realism." *Social Philosophy and Policy* 30 (2013): 259–79.

Huemer, Michael. *The Problem of Political Authority: An Examination of the Right to Coerce and the Duty to Obey.* New York: Palgrave Macmillan, 2013.

Hunt, Lester H. "Egoism in Nietzsche and Rand: A Somewhat Different Approach." *The Journal of Ayn Rand Studies* 10 (2009): 293–311.

Hunt, Lester H. "Thus Spake Howard Roark: Nietzschean Ideas in *The Fountainhead.*" *Philosophy and Literature* 30 (2006): 79–101.

Hunt, Lester H. *Nietzsche and the Origin of Virtue.* New York: Routledge, 1991.

Hunt, Lester H. "Politics and Anti-Politics: Nietzsche's View of the State." *History of Philosophy Quarterly* 2 (1985): 453–68.

Irwin, William. "Death by Inauthenticity: Heidegger's Debt to Ivan Il'ich's Fall." *Tolstoy Studies Journal* 25 (2013): 15–21.

Irwin, William. "Unbearable *Godot*: How an Existentialist Can Make Meaning and Find Happiness in Repetition." *Philosophy Today* 56 (2012): 84–9.

Irwin, William. "Prufrock's Question and Roquentin's Answer." *Philosophy and Literature* 33 (2009): 184–92.

James, Scott M. *An Introduction to Evolutionary Ethics*. Malden, MA: Wiley-Blackwell, 2011.

James, William. *The Principles of Psychology*. New York: Henry Holt and Company, 1890.

Jay, Martin. *Marxism and Totality: The Adventures of a Concept from Lukács to Habermas*. Berkeley: University of California Press, 1986.

Johnson, David Kyle. "Do Souls Exist?" *Think* 35 (2013): 61–75.

Joyce, Richard. *The Evolution of Morality*. Cambridge, MA: MIT Press, 2007.

Joyce, Richard. *The Myth of Morality*. Cambridge: Cambridge University Press, 2001.

Joyce, Richard, and Simon Kirchin, eds. *A World without Values: Essays on John Mackie's Moral Error Theory*. Dordrecht: Springer, 2010.

Kahan, Alan S. *Mind vs. Money: The War between Intellectuals and Capitalism*. New Brunswick, NJ: Transaction Publishers, 2010.

Kahane, Guy. "Evolutionary Debunking Arguments." *Nous* 45 (2011): 103–25.

Kelley, David. *A Life of One's Own: Individual Rights and the Welfare State*. Washington: The CATO Institute, 1998.

Kierkegaard, Søren. *Either/Or*, Vol. II. Howard V. Hong and Edna H. Hong trans. Princeton, NJ: Princeton University Press, 1987.

Kierkegaard, Søren. *Fear and Trembling/Repetition*. Howard V. Hong and Edna H. Hong trans. Princeton, NJ: Princeton University Press, 1983.

Kierkegaard, Søren. *Either/Or*, Vol. I. David F. Swenson and Lillian Marvin Swenson trans. Princeton, NJ: Princeton University Press, 1959.

Kinsella, N. Stephan. *Against Intellectual Property*. Auburn, AL: Ludwig von Mises Institute, 2008.

Kitcher, Philip. *Life after Faith: The Case for Secular Humanism*. New Haven: Yale University Press, 2014.

Koepsell, David. *Who Owns You?: The Corporate Gold Rush to Patent Your Genes*. Malden, MA: Wiley-Blackwell, 2009.

Kukathas, Chandran. *The Liberal Archipelago*. Oxford: Oxford University Press, 2003.

Kukathas, Chandran, and Philip Pettit. *Rawls: A Theory of Justice and Its Critics*. Stanford, CA: Stanford University Press, 1990.

Kymlicka, Will. *Contemporary Political Philosophy*, 2nd edn. Oxford: Oxford University Press, 2002.

Lawler, James. *The Existentialist Marxism of Jean-Paul Sartre*. Amsterdam: B.R. Grüner, 1976.

Leiter, Brian. "Moralities Are a Sign-Language of the Affects." *Social Philosophy and Policy* 30 (2013): 237–58.

Lemos, John. *Commonsense Darwinism: Evolution, Morality, and the Human Condition*. Chicago: Open Court, 2008.

Levitt, Steven D., and John A. List. "What Do Laboratory Experiments Measuring Social Preferences Reveal about the Real World." *Journal of Economic Perspectives* 21 (2007): 153–74.

List, John A. "On the Interpretation of Giving in Dictator Games." *Journal of Political Economy* 115 (2007): 482–94.

Locke, John. *The Second Treatise of Government and A Letter Concerning Toleration*. Mineola, NY: Dover Thrift Editions, 2002.

Loeb, Don. "The Argument from Moral Experience," in Richard Joyce and Simon Kirchin, eds., *A World without Values: Essays on John Mackie's Moral Error Theory*, pp. 101–18. Dordrecht: Springer, 2010.

Lomasky, Loren E. "Libertarianism at Twin Harvard." *Social Philosophy and Policy* 22 (2005): 178–99.

Lomasky, Loren E. "Libertarianism as if (the Other 99 Percent of) People Mattered." *Social Philosophy and Policy* 15 (1998): 350–71.

Machan, Tibor R. *Classical Individualism*. London: Routledge, 1998.

Mack, Eric. "Nozick's Anarchism," in J. Roland Pennock and John W. Chapman, eds., *Anarchism*, pp. 43–62. New York: New York University Press, 1978.

Mackie, J.L. *Ethics: Inventing Right and Wrong*. New York: Penguin, 1977.

Marks, Joel. *Bad Faith: A Philosophical Memoir*. Lexington, KY: CreateSpace, 2013.

Marks, Joel. *Ethics without Morals: A Defense of Amorality*. New York: Routledge, 2013.

Marks, Joel. *It's Just a Feeling: The Philosophy of Desirism*. Lexington, KY: CreateSpace, 2013.

Marx, Karl. *Karl Marx: Selected Writings*. David McLellan ed. Oxford: Oxford University Press, 1977.

Marx, Karl, and Friedrich Engels. *Marx/Engels: Selected Works in One Volume*. London: Lawrence and Wishart, 1968.

May, Larry. *Sharing Responsibility*. Chicago: University of Chicago Press, 1992.

McBride, William L. *Sartre's Political Theory*. Bloomington: Indiana University Press, 1991.

McCloskey, Deirdre Nansen. "Measured, Unmeasured, Mismeasured, and Unjustified Pessimism: A Review Essay of Thomas Piketty's *Capital in the Twenty-First Century*." *Erasmus Journal of Philosophy and Economics* 7 (2014): 73–115.

McLellan, David, ed. *The Eighteenth Brumaire of Louis Bonaparte*, in *Karl Marx: Selected Writings*. Oxford: Oxford University Press, 1977.

Meadowcroft, John. "Nozick's Critique of Rawls: Distribution, Entitlement, and the Assumptive World of *A Theory of Justice*," in Ralf M. Bader and John Meadowcroft, eds., *The Cambridge Companion to Nozick's Anarchy, State, and Utopia*, pp. 168–96. Cambridge: Cambridge University Press, 2011.

Mitchell, Gregory. "Libertarian Paternalism Is an Oxymoron." *Northwestern University Law Review* 99 (2005): 1245–77.

Moeller, Hans-Georg. *The Moral Fool: A Case for Amorality*. New York: Columbia University Press, 2009.

Morgan-Knapp, Christopher "Economic Envy." *Journal of Applied Philosophy* 31 (2014): 113–26.

Muller, Jerry Z. "Capitalism, Socialism, and Irony: Understanding Schumpeter in Context." *Critical Review* 13 (1999): 239–67.

Murphy, Liam, and Thomas Nagel. *The Myth of Ownership: Taxes and Justice*. Oxford: Oxford University Press, 2002.

Nagel, Thomas. *Mind and Cosmos: Why the Materialist Neo-Darwinian Conception of Nature Is Almost Certainly False*. New York: Oxford University Press, 2012.

Nagel, Thomas. "Libertarianism without Foundations." *The Yale Law Journal* 85 (1975): 136–49.

Narveson, Jan. *The Libertarian Idea*. Philadelphia: Temple University Press, 1988.

Neumann, Craig S., and Robert D. Hare, "Psychopathic Traits in a Large Community Sample: Links to Violence, Alcohol Use, and Intelligence." *Journal of Consulting and Clinical Psychology* 76 (2008): 893–9.

Neumark, David, and William Wascher. "'Minimum Wages and Employment: A Case Study of the Fast-Food Industry in New Jersey and Pennsylvania': A Comment." *American Economic Review* 90 (2000): 1362–96.

Nietzsche, Friedrich. *Beyond Good and Evil*. Walter Kaufmann trans. New York: Vintage, 1989.

Nietzsche, Friedrich. *The Gay Science*. Walter Kaufmann trans. New York: Vintage, 1974.

Nietzsche, Friedrich. *Thus Spoke Zarathustra*. Walter Kaufmann trans. New York: Penguin, 1966.

Nolan, Daniel, Greg Restall, and Caroline West. "Moral Fictionalism versus the Rest." *Australasian Journal of Philosophy* 83 (2005): 307–30.

Norton, David L. *Personal Destinies: A Philosophy of Ethical Individualism.* Princeton: Princeton University Press, 1976.

Nozick, Robert. *Anarchy, State, and Utopia.* New York: Basic Books, 1974.

Oddie, Graham, and Daniel Demetriou. "The Fictionalist's Attitude Problem," in Richard Joyce and Simon Kirchin, eds., *A World without Values: Essays on John Mackie's Moral Error Theory,* pp. 199–215. Dordrecht: Springer, 2010.

Olson, Jonas. *Moral Error Theory: History, Critique, Defence.* Oxford: Oxford University Press, 2014.

Pascal, Blaise. *Pensées.* A.J. Kreilsheimer trans. Harmondsworth, UK: Penguin, 1966.

Pascal, Blaise. *Pensées.* W.F. Trotter trans. New York: Modern Library, 1941.

Perry, Ralph Barton. *The Thought and Character of William James.* Cambridge: Harvard University Press, 1948.

Pew Research Center. *Second-Generation Americans: A Portrait of the Adult Children of Immigrants.* Washington, DC: Pew Research Center, 2013.

Pidgen, Charles. "Nihilism, Nietzsche, and the Doppelganger Problem." *Ethical Theory and Moral Practice* 10 (2007): 441–56.

Piketty, Thomas. *Capital in the Twenty-First Century.* Arthur Goldhammer trans. Cambridge, MA: Harvard University Press, 2014.

Poellner, Peter. "Early Sartre on Freedom and Ethics." *European Journal of Philosophy* (2012): 1–27. DOI: 10.1111/j.1468-0378.2012.00532.x.

Poster, Mark. *Existential Marxism in Postwar France: From Sartre to Althusser.* Princeton: Princeton University Press, 1975.

Rand, Ayn. *Atlas Shrugged.* New York: Signet, 1957.

Rand, Ayn. *The Fountainhead.* New York: Signet, 1952.

Rasmussen, Douglas B., and Douglas J. Den Uyl. *Norms of Liberty. A Perfectionist Basis for Non-Perfectionist Politics.* University Park, PA: Penn State University Press, 2005.

Ratner-Rosenhagen, Jennifer. *American Nietzsche: A History of an Icon and His Ideas.* Chicago: University of Chicago Press, 2012.

Rawls, John. *A Theory of Justice.* Cambridge, MA: Harvard University Press, 1971.

Richardson, James D., ed. *A Compilation of the Messages and Papers of the Presidents,* Vol. 7. New York: Bureau of National Literature, 1897.

Robin, Corey. "Nietzsche's Marginal Children: On Friedrich Hayek." *The Nation,* May 27, 2013, pp. 27–36.

Rochefoucauld, Francois de la. *Maxims,* in Kevin Jackson, ed., *The Oxford Book of Money.* Oxford: Oxford University Press, 1996.

Romar, Edward J. "Noble Markets: The Noble/Slave Ethic in Hayek's Free Market Capitalism." *Journal of Business Ethics* 85 (2009): 57–66.

Rosenberg, Alex. *The Atheist's Guide to Reality: Enjoying Life without Illusions*. New York: Norton, 2011.

Rothbard, Murray N. *For a New Liberty*, 2nd edn. Auburn, AL: Ludwig von Mises Institute, 2006.

Rumbaut, Rubén G. "The Coming of the Second Generation: Immigration and Ethnic Mobility in Southern California." *The Annals of the American Academy of Political and Social Science* 620 (2008): 196–236.

Ruse, Michael. *Taking Darwin Seriously*. Oxford: Blackwell, 1986.

Ruse, Michael, and E.O. Wilson. "Darwinism as Applied Science," in Elliott Sober, ed., *Conceptual Issues in Evolutionary Biology*, 2nd edn, pp. 421–38. Cambridge: MIT Press, 1994.

Sartre, Jean-Paul. *Notebooks for an Ethics*. David Pellauer trans. Chicago: University of Chicago Press, 1992.

Sartre, Jean-Paul. *No Exit and Three Other Plays*. New York: Vintage International, 1989.

Sartre, Jean-Paul. *Life/Situations: Essays Written and Spoken*. Paul Auster and Lydia Davis trans. New York: Pantheon, 1977.

Sartre, Jean-Paul. *Critique of Dialectical Reason*. Alan Sheridan-Smith trans. London: New Left Books, 1976.

Sartre, Jean-Paul. *Between Existentialism and Marxism: Sartre on Philosophy, Politics, Psychology, and the Arts*. John Matthews trans. New York: Pantheon, 1974.

Sartre, Jean-Paul. *The Communists and Peace, with A Reply to Claude Lefort*. Martha H. Fletcher and Phillip R. Berk trans. New York: George Braziller, 1968.

Sartre, Jean-Paul. *Search for a Method*. Hazel E. Barnes trans. New York: Random House, Vintage Books, 1968.

Sartre, Jean-Paul. *The Transcendence of the Ego*. Forrest Williams and Robert Kirkpatrick trans. New York: Hill and Wang, 1957.

Sartre, Jean-Paul. *Being and Nothingness*. Hazel Barnes trans. New York: Washington Square Press, 1956.

Sartre, Jean-Paul. *Anti-Semite and Jew*. George J. Becker trans. New York: Schocken Books, 1948.

Sartre, Jean-Paul. *The Emotions: Outline of a Theory*. Bernard Frechtman trans. New York: Philosophical Library, 1948.

Sartre, Jean-Paul. *Existentialism*. Bernard Frechtman trans. New York: Philosophical Library, 1947.

Sartre, Jean-Paul. *Situations*. Vols. 1–10. Paris: Gallimard, 1947–76.

Sartwell, Crispin. *Against the State: An Introduction to Anarchist Political Theory*. Albany: State University of New York Press, 2008.

Schmidtz, David. "The Right to Distribute," in Ralf M. Bader and John Meadowcroft, eds., *The Cambridge Companion to Nozick's "Anarchy, State, and Utopia,"* pp. 197–229. Cambridge: Cambridge University Press, 2011.

Schmidtz, David, and Robert E. Goodin. *Social Welfare and Individual Responsibility: For and Against.* Cambridge: Cambridge University Press, 1998.

Schoenblum, Jeffrey A. "Tax Fairness or Unfairness?: A Consideration of the Philosophical Bases for Unequal Taxation of Individuals." *American Journal of Tax Policy* 12 (1995): 221–71.

Schumpeter, Joseph A. *Capitalism, Socialism and Democracy*, 3rd edn. New York: Harper Perennial Modern Classics, 2008.

Schutte, Ofelia. "Nietzsche's Politics." *Journal of the British Society for Phenomenology* 14 (1983): 139–57.

Skoble, Aeon J. *Deleting the State: An Argument about Government.* Chicago: Open Court, 2008.

Solomon, Robert C. "Pessimism vs. Existentialism." *The Chronicle Review*, January 26, 2007. http://chronicle.com/article/Pessimism-vs-Existentialism/8935/.

Solomon, Robert C. *Dark Feelings, Grim Thoughts: Experience and Reflection in Camus and Sartre.* Oxford: Oxford University Press, 2006.

Spurling, Laurie. "Marx and the Existentialists." *Journal of the British Society for Phenomenology* 7 (1976): 131–7.

Stagg, J.C.A. *The Papers of James Madison Digital Edition.* Charlottesville: University of Virginia Press, Rotunda, 2010.

Stamos, David N. *Evolution and the Big Questions: Sex, Race, Religion, and Other Matters.* Malden, MA: Blackwell, 2008.

Street, Sharon. "A Darwinian Dilemma for Realist Theories of Value." *Philosophical Studies* 127 (2006): 109–66.

Sturgeon, Nicholas L. "Harman on Moral Explanations of Natural Facts." *The Southern Journal of Philosophy* 24, Supplement (1986): 69–78.

Sullivan, Missy. "Lost Inheritance." *The Wall Street Journal*, March 8, 2013. http://online.wsj.com/news/articles/SB10001424127887324662404578334663271139552.

Thaler, Richard H., and Cass R. Sunstein. *Nudge: Improving Decisions about Health, Wealth, and Happiness*, revised and expanded edn. New York: Penguin, 2008.

Thaler, Richard H., and Cass R. Sunstein. "Libertarian Paternalism." *American Economic Review Papers and Proceedings* 93 (2003): 175–9.

Thoreau, Henry David. *Walden*, in Carl Bode, ed., *The Portable Thoreau*. New York: Penguin Viking, 1982.

Tomasi, John. *Free Market Fairness.* Princeton: Princeton University Press, 2012.

Turgenev, Ivan. *Fathers and Sons.* Richard Freeborn trans. Oxford: Oxford University Press, 2008.

Select Bibliography

Walsh, George V. "Rawls and Envy." *Reason Papers* 17 (1992): 3–28.

West, Caroline. "Business as Usual?: The Error Theory, Internalism, and the Function of Morality," in Richard Joyce and Simon Kirchin, eds., *A World without Values: Essays on John Mackie's Moral Error Theory*, pp. 183–98. Dordrecht: Springer, 2010.

White, Mark D. *The Manipulation of Choice: Ethics and Libertarian Paternalism.* New York: Palgrave Macmillan, 2013.

White, Mark D. *Kantian Ethics and Economics: Autonomy, Dignity, and Character*. Stanford, CA: Stanford University Press, 2011.

Wielenberg, Erik J. "On the Evolutionary Debunking of Morality." *Ethics* 120 (2010): 441–64.

Wielenberg, Erik J. "In Defense of Non-Natural, Non-Theistic Moral Realism." *Faith and Philosophy* 26 (2009): 23–41.

Index

The Free Market Existentialist: Capitalism without Consumerism, First Edition. William Irwin.
© 2015 John Wiley & Sons, Ltd. Published 2015 by John Wiley & Sons, Ltd.

Index

Index